BIG INCLUSIVE **SEND CAREERS** HANDBOOK

Jenny Connick FRSA

trotman | t

Big Inclusive SEND Careers Handbook

This first edition published in 2024 by Trotman, an imprint of Trotman Indigo Publishing Ltd, 18e Charles Street, Bath BA1 1HX

© Trotman Publishing Ltd 2024

Author: Jenny Connick

British Library Cataloguing in Publication Data
A catalogue record for this book is available from the British Library.

ISBN 978 1 911724 22 3

All rights reserved. This book is sold subject to the condition that it shall not, by way of trade or otherwise, be lent, resold, hired out or otherwise circulated without the publisher's prior written consent in any form of binding or cover other than that in which it is published and without a similar condition including this condition being imposed on the subsequent purchaser. No part of this publication may be reproduced, stored in a retrieval system or transmitted in any form or by any means, electronic and mechanical, photocopying, recording or otherwise without prior permission of Trotman Indigo Publishing.

Every effort has been made to trace copyright holders and to obtain their permission for the use of copyright material. The publisher apologises for any errors or omissions, and would be grateful to be notified of any corrections that should be incorporated in future editions of this book.

Cover design by Anna Liddeatt

Printed and bound in the UK by 4Edge Ltd, Hockley, Essex

All details in this book were correct at the time of going to press. To keep up-to-date with all the latest news and updates and to access the online resources that accompany this book, use the QR code or visit **trotman.co.uk/pages/big-inclusive-send-careers-handbook-resources**

Contents

List of figures	vii
About the author	viii
Dedications and thanks	ix
Why is this book important and how can you get the best out of it?	xi
Foreword	xiii

1 Introduction to SEND and inclusion and early career development   1

SEND and inclusion and early career development   1
- Introduction   2
- Inclusion, what does it mean, what could it mean   2
- An introduction to young people with SEND or who are vulnerable and/or disadvantaged   4
- Educational settings and young people with SEND   5
- Types of barriers to achieving optimal career outcomes   6

Anxiety around Difference and Diversity and the impact on career outcomes   11
- Introduction   11
- Social and medical models of disability   12
- Where does anxiety come from?   12
- Unconscious bias and the implications for outcomes   13
- Stereotypes   13
- Ableism   14
- Employer confidence   14
- The importance of language and communication   15
- The impact on outcomes of treating those with additional needs less favourably   16
- Building our confidence and reducing our anxiety around diversity   16

2 Who *are* young people with SEND?   23

- Introduction   23
- The legal framework surrounding SEND – SEND Code of Practice   24
- Short descriptions of the characteristics of different SEND groups   25
- Education, Health and Care Plans – what do they have to do with career development and the definition of young people with SEND?   30
- Optimum career outcomes   32
- Defining the two Career SEND Groups – Career SEND Group One and Career SEND Group Two   32
- Intersectionality between Career SEND Groups One and Two   36
- Where do vulnerable and disadvantaged young people meet SEND?   36

Contents

3 The organisation of career development for young people with SEND – the people — 43

Appreciating the influences and influencers on career decisions, positive and negative — 44

A short history of career development and SEND — 45

The Careers and Enterprise Company — 48
- Introduction — 48
- Improvements in career development and SEND made by the CEC since 2016 — 50
- How the Careers and Enterprise Company can support you — 51

Careers leaders — 57
- Introduction — 57
- The careers leader role — 58
- #sameanddifferent – a career delivery model for SEND and inclusion — 59
- Strategic careers health check for SEND — 62

Careers advisers – creating an inclusive careers guidance space — 69
- Introduction — 69
- The careers adviser's impact on improving career/life outcomes — 70
- Working as part of the Careers Team — 70
- Creating an inclusive careers guidance environment — 70
- Trauma-informed therapeutic personal careers guidance and ACEs (adverse childhood experiences) — 73

4 The organisation of career development and young people with SEND – the process — 79

Gatsby Benchmarks — 79
- Introduction — 79
- The eight Gatsby Benchmarks — 80
- Looking at the eight Gatsby Benchmarks from a SEND perspective — 81
- SEND Gatsby Toolkit – what good looks like for Career SEND Groups One and Two — 82

Career development process at schools, special schools and colleges — 95
- Introduction — 95
- Key stakeholders and perspectives — 95
- The organisation of early career development at school — 97
- Funding plays a part — 98
- Quality and standards of career development — 98

The career development process — 104
- Introduction — 104
- Understanding the career development process — 104
- Raising aspirations — 105

The importance of starting early and young people with SEND	106
The career development process in detail	106
Personal development	110
How to compete for the career of choice – personal brand and how to stand out	111

5 The career journey of a young person with SEND/additional needs — 117

Career pathways and destinations explained – Career SEND Group One and Career SEND Group Two — 117
Introduction	118
Career pathways	118
Career destinations	121

Career destinations – discuss! — 128
Introduction	128
Destinations – key questions – the challenge!	129
Supply and demand – what influences destinations?	130
Travel	131
Infrastructure	131
Recording destinations	131

Youth voice – hearing from young people — 136
Introduction	136
Oracy	137
Youth Voice – Billy	138
Youth Voice – Emily	140

6 Increasing employer engagement, enterprise and skills — 145

Increasing employer engagement — 145
Introduction	145
Why aren't employers engaging in the numbers needed?	146
What do special schools, schools and colleges want from employers?	146
Ways to attract more employers – what can you offer employers?	147
Training for employers	148
Employer standards	148
Getting ready for the challenge!	148

The value of enterprise for young people with SEND — 154
Introduction	154
The essence of enterprise	155
Enterprise and entrepreneurship (intrapreneurship)	155
Enterprise skills	155
Enterprise and SEND	156
How to bring enterprise into your school, special school and college	157

Contents

Skills and skills development	**161**
Introduction	161
Explore the difference between skills, knowledge and behaviours	161
Skills development levels	162
Exploring different skills frameworks	162
Skills focus for Career SEND Group One	166
Skills focus for Career SEND Group Two	166
The impact of disadvantage on the acquisition of skills, positive and negative	167
Planning for skills using the Gatsby Benchmarks	167

7 Making the difference — 173

Transition and why it is vital to get it right	**173**
Introduction	174
The importance of getting transition right	174
What happens when transition goes wrong?	175
Different types of transitions	175
Preparation for transition	175
Support and reasonable adjustments	177
Parents, carers and families perspective	178
Post transition	179
Engaging parents, carers and families	**182**
Introduction	185
Further ideas for effective parent, carer and family engagement	187
Evaluating the impact of your careers programme: answering the question, 'so what?'	**193**
Introduction	193
What are you evaluating?	194
Who are you evaluating for?	194
How are you evaluating?	194
Ways to secure evidence	194
Nesta's Standards of Evidence	195
What will you do with the data?	196

8 The value chain of early career development for inclusion #differentandbetter — 201

So, how do we put all your learning together?	203
Epigraph	**213**
Afterword	**215**
Glossary of Key Terms	**217**

List of figures

chapter 3 #sameandifferent	46
chapter 3 SEND Careers health check checklist	56
chapter 3 National Careers Strategy 2017	60
chapter 4 Gatsby Benchmarks framework	94
chapter 6 Skills frameworks	163
chapter 8 #differentandbetter	206

About the author

Jenny Connick FRSA is the founder of Talentino, an independent early career development company founded in 2011 that specialises in the early career development of young people with special needs and those who are vulnerable and disadvantaged. The Talentino SEND careers development programmes can be found in over 400 special schools, schools and colleges across England.

Connick's background is as an HR director both in the UK and internationally latterly for Siemens, focusing on strategy, organisational development and design.

However, it is her experience with Talentino that has enabled her to create this book having listened to thousands of careers practitioners, teaching staff, young people, parents and families, and employers. Talentino's vision is and always has been to improve outcomes through raising the quality and relevance of early career development for young people with additional needs.

Leading Talentino, which has been the strategic partner for SEND and Inclusion for the Careers and Enterprise Company since December 2018, has also given Connick the chance to contribute to national SEND careers initiatives like writing the SEND Gatsby Toolkits. And it has been a transformative partnership. Connick is considered a thought leader in the field of SEND and early career development.

Award-winning for many years, Connick was recognised for services to education by being invited to the late Queen's Garden Party at Buckingham Palace in 2017.

She wrote the *Little SEND Careers Handbook* in 2022 predominantly for her customers, but it became a hit with over 4,000 copies sold after self-publishing. This new book captures many voices and opinions as well as her learning over the last 13 years and is shared with love and respect but most of all with the fervour she has shown for many years to improve career outcomes for all young people but particularly those with any additional need.

Outside of writing and running Talentino, Connick can be found in the company of her close and extensive family and has just welcomed her first granddaughter as well as growing vegetables but is still at a loss as to how to grow sizeable celeriac!

Dedications and thanks

It has been a privilege to be commissioned to write this book, but I could not have done without the thousands of people I have met during the 13 years of working with consummate and passionate professionals, and young people and their families. I would especially like to name the 'career chums' who have contributed to each chapter with their own perspective, namely:

- Oli de Botton, CEO of the Careers and Enterprise Company
- Wayne Norrie, CEO of Greenwood Academies Trust
- Nana Marfo, Founder of Unique Abilities and disability activist
- Dan Pikett, Founder of Spatial Careers
- Nicola Hall, Director of Education at the Careers and Enterprise Company
- Kelly Dillon, Head of Inclusion at the Careers and Enterprise Company
- David Morgan, CEO of Career Development Institute
- Amanda Cheney, National SEND Education Manager at Talentino
- Dame Christine Lenehan, CEO of the Council for Disabled Children (Retired)
- John Yarham, Deputy CEO of the Careers and Enterprise Company
- Dr Deirdre Hughes, Associate Professor and Co-Founder of CareerChat Ltd
- Julie Grant, Employer Engagement Manager at Brookfields Special School
- Bill Muirhead, Managing Director of the Peter Jones Foundation
- Brandon Mills and Sara Attra, Head Teachers
- Hardeep Rai and Eshan Rai
- Billy Mills
- Emily Pearse
- Laura-Jane Rawlings MBE, CEO of Youth Voice UK
- Dr Emily Tanner, Head of Post-14 Education and Skills at Nuffield Foundation
- Tom Ravenscroft, CEO of Skills Builder

Dedications and thanks

- Gareth Ivett, Principal at Creating Tomorrow College
- Helen Hannam, Deputy Head Teacher at Manor Green

Throughout my journey with Talentino I could not have achieved what I have without the love and support of my husband, Alan, and family – Josh and Taylor, Toby and Emma, Aoife, Harry Man, Kit and Harri Dog; my twin Paul; and numerous Talentino colleagues and chums including Helen, Toby, Brandon, Sally, Jack, Amanda – past and present.

Why is this book important and how can you get the best out of it?

This book has been written for anyone and everyone who has an interest in ensuring that the most disadvantaged and vulnerable young people in our society get the best chance to enjoy an optimal career outcome after leaving school. I use the word 'career' to mean 'learning new stuff over a period of time', so whether as a careers practitioner you are supporting someone who is destined for a Supported Internship, extended work placement, accessible apprenticeship, starting as an entrepreneur, starting FE college, or the dizzy heights of Oxford or Cambridge, this book is for you.

Inclusion is about everyone having equal opportunities to succeed; not the same opportunities and not the same outcomes but one that is parous to their peers and gives life purpose. This book takes you through every aspect of thinking this through – who are these young people, what is possible for them, what gets in the way, and how careers practitioners individually and collectively can create careers models and landscapes which improve outcomes at a granular and strategic level.

Whether you are a careers leader; careers adviser; member of the senior leadership team (SLT); a training provider; hail from an FE college or university; an employer, parent, carer or family member; have SEND responsibility in a local authority, or even a policymaker – there is something in this book for you, I promise you.

Each chapter is structured in the same way with an introduction, key content, a guest contributor's perspective and lots of top tips. Some chapters are a little bit heavier than others, but take your time; it is packed with ideas for you to think about.

Every chapter includes an action checklist. This has questions and pointers for you to think through your work now and how to make it more inclusive and deliver better outcomes in the future. You could even put them all together like an Inclusive Careers Action book so they will enable you to deliver a focused, results-driven Inclusive SEND career strategy and programme for your students with additional needs. They are called 'My little checklist' and I have to be honest, I can't say that without humming 'My Little Pony' in my head, but the publisher said no . . .

Why is this book important and how can you get the best out of it?

Each chapter has been written to build on the previous one, but if you are a bit of a rebel like me, you can just dip into what you fancy at any time.

> ♥ There are two types of people who come into the world of special needs: those who run for the hills after a week and those who become compelled and committed to stay the distance to support the improvement of outcomes. Who will you be?

Foreword

I believe strongly in helping all young people find their voice and passion so they can lead lives of choice and opportunity.

Sometimes – and certainly too often – young people with additional needs have the highest barriers to this future. Our goal should be to create a system around them that is as deft at meeting their needs as it is at appreciating the strengths they have. We are seeing progress, but there is undoubtedly further to go. Fortunately, there are beacons to guide us.

Talentino is one of these. Their work shows what it is possible to achieve for young people if the approach is right. That is why the Careers and Enterprise Company (CEC) – the national body for careers education in England – is a proud partner in our collective mission to help every young person find their 'best, next step'. With Talentino, we are helping to support young people with additional needs for the world beyond education and on their career journeys.

Our 'Careers Health Checklist' is one example. The checklist is a straightforward way for settings to identify the steps that will make the most difference to pupils. Best practice is having a senior person take the lead on careers, with support from a link governor and the ambition to take a whole-school approach.

The Gatsby Benchmarks have been used to define and measure the right actions for schools and colleges to take on careers education for 10 years now. So, we can say with confidence that when they are applied effectively, they can be a great driver for enabling all young people to be successful and have a positive career outcome. Where the benchmarks are fully embedded with buy-in across the school or college community, inclusion is the norm and not an add-on.

It is promising to note that when I looked at what's happening on the ground for our recently published 'New & Next' annual report, I found that some of the best careers practice in the country comes from settings which work with pupils with additional needs.

The tailored support for young people in these settings means that they achieve well on the Gatsby Benchmarks (5/6/8 – above the national average) and outperform the mainstream when it comes to workplace experiences and interactions with further and higher education.

Foreword

Encouragingly, we are seeing employers make a difference too. In fact, the more inclusive the recruitment practices, the more young people and businesses benefit.

Many employers who have used careers education to meet and get to know students with additional needs have been better able to recognise their talents and have now identified them as groups they specifically want to bring into their workplaces. This work cannot start early enough.

Working nationally and locally, with young people at the centre of our model and embracing new ideas like reinventing work experience for the 21st century, we are working hard to make sure that improvements in the careers system are durable and sustained.

Increasingly, young people are finding their voice in this system, and feeling the benefits. But there is still a long way to go if we are to achieve that for everyone.

Our commitment to every young person in England is that I will never stop searching for and sharing ways to break down the barriers to success that they face.

This book is one such method. It contains helpful information for careers leaders and employers alike. I'd encourage anyone who is aspirational for the lives of young people to draw from the wisdom and best practise in its pages.

Oli de Botton,
CEO, The Careers and Enterprise Company

Chapter 1
Introduction to SEND and inclusion and early career development

SEND and inclusion and early career development

- Inclusion, what does it mean, what could it mean
- An introduction to young people with SEND or who are vulnerable and/or disadvantaged
- Educational settings for young people with SEND, or who are vulnerable and/or disadvantaged
- Types of barriers to achieving optimal career outcomes
- Guest contributor – Wayne Norrie, CEO of Greenwood Academies Trust

The Big Inclusive SEND Careers Handbook

Introduction
Welcome to the *Big Inclusive SEND Careers Handbook.* And there they are, our first important two words – 'Inclusive' and 'SEND' – side by side. But what is the difference? Did I need to use both or are they interchangeable? Do they mean the same thing? How do I incorporate them into my practice?

At the simplest level, **SEND stands for special educational needs and disabilities**. It is sometimes described as SEN(D) as not all children and young people have disabilities *and* special needs. The term SEND is derived from legislation called the SEND Code of Practice, which was introduced in 2014 to enable a new planning process to move from statements to Education, Health and Care Plans (EHC Plans) for children and young people aged 0–25 years (more of this in Chapter 2). SEND is a term used in education, by local authorities, by families and in career development arenas, but importantly it is *not* a term used in business or by employers who would instead use words such as Diversity. Thereby hangs a tail when it comes to employers understanding (or not) who these young people are.

> ♥ One of the functions of this book I really want you to take on board is better understanding the obvious and less obvious barriers young people with additional needs face. You can be part of the community that improves life outcomes in every aspect – health, mental health, financial wellbeing, quality of life and even longevity. To emphasise this, there will be boxed text, like this one, with the changing lives icon ♥. I make no apology for being evangelical and I promise you will feel the same by the end of the book!

Throughout this book, the language will change to get you used to the myriad of terms and abbreviations. The standard term for me has always been young people with SEND and/or vulnerable and/or disadvantaged. There have been challenges to this, but as you will find, this is not unusual, and everyone needs to listen hard when it is the young person telling us what nomenclature they prefer. There are multiple ways of referring to different groups of young people who experience the widest range of barriers to future career success, and it can feel like a minefield at times. You can find out more about the use and impact of language later in this chapter.

Inclusion, what does it mean, what could it mean
One definition of inclusion is (and I like this as it moves the debate away from special schools versus mainstream to what really matters) **100% of children learning and having needs met in high-quality education 100% of the time.**

Introduction to SEND and Inclusion

Every child, every lesson, every day, every week. Inclusion is aspiration, progression and success for all.

I would urge you to generate discussion and debate in your own environment about what Inclusion means to you and your team. What does it look like when you get it right and conversely what happens when you don't? Think about:

- How is Inclusion interpreted in your education setting?
- What does exclusion look like, formal and informal?
- What could Inclusion look like at its best in your context?

Inclusion is a very interesting, evocative and emotive word. It is often *interpreted* as all children and young people being educated in the same school, usually mainstream. It is nowhere near as simple as this supposedly innocent assumption!

My favourite definition of inclusion in relation to careers is:

Inclusion is about ensuring that *all* young people are prepared for whatever optimum career and life outcome looks like for them – leading a purposeful life that is well supported or being at the highest levels of education or employment and everything in between.

> ♥ I would like inclusion to be defined by all careers practitioners as the practice of identifying and supporting *any* and *every* young person who needs additional support and encouragement in whatever way possible, whether this is defined through a statutory process or plan or by noticing intuitively or via an inclusive career's strategy that a young person just needs a bit more support.

Right now, you might be feeling the enormity of the task and responsibility of ensuring you are doing the very best for all the diverse young people you work with to achieve optimum career outcomes. Feeling out of our depth can prevent us from jumping in and providing more support in case we get it wrong.

> ♥ I promise you, when you have waded through this book, created your checklists, and shared tools and resources, particularly if you eat as many biscuits as I have while writing it (!), you will feel totally compelled to support these young people to achieve *more*, and any feelings of anxiety you had will disappear and be replaced by concrete ambitions.

An introduction to young people with SEND or who are vulnerable and/or disadvantaged

It is not unusual for often well-meaning individuals who are not familiar with SEND and/or disability to focus on the diagnosis – what is 'wrong' with them, what they can't do – instead of focusing on what is possible and increasing the probability of making the possible happen. Personally, I think that comes from a place of anxiety, but focusing on what someone can do always leads to a more positive dialogue. After this conversation, identifying any reasonable adjustments that are required is the time to cover off any conversation around additional needs.

Some of those definitions are enshrined in legislation, for example within the SEND Code of Practice 2014 where four key groups are identified (you can find out more in Chapter 2):

- cognition and learning needs
- communication and interaction needs
- social, emotional and mental health difficulties (SEMH)
- sensory and/or physical needs.

Being inclusive means not stopping at the definitions in the SEND Code of Practice but including other groups, for example young people defined by what is happening in their lives, for example young carers. For some, it is about what isn't happening in their lives and what needs to be in place to thrive, for example young people eligible for free school meals or defined by a local authority as a 'child in need' or identified as a student targeted by Pupil Premium funding.

The term 'vulnerable and disadvantaged' covers a very broad range of young as exemplified by the explanation in the YoungMinds Amplified project including those we haven't mentioned yet:

Young people from low-income families • Children with experience of the justice system • Young people who have been sexually abused and/or exploited • Substance misusing young people • Lesbian, gay, bisexual young people • Trans young people • Young people who have experienced abuse/neglect in any form • Black, Asian and minority ethnic (BAME) • Children with refugee and asylum seeker status • Children and young people who have experienced domestic violence in the home • Children and young people whose parents are affected by drug/alcohol abuse • Children and young people who have experienced loss/bereavement • Young people whose parents are affected by mental health issues • Children and young people whose parents are in prison • Teenage parents.

Introduction to SEND and Inclusion

A disability might be acquired too, for example an acquired injury/brain injury; they may have experienced trauma at birth (see Chapter 7 and Hardeep Rai's guest contribution); have been premature or have foetal alcohol syndrome; or have a genetic or chromosomal aspect, e.g. Down's syndrome.

Neurodiversity, which is a very broad term and can include, for example autism, ADHD, Tourette's, and specific learning difficulties such as dyslexia, dyspraxia and dyscalculia, is a specific group of additional needs, and a young person may often be neurodiverse in conjunction with having other additional (special) needs. One in 100 are autistic with around 16% in employment.

> ♥ Careers professionals need to understand the widest range of groups of young people who are impeded from achieving their optimum career outcome so they can be supported to navigate the barriers they face, raise their aspirations and co-create pathways that enable them to lead happy and successful lives where they flourish in every way with purpose.

It's worth highlighting early on in our relationship dear reader that language is a very powerful enabler in our SEND and inclusion world, *but* it can equally be divisive and offensive and play a part in denying opportunities to young people with additional needs. The term 'additional needs' can be helpful when considering different groups.

It is important to remember that many young people with special needs may have a dominant need, but it would not be unusual to have other needs which could be physical, behavioural, speech and language, social, emotional, medical, health or mental health among others.

Educational settings and young people with SEND

All educational settings, including schools, special schools, mainstream schools, units within mainstream, SEMH schools (also called special schools), alternative provisions (APs), pupil referral units (PRUs), residential schools and colleges, independent special schools (both day and residential), virtual schools, hospital schools, home education, sixth-form college, further education (FE) colleges, and universities, will have learners with SEND/additional needs. Some young people may not be at school and waiting for a place too.

In January 2024, there were 1.61 million children and young people with SEND; around 16% of students in mainstream schools are defined as having SEND, which is sometimes a surprise. But don't forget to extend your thinking outside of those defined via the SEND Code of Practice to those vulnerable and disadvantaged groups too.

Recognise as well that there will also be learners with undiagnosed special needs. For example, girls have been historically underdiagnosed with regard to autism and have developed effective masking techniques.

Many young people continue to be impacted by their experiences during the Covid pandemic such as experiencing heightened anxiety, depression, developmental setbacks, speech and language challenges, mental health issues, physical health issues such as asthma, and low levels of school attendance.

The SEND Reforms have the potential to impact career outcomes both negatively and positively. Although nothing has been confirmed or firmed up and is still being consulted on, there are some suppositions which can be drawn, such as the impact around 'inclusion' in mainstream – meaning that more young people with a higher level of additional needs will be placed in mainstream schools, which doesn't necessarily mean inclusion in the classroom, it might be a separate unit. It doesn't mean the school staff are trained or confident or the school is sufficiently funded to meet the young person's needs. It has the potential for more exclusions to take place and the negative impact that has. Both main political parties support more inclusion in mainstream schools and my experience is that this is already happening.

The impact of having special/additional needs is that young people can be:

- less likely to achieve qualifications
- more likely to be NEET (not in education, employment or training)
- more likely to suffer from mental health problems
- more likely to be represented in the homeless community
- more likely to be represented in the criminal justice system
- many experience **disadvantages** due to their special needs.

Types of barriers to achieving optimal career outcomes

For young people with SEND or who are vulnerable or disadvantaged, there are multiple barriers to achieving optimum career outcomes – some are obvious and some are more subtle. Barriers could include:

- lack of understanding about *who* these young people are and what their backgrounds look like
- not achieving qualifications at the usual milestones, which means opportunities cannot be pursued
- achieving qualifications which employers don't understand, particularly the case for those working below Level 2/GCSEs
- not having access to qualified careers advisers who understand their additional needs and what they *can* do

Introduction to SEND and Inclusion

- missing vital signs that a young person might need more support to engage in career development activities
- lack of opportunities such as supported training and employment options for school leavers
- FE college courses which repeat content and do not enable a young person to secure employment
- a lack of support such as trained job coaches available locally
- transport policies which don't support employment such as providing free passes (great), but they can't be used until after 9 am when the working day has already started
- funding like benefits which are cut when a young person takes up an opportunity but aren't reinstated if the opportunity breaks down making a family reticent to support the young person to train or work in the first place
- application processes which are difficult to navigate due to specific personal barriers.

Summary of key points

This is a tough section if you are not familiar with special needs/SEND and the debates around inclusion, so well done for getting to this page! You have been given a broad description of the wide range of learners you may be working with and the factors that could impede their potential destinations – some personal, some systemic. You have considered the widest range of young people who you need to include despite the legal definition being specific to SEND and in relation to achieving an EHC Plan. They all need us all to be inclusive. You have considered what gets in the way of potential career success, looking at external factors and those that sit within all of us, unconscious biases, which is a tough one. Tackling the different facets of inclusion to the ground, what it means in your context and what could it mean in every educational setting.

Resources

https://assets.publishing.service.gov.uk/media/63ff39d28fa8f527fb67cb06/SEND_and_alternative_provision_improvement_plan.pdf

www.gov.uk/government/publications/dedicated-schools-grant-very-high-deficit-intervention

♥ If you are feeling buried under the weight of the task, I urge you to read Wayne Norrie's inspirational story, coming up next. And I promise you, this book and your work are totally worth the time and consideration and you *can* change lives.

GUEST CONTRIBUTOR – WAYNE NORRIE, CEO OF GREENWOOD ACADEMIES TRUST

A personal story of inclusion. Our first guest contributor is Wayne Norrie, the CEO of Greenwood Academies Trust (GAT) with 37 schools, serving the most deprived communities in the East Midlands. He manifests inclusion in everything he does and always has. His childhood was tough; he understands inclusion (or the lack of it) from the inside out. His contribution is taken from an interview he did at the time of writing with Schools Week and if you don't know him, you should reach out. Wayne is truly inspirational. He puts his learners first before anything or any external body. Wayne Norrie says he's not accountable to the Department for Education or Ofsted but only to the children he serves.

I first met Wayne when he described his 'journey' at the GAT SEND Conference. He talked about leaving primary school not being able to read or write, 'slipping through the net'. His head teacher at his senior school told him he would amount to nothing, so imagine their surprise when he turned up as an HMI Schools Inspector a few years later! He emphasised the importance of teachers teaching everyone in their classroom, not hiving off (excluding) children to be taught elsewhere in school. He said they are paid to teach all the class, not 75% of it. Inclusion means inclusion for all children for Wayne.

His childhood was tough, his education patchy, his initial results poor and yet he casts no blame on his parents – or those of GAT's children facing similar challenges. 'Parents do the best job they know how'. His mum was a pit wagers' clerk. His dad and grandad were both miners, who never spoke to each other again after the latter chose not to strike. After the pits closed, their world 'crumbled around them'.

'I know what it's like to wake up and see your own breath, and for your mum to start buying tinned food in September, so you could have a half-decent Christmas'.

The children-first ethos has improved Progress 8 scores significantly since he took over and now match the national average. Inclusion means just that; exclusions are rare and only after everything else has been considered. The proportion of 'good' and 'outstanding' schools has risen from 57% to 84%.

Wayne says knowing 'what makes kids tick' in the communities where the trust works. He enables his schools to roll out curriculums 'built out from the needs of their community. It takes much longer to do that, but I do it properly'. He compares being a MAT (multi-academy trust) chief to 'changing a car engine while going at 90 mph down the M1. I must keep these schools running, but at the same time, things are so broken in so many communities'.

Ingoldmells Academy, near Skegness's sprawling caravan parks, is a GAT school and because so many parents rely on seasonal work, some of its pupils live in caravans nine months a year and bed and breakfasts the other three (as caravan parks are not open year-round). School staff pick up the pupils from their accommodations in those three months. 'Otherwise, they might not come back', says Wayne. Inclusion in action.

At 14, Wayne was caught joyriding by a police officer who drank in the same miner's welfare club as his dad. He took Wayne home, but such was his dad's fury that Wayne 'wished he'd put me in a cell'. When Wayne failed all his GCSEs, his dad had a 'stroke of genius' by getting him a gruelling job as a hod carrier, carrying bricks up and down scaffolding. 'It knocked all the cockiness out of me. I begged him to send me back to school'.

He retook his exams, and while doing community volunteering at Bulwell's Rufford Junior School, 'caught the teaching bug'. Despite failing GCSE maths three times, he now runs a trust with a £150 million budget.

He says inclusion is 'at the heart' of GAT's ethos. He takes on a greater share of children with challenging needs. Wayne says more than half of GAT's pupils are on free school meals, which is a huge rise from the 34% last year.

To prevent off-rolling, Wayne believes schools should be made to 'carry a proportion' of excluded pupils' eventual grades. He commits to spending three days a week in GAT's schools, arguing it is 'very easy as a CEO to get detached from those children you serve'.

Wayne also helps 'struggling' MATs. He was brought in by the DfE as the interim chief executive of the four-school Evolve trust in 2022 after Ofsted found special needs pupils at its Harlow Academy, in Nottinghamshire, were 'at imminent risk of harm'.

I believe it is his authenticity, refusal to accept anything but the best for his children, his personal experience and standing behind what he thinks inclusion looks like that all come together to illuminate this man; his light just shines. It is a privilege to know you, Wayne. Thank you for sharing your story of inclusion.

My little checklist – Top tips to improve your understanding of SEND and inclusion

Top tips to improve your understanding of SEND and inclusion	How you can improve your understanding of SEND and inclusion	Planned action	Tick action completed
How can I ensure my colleagues understand the term SEND and where it comes from?	Make yourself familiar with the SEND Code of Practice and keep up-to-date with the SEND Reforms.		
What do I think inclusion means?	Become familiar with diverse reference sources to form your own view of inclusion and how it relates to your work.		
Which Career SEND Group(s) are my learners in?	Appreciate you may have learners in both groups and will need to create a careers strategy that reflects this.		
What are the optimum career outcomes for my learners currently?	Use your destinations data to establish what the optimum outcomes are for learners *now*.		
What *could* the optimum career outcomes be for my learners in the future?	Use the list on page 33 to correlate what your learners *could* access in terms of other career outcome possibilities. At this stage don't think about local supply and demand issues.		
Could I articulate the key barriers to achieving optimum career outcomes?	Talk to your key stakeholder groups – SENCO, parents/carers and families, staff/employers, careers advisers/careers leaders, FE – and establish a shortlist.		
How can I use the PALs activities to raise the aspirations of my learners?	Be strategic and triangulate data from EHC Plans, young people directly, the careers team, potential career outcomes on offer locally, local employers and FE, and be more targeted about organising PALs related activities.		
How can I use #sameanddifferent to enhance the delivery of careers?	Remember the three tenets – aspects that are the same as anyone else without SEND leaving school, same and different aspects which are the same but need to be delivered differently and different aspects. You can use aspects of your own too.		
What ideas can I take from the case study and integrate into my practice?	The case studies in this chapter are videos which you could use with employers and other stakeholders, especially employers, to generate discussion around diversity.		
What do I need to think about in terms of my practice when considering the 'achieving change/future focus' commentary?	Try to keep in front, use social media more, follow careers leaders and careers hubs on LinkedIn, check the DfE website for updates, use the Resource Directory on the CEC website. Create a timetable of upcoming changes.		
Consider your whole school in inclusive teaching practices	Ensure your careers practice reflects this.		

Introduction to SEND and Inclusion

Anxiety around Difference and Diversity and the impact on career outcomes

- Social and medical models of disability
- Where does anxiety come from?
- Unconscious bias and the implications for outcomes
- Stereotypes
- Ableism
- Employer confidence
- The importance of language and communication
- The impact of treating those with additional needs less favourably on outcomes
- Building our confidence and reducing anxiety around Diversity
- Guest contributor – Nana Marfo, founder of Unique Abilities

Introduction

The anxiety that exists around differently abled people has a major impact on the possibility of young people achieving optimal career outcomes whatever that looks like for them. There are multiple reasons why this anxiety exists but no argument that any should persist.

♥ Whatever your standpoint, whether you are an economist, an ethicist, a careers leader or an employer looking to benefit from a diverse workforce, it makes absolute sense to include all people of all abilities to ensure they benefit from a world that welcomes them into every corner of society and work*ing* is central to this. I spell work*ing* like this because for some people it is about using work-related skills and benefiting from the positive feelings gained by being in a working environment as opposed to travelling independently and working full time.

Social and medical models of disability

The **medical model of disability** was the original 'lens' through which disability was viewed. It:

- looks at a person's impairment first and focusing on the impairment as the reason they are not able to participate fully in society (Example: 'they can't read that newspaper because they are blind')
- focuses on the impairment and what can be done to 'fix' the disabled person or provide special services for them as an individual
- focuses on the individual as the problem rather than looking more widely at society enabling all people.

The **social model of disability** was created by disabled people themselves. It:

- looks at the **barriers erected by society** in terms of disabled people being able to participate fully in day-to-day life
- seeks to remove unnecessary barriers which prevent disabled people from participating in society, accessing work and living independently
- recognises that attitudes towards disabled people create unnecessary barriers to inclusion barriers ranging from prejudice and stereotyping to unnecessary inflexible organisational practices and procedures and seeing disabled people as objects of pity/charity
- understands a person does not 'have' a disability – disability is something a person experiences. (This is an interesting notion when it comes to thinking about language, see page 15.)

However, there are occasions when both models overlap. For example, if someone needs a reasonable adjustment made at work or in education, you could argue that the medical model which talks about 'fixing' the person or providing special services is the same thing. However, the intention behind a reasonable adjustment is different, as it is about ensuring everyone can fully participate in society.

> ♥ For young people with SEND/additional needs or who are vulnerable and/or disadvantaged, it is about what they *can* do, not what they can't. Focus on the career possibilities and what support needs to be put in place to achieve career aspirations. Whole of society, all people.

Where does anxiety come from?

Anxiety around difference can come from multiple sources, such as being more comfortable around 'people like me' and the converse; being worried about doing or saying the wrong thing, so not engaging at all; believing people who have different needs are someone else's responsibilities and are somehow hived off from people without apparent additional needs; or applying a kind of hierarchy to different disabilities, for example physical disabilities are somehow more acceptable than those related to mental health. In some cultures, disability is seen as a punishment for wrongdoing of some kind. None of these explanations is an excuse for a lack of engagement or support, but acknowledging how impactful these anxieties can be is important, and improved information sharing and education can make a big dent in these anxieties.

Unconscious bias and the implications for outcomes

One of the most significant barriers is 'unconscious biases', which are formed by our experiences, our socialisation and our education. Collectively they create unintentional mental associations which determine our response to a person/situation and can include a bias which consciously we would not believe ourselves to have. We may truly believe ourselves to have the most altruistic beliefs, but our unconscious biases would contradict this.

Unconscious biases might include gender, race, religion, disability, sexuality, ageism (in our case young people), names, halo/horns and many others. These biases operate at a subconscious level and can run contrary to our conscious beliefs. These biases shape and mould our behaviours, and in acknowledging them, doing some deliberate work to firstly understand them and secondly to try and overrule them, is paramount. There are tools that can help us understand more about our personal biases.

> ♥ When you are in a situation where your unconscious bias could work against a young person (and you won't consciously know it is!) adopt a rule of thumb in which you are taking multiple factors into account, considering multiple views, applying multiple data points, creating standardised processes and anonymising personal data. Lastly, set up a bias challenge chum set; challenge each other if you see biases creeping in.

Stereotypes

Stereotypes are a way of describing groups as having (usually) negative characteristics and come from (apparently) a basic human need to categorise or make things simpler to explain in a world that is more complicated than most can deal with and is 'grounded in the observations of everyday life' (Alice Eagly). These groups will often consist of people with whom most have no relationships or prior knowledge. Stereotypes in our career world may be around age (young people are lazy); gender (boys are better at maths than girls); disability (they can't . . .). Ensuring that you challenge your own practices and outcomes around learners who belong to diverse groups will help you resist negative stereotyping.

Ableism

According to SENSE UK, **ableism** is a word for:

> unfairly favouring non-disabled people. Ableism means prioritising the needs of non-disabled people. In an ableist society, it's assumed that the "normal" way to live is as a non-disabled person. It is ableist to believe that non-disabled people are more valuable to society than disabled people.

Ableism can be overt, for example not ensuring that communication methods embrace all types of communication needs; or more covert, for example, choosing an inaccessible meeting room which could preclude some people from attending. At the launch of Disability Confident, the keynote speaker was a wheelchair user, but the lectern was on a platform with no ramp. To avoid being ableist or as some disabled people prefer, disablist, we need to ensure all our work and methods of work are inclusive.

Employer confidence

The largest group that could make a huge dent in achieving economic and societal inclusion is, of course, employers. However, employers are people and need to raise their confidence. It has been recognised that although there is some good work going on within the (currently) 22,000 'disability confident employers', many continue to lack the confidence to take their work further. Professor Kim Hoque carried out research demonstrating that disability confident employers had minimal impact on employing disabled people. He created the Disability Employment Charter, which more than over 200 organisations have signed. Lord Shinkwin said in May 2024:

> of the 129,000 jobs listed on the DWP's Find a Job service, only 0.51% are fully remote and just 2.75% are listed as being hybrid remote? As Professor Hoque said when he gave evidence to the Work and Pensions Select Committee in the other place in June 2024: "The idea that there are all of these working from home opportunities out there for disabled people . . . is just a complete myth".
>
> *(www.parallelparliament.co.uk/lord/lord-shinkwin/debate/2024-05-16/lords/lords-chamber/people-with-disabilities-access-to-services)*

At the time of this writing, there was a plan to provide training through the Careers and Enterprise Company in partnership with BASE (British Association of Supported Employment) to build their confidence with a new programme of training – Disability Confidence in Action – as part of their Employment for All Mission.

The importance of language and communication

Language and methods of communication can feel like a minefield, but following a few simple principles can prove our best ally. Many people, and I suspect employers are a significant group here, are worried about using the wrong words, disrespecting people, not being politically correct (is that a thing anymore?) or causing offence.

Language and communication can be considered through simple principles. Feel more confident about engaging with a diverse range of individuals because it is the lack of engagement that can lead to poor outcomes. You can find out more at Scope (www.scope.org.uk/about-us/house-style-guide/).

Try not to think about hard and fast rules. What is appropriate one week might change. The terms around autism are a great example. Autism, autistic spectrum and neurodiverse are all terms that are used. Charities are always great references; try to keep up to date with the latest thinking (www.ambitiousaboutautism.org.uk/information-about-autism/understanding-autism/how-to-talk-about-autism).

The whole debate around person or disability first can generate quite a discussion! The two terms 'SEND student' and 'student with SEND' have two different implications. Putting 'SEND' first places the additional need before the person and therefore defines them first and foremost as having special needs. The word 'person' coming first defines their needs second. Individuals with special needs may say their additional need is part of their identity, as someone I worked with told me 'My autism is not like my Apple Watch which I take off at night and out on in the morning, it is always part of me'. I think this debate could be a useful one for your team.

Language evolves fast and *individuals will have preferences themselves* which may not be what you thought was appropriate. I was listening to four autistic adults describing what they would like to be called and there were four different terms. A friend of mine who has MS describes herself as a 'crip' which she was happy with, but her husband wasn't. Check out https://geniuswithin.org/what-is-neurodiversity/autism/. Ask your students what they would prefer.

There are some terms that are definite no-no's such as handicapped, crippled, spastic, mental, normal. Government advice on language can be found at www.gov.uk/government/publications/inclusive-communication/inclusive-language-words-to-use-and-avoid-when-writing-about-disability.

Consider all groups' communication needs when planning such as adjustments for hearing or visual impairments; visual cues like symbols, and sensory needs such as dimming the external sensory environment or providing fidgets. Also ensure physical access is comfortable; take breaks; provide clear, unambiguous content;

enable space to move around in between seated areas; consider duration; and so on.

The impact on outcomes of treating those with additional needs less favourably

I have heard countless times employers who are key to offering opportunities talk about the reasons they don't engage with a more diverse range of young people, the reasons for which could include some of the attitudes described in the last few sections.

There is absolutely no doubt this a negative impact on outcomes. If you look at any group that would be defined as diverse, the range of educational and employment outcomes is not parous with their peers who would not be considered to have additional needs. Two examples bear this out:

- Of the adults with learning difficulties, 86% want to work and 4.7% have a job (this has increased from 65% 10 years ago) so the impact of career development at school is working. The employment rate of disabled people is around 52% against 86% for non-disabled people.
- The Buckland Review 2024 identified that:

    Autistic people face the largest pay gap of all disability groups, receiving a third less than non-disabled people on average. Autistic graduates are twice as likely to be unemployed after 15 months as non-disabled graduates, with only 36% finding full time work in this period. Autistic graduates are most likely to be overqualified for the job they have, most likely to be on zero-hours contracts, least likely to be in a permanent role.

♥ If bias generates stigma, exclusion and/or discrimination, whether overt or covert, it is a fair assumption that it will contribute to a negative impact on outcomes. This needs to be challenged and addressed. I have seen employers unfold and become creative and committed to more diverse groups of young people when their anxieties have dissipated through education, inclusion and encouragement. Let's not judge but seek to understand why these anxieties exist and work to dissolve them.

Building our confidence and reducing our anxiety around diversity

We can all build and increase our and others' confidence around diversity by taking some simple steps:

Introduction to SEND and Inclusion

- Do some homework about the different groups your students will come from, such as those with special needs (learning difficulties, physical/mobility challenges, mental health issues, anxiety, neurodiversity, ADHD, speech and language difficulties, behavioural challenges, socio-economic factors, adverse childhood experiences [ACEs]). Don't worry if you are not familiar with these terms, Chapter 3 is about who young people with SEND are. Then move towards looking at optimal career outcomes and away from the diagnoses.
- Try to uncover your unconscious biases and check your planning and decisions to make sure they are inclusive.
- Reframe the diagnosis to help you identify reasonable adjustments that can be made in your careers practice and in others' (e.g. employers) work experience and work insights.
- Use the many charities that focus on different groups and keep yourself up to date on language and ideas.
- Ensure that you consider each individual child/young person and don't assume they don't have an additional need or need for additional support because they 'don't look like it'.
- Help other stakeholders like employers to become more inclusive. Your confidence will build theirs!

Summary of key points

In many ways, this is a difficult chapter to think through. However, there is no doubt we all have to reduce our anxiety around diversity and build our confidence no matter how clumsy our initial attempts might be. It is vital to our young people that we do this to enable them to have the highest probability of not becoming statistics that demonstrate a gap between them and their peers.

Knowing where anxiety comes from, challenging our biases, appreciating the part that language and communication methods play and building our own competence are really helpful.

Understanding that reducing the anxiety of ourselves and the stakeholders around us and building our collective confidence makes everyone more compelled to engage authentically and respectfully for the benefit of millions, yes millions of young people. As I said at the beginning, whether you are an economist or ethicist or simply believe in doing the right thing, conquering anxiety is a very powerful enabler.

💻 Resources

A model for diverse careers guidance, simple tips: www.linkedin.com/advice/0/how-can-you-work-more-effectively-diverse-populations

Scope: www.scope.org.uk/about-us/social-model-of-disability/

There is a wide range of reference reading material from the CDI's Library of resources concerning Equality, Diversity and Inclusion. See www.thecdi.net/resources/cdi-resources/diversity-resources

A series of short films portraying disability: https://shortfilmsmatter.com/subject/disability

Crip Camp:A Disability Revolution: www.netflix.com/gb/title/81001496

Introduction to SEND and Inclusion

 GUEST CONTRIBUTOR – NANA MARFO, DISABILITY ACTIVIST AND FOUNDER OF UNIQUE ABILITIES

Nana Marfo has been a friend for a few years now. I love his perspective on his disability which he reframes as 'unique abilities' and has a consultancy by the same name. His contribution describes his life and how he has used his experiences from early on to change the mindsets and understanding of others around diversity. Thank you, Nana.

My name is Nana Marfo, and I am an advocate for improving the rights of individuals with disabilities. While society likes to use the term 'disability', I prefer to view this as a unique ability. Why should it be seen as a disadvantage? Society may think that disabled people are losing the battle of living a normal life, but we are living our best life, just in a unique manner.

Throughout my life, I have seen first-hand how individuals with disabilities are treated differently, often without proper justification. Do not get me wrong, I have faced more adversity than most and I have had to show remarkable resilience. At birth, I was born into an incubator needing a tracheotomy which I still have and so far, have had over 210 operations in my life. Surely the ability to take on, and beat, these challenges should be viewed as a unique ability.

To fully illustrate why I am so passionate about reform, I need not look past my own experiences. I was placed at a school for individuals with Special Educational Needs (SEN), despite my mother's protests. Now, the objection to this may not seem obvious at first glance but becomes crystal clear when the impact of my condition is examined. Notably, while I experienced speaking and breathing difficulties, my brain capacity was not impacted. As a result, it was inappropriate for me to be placed within a SEN school. For me, this illustrated that disabilities are often viewed together as a collective, despite the huge differentiations within varying conditions. Even then, during primary school, I could see that change was needed.

Very few of my peers understood my disability and I ended up getting excluded after getting into a couple of fights. I wanted my peers to look past my disability and, in doing so, I ended up trying to be the class clown.

It took me a long time to accept and understand my condition. I feel like I went through World War III with my medical treatment as a child. Aside from the surgeries, I also had lots of skin grafting and I was in and out of Great Ormond Street every three to six months for speech therapy and check-ups. Eventually, I came to realise that there was light at the end of the tunnel. At the end of the day, life can be hard, but this was not going to stop me from living my life to the fullest, alongside my unique ability.

Following education, I worked in the civil service for nine years. While this built up my confidence, it again became clear that I had to face complex challenges that were not presented to many of my peers. I needed reasonable adjustments that were not being accepted. Eventually I had to go to a tribunal to get extra rest days to compensate for additional health challenges. It was at this point that I first realised the power advocacy can have in making a difference. I wanted to be the voice that could help others overcome the challenges that I had to fight alone.

Previously, members of the department had even mocked me on a national platform by comparing my voice to that of Darth Vader. This injustice, however, only provided further motivation for me to become a voice for others.

I began to voice my frustrations and gradually I gained momentum. More and more people recognised that this was not an isolated issue and stretched across several sectors. I received contact from BBC London and was nominated for a national diversity award. I now try to push for reform through my freelance work with Scope and through writing articles for *The Independent*.

I created Unique Abilities to give a voice to people with different disabilities and I encourage people to be themselves without repercussions. I strive towards ending the stigma around disabilities and instead celebrate the ways in which we are all unique. Despite my individual efforts, there needs to be structural reform. The welfare system needs to move beyond a tick-box exercise. Aside from the degrading format, it can be extremely difficult to quantify impact, and this should not result in the withdrawal of support. Instead, more time needs to be spent speaking to people rather than just completing surveys.

It was difficult growing up feeling like the duality of my identity was a massive taboo (even among people of the same ethnicity) due to society's lack of understanding about disability and the far-reaching impacts of ableism. But it opened my eyes to the importance of doing what I do today.

I've learnt that there is an incredible lack of understanding from workplace policy, law enforcement, local authorities and more – all of which still have yet to figure out how to fairly work with and represent black disabled people.

Since 2021, I have been continuing my work, delivered a TED talk and am continuing my advocacy work locally and nationally. If Black Lives Matter, disabled black lives should too. The sooner society wakes up to that, the more freedom we'll all be able to enjoy like everyone else.

My little checklist – Top tips to improve your understanding of anxiety around diversity

Top tips to improve anxiety around Diversity	How to improve anxiety around Diversity	Planned action	Tick action completed
Be honest with yourself and identify if you have any anxiety around difference and where that might come from	Create a little action for yourself concerning how you will improve your confidence around diversity. You don't need to share it if you don't want to.		
What is the medical model of disability?	Think about the elements and your practice. Establish if you need to adapt your practice in any way.		
What is the social model of disability?	Think about the elements and your practice. Establish if you need to adapt your practice in any way.		
Where and how do the two models overlap?	Identify ways to integrate the elements respectfully into your practice.		
Think about your own unconscious biases	If you feel you may have bias, maybe use some tools to establish this.		
Analyse the career journeys of current students with different profiles	Are their career journeys the same but potentially delivered differently with reasonable adjustments or are there unexplained differences?		
Analyse the career destinations of past students with different profiles	Are their career destinations parous or are their unexplained differences?		
Identify the language and communication methods used every day around diverse groups of students	Decide if the language and communication methods are the optimum methods. Make changes, if necessary; signpost too if helpful to other staff.		
Notice how employers are talking to you about diversity	Offer a short training session to employers about language and the impact of language.		
Utilise the CDI library of resources to help inform your practice	Share new initiatives with other staff and your team to lead the way.		
Find out if your organisation has an inclusion strategy and if it references the content expressed in this chapter	If it doesn't, approach the leadership team or lead an initiative yourself that seeks to improve confidence and commitment to success around diversity.		

Chapter 2
Who *are* young people with SEND?

- The legal framework surrounding SEND – SEND Code of Practice
- Short description of the characteristics of the SEND groups
- Education, Health and Care Plans
- Optimum career outcomes
- Defining the two career SEND groups – Career SEND Group One and Career SEND Group Two
- Intersectionality between the two career SEND groups
- Where do vulnerable and disadvantaged young people meet SEND?
- Guest contributor – Dan Pikett, Founder of Spatial Careers

Introduction

One of the key reasons, in my opinion, for poor outcomes for many young people with SEND/additional needs is the anxiety which many people have who do not understand who these young people are and want to avoid offending them or saying and/or doing the wrong thing. This can result in a lack of engagement with key stakeholders like employers, careers leaders and careers advisers, which means opportunities are lost. Everyone misses out. Teacher training often has very little content around SEND and inclusion, although there are plans to improve this. My son had half a day on SEND during his one-year PGCE; happily, he was based in a special school, though. Research shows that staff in mainstream schools can be apprehensive about teaching young people with SEND. The start of the conversation when it comes to early career development should focus on what someone *can* do, not what they can't. We get to this by understanding who they *are*.

> ♥ If you prefer speed reading, this is *not* the chapter to do it! Understanding who these young people are will be the single most important aspect of improving outcomes! More biscuits please!

The legal framework surrounding SEND – SEND Code of Practice

The legal definition of a young person with SEND is enshrined in the **SEND Code of Practice,** which was created in 2014 and covered in Chapter 1.

Specifically, the SEND Code of Practice states:

> **A child or young person has SEN[D] if they have a learning difficulty or disability which calls for special educational provision to be made for him or her.** A child of compulsory school age or a young person has a learning difficulty or disability if he or she has a disability which prevents or hinders him or her from making use of facilities of a kind generally provided for others of the same age in mainstream schools or mainstream post-16 institutions.

There are four areas of need and support:

> **Communication and interaction** – Speech, language and communication needs; those with autistic spectrum disorder (ASD; neurodiverse)
> **Cognition and learning** – Specific learning difficulty, moderate or severe difficulty, or profound and multiple learning difficulty (PMLD)
> **Social, emotional, and mental health (SEMH) difficulties/behaviour sensory**

Physical needs, including visual impairment, hearing impairment, multi-sensory impairment, physical disability, Down's syndrome, chromosomal and genetic disorders

> ♥ Although I have reiterated the notion of focusing on what someone can do, not what they can't, I am including a set of descriptors so you have a fuller explanation of different special needs. Remember, it is not always about a single need. Often, a young person can experience multiple additional needs, for example have a learning difficulty and speech and language challenges as well as mental health challenges. There may be a dominant need, but as with all young people, a holistic approach needs to be taken.

It is worth saying, too, that young people in either Career SEND Group often have more than one additional need. For example, they may have a dominant special

Who *are* young people with SEND?

need, such as learning difficulties, but they might have behavioural issues, speech and language needs, be autistic, have medical or health needs, face challenges because of their socio-economic background, or be a looked after child/care experienced. They may have experienced an adverse childhood experience (ACE) and have a physical disability or mental health and anxiety challenges. It would be very rare for a child or young person with special needs and/or disabilities to have just one aspect of their special needs.

Short descriptions of the characteristics of different SEND groups

Although I want us to focus on what young people CAN do, there is a place for a conversation about what gets in the way and the barriers that are faced to securing their optimal career/life outcomes. That conversation comes into play when identifying ways to tackle barriers and create reasonable adjustments to ensure full participation.

I have taken information from expert sources including Mencap, The Genius Within, The British Dyslexia Association, NHS, MIND and recommended definitions of SEND for the purposes of completing the recent Census. The SEND Code of Practice cites four groups:

- **Communication and interaction** – *Speech, language and communication needs, Autistic Spectrum Disorder (ASD, neurodiverse)*
- **Cognition and learning** – *Specific learning difficulty, moderate or severe learning difficulty or profound and multiple learning difficulty (PMLD)*
- **Social, emotional, and mental health difficulties (SEMH)/ behaviour sensory**
- **Physical needs**, *including visual impairment, hearing impairment, multi-sensory impairment, physical disabilities*

Please remember that many young people with special needs will have more than one dimension of need, impacting in different ways. Some additional needs might be transitory – for example, the exceptionally high number of young people with anxiety following Covid are treatable assuming services are available. CAMHS (children and adult mental health services), for example, is currently overstretched.

We are starting with Mencap which helpfully describes the difference between a learning disability and a learning difficulty.

Learning disabilities have an impact on intellectual ability and are permanent. They might be moderate, severe or profound determining the extent of support needed and the level of independence expected. Learning disabilities might exist on their own or in conjunction with another condition such as autism. Around 50% of autistic people will have a learning disability too. Other conditions where people may have learning disabilities include cerebral palsy (around 45%) and global developmental delay or an acquired brain injury. Chromosomal disorders can impact differently for individuals – for example, Down's syndrome. The Down's Syndrome Association UK talks about young people having their own personalities, likes and dislikes, and things that make them who they are – like everyone, with different levels of learning disabilities, support needs and potential for employment. There are some great role models, children's TV presenters, TV actors, Gucci models, airline staff – think beyond the obvious!

Learning disabilities exist at different levels described as 'Moderate (MLD)', 'Severe (SLD)' or 'Profound and multiple (PMLD)'.

Young people with moderate learning disabilities achieve at a lower level than their peers of a similar age in the core subjects because of their intellectual learning disability. They may be educated in special schools or in mainstream and there is more of a push for this currently. Many young people who have been excluded are often found to have special needs that have not been diagnosed and may 'belong' to this group. These young people may also experience speech and language delay, low self-esteem, low levels of concentration and under-developed social skills. Effective early career development programmes with personal and social development and employability skills development elements can make a positive impact on the level of these skills although they do not raise someone's inherent intellectual ability. Positive optimal career outcomes, including full-time employment, for this group is totally possible.

Young people with severe learning disabilities will have significant intellectual or cognitive impairments. These young people will need a higher level of support than those with moderate learning difficulties. They may also have difficulties in mobility and coordination, communication and perception and the acquisition of self-help skills. Learners with severe learning difficulties will need support across the curriculum. They may require teaching around independence and social skills. Symbol language and sign language could be used to supplement communication and many will be able to communicate verbally with simple conversations. Levels of support required will vary. They may have additional needs they may be Autistic, have a sensory impairment such as visual or hearing, difficulties with appropriate social interaction and understanding, associated challenging behaviours, a lack of awareness around risk and personal risk, and be travel dependent. Part-time/supported employment is possible for many.

Young people with PMLD – Profound & Multiple Learning Disabilities – have profound and multiple learning difficulties and have complex learning needs. In addition to very severe learning disabilities, these young people may have other significant disabilities, such as physical disabilities, sensory impairment or a severe medical condition. Learners require a high level of support and will have needs that may require many services to be involved, and their progression will follow a pathway of small but very important steps. They need helpers for the majority / all needs including personal care, very little awareness of risk. They are likely to need sensory stimulation and a curriculum broken down into very small steps. Some learners communicate by gesture, eye pointing or symbols, while others by very simple language. Progress is identified through the Engagement Model. These young people would follow the third 'sensory pathway' within the Career SEND Group One Group.

It is important to stress that in the same way that people without special/additional needs are individuals, so are young people with special needs with strengths and different needs so please don't think of defining them in a single way. All of us are individuals.

Learning difficulties are not the same as learning disabilities as they do not impact a person's intellectual capability. A person with a learning disability could also have a learning difficulty though. They are sometimes described in education as SPLD – Specific Learning Difficulties – and include:

- **Dyspraxia** – 'affects fine motor coordination in children and adults'
- **Dyscalculia** – a 'specific and persistent difficulty in understanding numbers resulting in difficulties with maths and happens across all ages and levels of education'
- **Dyslexia** – 'primarily affects reading and writing skills, information processing, remembering information they see and hear which can affect the acquisition of literacy skills and other skills like organisational'. It can be different for everyone.
- **Dysgraphia** – it is a neurological condition in which someone has difficulty turning their thoughts into written language.

Neurodiversity

'Genius Within' identifies neurodiversity as 'the concept that all humans vary in terms of our neurocognitive ability. Everyone has both talents and things they struggle with. However, for some people the variation between those strengths and challenges is more pronounced, which can bring advantage but can also be disabling. Neurodivergent people tend to find some things very easy and other things incredibly hard. This usually leads to an inconsistent performance at school or work.' They identify *neurominorities* as follows:

Autism and ASD (autistic spectrum disorder) – 'Autism affects the way a person experiences their environment and influences the way they communicate. Autistic people often experience their senses more intensely than others meaning the world can feel overwhelming at times. There are many skills associated with Autism such as honesty and directness, attention to detail, an ability to find or create patterns, processing information and memory'. Note that the term Asperger's syndrome is no longer acceptable. An autistic person may have learning disabilities and/or other additional needs.

ADHD – attention deficit hyperactivity disorder (ADHD) – affects behaviour and can cause restlessness, acting on impulse and difficulty in concentrating, often starting in childhood and continuing into adulthood. Having ADHD means you could experience other challenges including anxiety, depression, conduct disorder (persistent patterns of antisocial, aggressive or defiant behaviour), substance abuse or sleep problems.

SEMH – Social, Emotional and Mental Health (SEMH) This is the third group defined within the SEND Code of Practice and those defined as having SEMH may also have other difficulties/disabilities. SEMH needs may be long-term, but these may also be short-term and transitory.

The 'emotional' aspect of SEMH refers to the awareness of and ability to self-regulate the emotions which sit alongside social behaviours.

The 'mental health' aspect of SEMH is not simply the absence of mental illness but is a broader indicator of social, emotional and physical wellness. It is influenced by the wider contexts within which a child or young person lives.

The 'social' aspect of SEMH refers to the relationships which the young person has with others, and their skills in being able to establish, maintain and repair these relationships.

There are dedicated SEMH schools with small numbers and very small classes or these young people may be educated in any educational setting.

Young people may experience a wide range of social and emotional difficulties including becoming withdrawn or isolated, as well as displaying challenging, disruptive or disturbing behaviour, reflecting underlying difficulties such as anxiety or depression, self-harming, substance misuse, eating disorders or physical symptoms that are medically unexplained.

It is really important to consider all the potential underlying reasons why these destructive behaviours are happening and more stakeholders need to understand the ACEs model (Adverse Childhood Experiences) and I would urge you to read pages 34–35.

Speech, language and communication (SLC) is the number one special need in England today (2024). These learners may have other special additional needs. They may have difficulty saying what they want to, understanding what is being said to them if they do not understand or using social norms of communication. Each young person with SLCN will have different needs which may change and improve over time.

Physical needs as identified in the SEND Code of Practice include visual impairment, hearing impairment, multi-sensory impairment and physical disabilities

Visual impairment refers to a range of difficulties from minor impairment through to blindness. Young people whose vision is corrected by wearing glasses or contact lenses are not considered as having a visual impairment; only those who need some kind of adaptation such as Braille and 3-D representations are visually impaired. The Thomas Pocklington Trust has some great resources (https://www.pocklington.org.uk/).

Hearing Impairment Young people with a hearing impairment range from those with a mild hearing loss to those who are profoundly deaf. They may require hearing aids or adaptations to their environment. Look at https://www.ndcs.org.uk/information-and-support/childhood-deafness/information-for-deaf-young-people/

Multi-Sensory Impairment Young people with multi-sensory impairment have a combination of visual and hearing difficulties. The combination can result in high anxiety and multi-sensory deprivation. Young people need teaching approaches which make good use of their residual hearing and vision, together with their other senses.

Physical Impairments

Contrary to what many people believe, and Google searches show (!), most physically disabled people do not use wheelchairs, the ratio actually being only 1:100. Physical disabilities could include challenges with mobility, sensory disabilities, any part of the body that doesn't work in an optimal way and requires some type of adaptation to fully participate in life. It could include challenges with digestion, breathing (asthma), movement, energy levels, coordination and immunity. Reasonable adjustments can mitigate the impact of physical disabilities, creating fuller participation in education, training and work.

Person first, disability second, full participation in life, education, and training and employment should be our daily mantra as career guidance professionals.

Education, Health and Care Plans – what do they have to do with career development and the definition of young people with SEND?

There were 1.61 million young people with SEND in England as of January 2024; 575,963 (35%) of young people have an EHC Plan, up 11.4% since 2023 and nearly 27% were new from 2022; and 65% will have an individual support plan (ISP).

Obtaining an EHC Plan is an extremely tough battle for many families as borne out by the incredibly high number of appeals being brought and won by families against local authorities. As stated by the Children's Commissioner on 29 January 2024, appeals had gone up by 24% in 2022/23 and appeals had been found in favour of 98% of families.

Education, Health and Care Plans – current and future

The spending on EHC Plans has escalated and by way of bringing the spending down, the process is being digitised. It has been stated that fewer will be needed as more young people will be in mainstream, in my view two disassociated facts. Just because you reduce the number of plans, the need doesn't reduce. Many local authorities turn down applications and spend huge sums on defending appeals, 98% of which are won by the family even if that is in part.

The 'Safety valve' scheme which is meant to reward local authorities that have overspent on their SEND budgets. In order to bring things back into line, they are given money/credit against their overspending, it is not new money. Some local authorities have stopped accepting new EHC plan application processes which they have legal responsibilities to engage in. Whatever way you look at it, young people's needs are not being met now and there is a danger this will get even worse.

Currently, a young person can only secure a place in a supported internship training programme if they have an EHC Plan. As of January 2024, only 35% of young people identified as having SEND had one, therefore 65% would be denied this opportunity, which has an employment rate of between 65% and 100%. The project being delivered by DFN Project Search, BASE and the NDTI will have delivered 4.500 new supported internships by 2025. There is some good news: there is a DfE project with Dynamic Training for 200 young people without an EHC plan to do a supported internship and the word on the street is that there is an appetite to expand this further.

An EHC Plan identifies the support a young person needs and should be focused on the future. Annual reviews take place with all stakeholders – parents, carers, families, the young person and any external agency staff such as social workers. In

Year 9, there should be a **Transition Review** where future plans for what comes next after school are discussed as well as the pathway to achieve them.

For me, it is very definitely not just about those young people defined through the acquisition of an EHC Plan, but I would want to include *all* young people with any type of additional need including vulnerable and disadvantaged young people who might not be included or covered by the SEND Code of Practice into the career development strategy and programme.

Many schools and colleges prioritise young people who have an EHC Plan, however only 35% have one so potentially it means the vast majority do not enjoy a full career development experience and the potential for not achieving an optimal career outcome is increased.

An EHC Plan is a valuable resource and can be accessed by SENCOs, careers leaders and careers advisers. It specifies a child/young person's:

- educational needs and identifies the potential/actual schools or educational settings they could attend
- health requirements
- social care requirements and support.

They are sometimes described as the 'golden thread' combining all the information to support the young person. When they work well, the young person thrives, families are confident their child is being supported effectively and services are in place. Career development can progress according to the employment outcomes identified in the EHC Plan.

However, there are multiple issues with EHC Plans. In recent years there has been a 'perfect storm' of the numbers of young people diagnosed with SEND increasing; the number of applications for EHC Plans exploding with high numbers of appeals being won when they are turned down by local authorities with overstretched budgets. It should be remembered that local authorities have legal obligations to comply with when it comes to EHC Plans and the application processes, and at times it appears these are being breached with little accountability. At the time of writing, there was a pilot to standardise the process of application by digitising it. Suffice it to say, achieving can be a stressful process, but when EHC Plans work well everyone benefits and the potential for optimum career outcomes is increased.

IEPs or Individual Education Plans are created by a school and identify support for young people and can created be before an EHC Plan is granted or as an alternative.

Optimum career outcomes

It is important to approach the definition of young people with SEND/additional needs from the perspective of understanding what is aspirational, what is possible and what the optimum career outcome could look like.

 Thinking about what someone CAN do and not what they can't means it:
- generates a conversation about optimum career outcomes
- is aspirational for everyone concerned
- focuses career development activities on the achievement and pathways to these outcomes
- reduces the focus on what someone can't do and focuses on what they can
- reduces the anxiety of careers practitioners and employers who then understand what is possible and then focus on delivering more activities
- deepens our thinking about the different groups of neurodiverse individuals, for example those who are autistic, ADHD, Tourette's
- extends our inclusion to those not specifically and legally defined as SEND but who are vulnerable or disadvantaged in other ways.

Putting the SEND Code of Practice groupings aside for a moment, a more positive approach is to start with the outcomes and establish in a broad sense what the entry point is to an early career. For many early careers, GCSEs/Level 2 qualifications are that starting point.

Establishing who would or would not work at Level 2/GCSE levels meant two groups were established. This is in no way disrespectful or derogatory or demeaning. The following terms have been used for over six years now, and I have found that career practitioners and employers relax, anxieties subside and they are then able to develop an offer/service which focuses on improving outcomes because they are compelled to support these young people:

- Career SEND Group One
- Career SEND Group Two
- Intersectionality between Career SEND Groups One and Two

Defining the two Career SEND Groups – Career SEND Group One and Career SEND Group Two

I know that when people are anxious about engaging with a more diverse group/individuals, they can focus on what someone can't do rather than what they can. The SEND Code of Practice is by definition a deficit model as the function and purpose is to establish what a young person needs because they need support

Who *are* young people with SEND?

in some way. Using it to drive the definition and organisation of early career development is not as useful as thinking it through in a different way.

> ♥ Most careers start with whether a young person will or can take the GCSEs. Using this as the starting point helps us define two groups of young people: those who could and do take GCSEs and those who do not and never will. This sounds brutal to some people, but what it should do is drive the careers conversation around what someone *can do* and what their optimal career outcome could be, encouraging them to aspire to those career destinations and provide concrete pathways to those destinations. So our two Career SEND Groups are divided into those young people who typically would take GCSEs/Level 2 qualifications and those who would not.

Career SEND Group One – typically will *not* take GCSEs/Level 2 qualifications and positive optimal career outcomes could include:

- supported employment
- pre-supported internships and supported internships
- inclusive apprenticeships
- T Levels/T Level Transition programme
- supported self-employment
- supported volunteering
- supported independent living
- activities based in the community and activities signposted via the local offer
- FE colleges
- specialist colleges.

> ♥ The key issue for the Career SEND Group One is supply and demand – there are not enough employer-led training and employment opportunities or high-quality community-based options.

Career SEND Group Two – young people in this group typically will or could take GCSEs/Level 2 qualifications and/or higher levels of qualifications. They should ideally enjoy the same career outcomes as their peers without additional needs, including:

- apprenticeships at various levels
- university
- FE college
- self-employment/entrepreneur

- employment
- T Levels.

> ♥ Key issues for Career SEND Group Two – invisible barriers unknown to key stakeholders and facing **multiple barriers** that key stakeholders are unaware of prevent them from achieving the optimum career outcomes.

To understand more about Career SEND Group Two let's look at the different 'membership' groups as they differ widely from each other. It is important to understand the barriers they may experience in their early career development, so the right ongoing support can be organised to enable them to succeed. There are three groups:

1. Young people who will require some type of reasonable adjustment in education or at work – These young people may have a visual impairment, hearing impairment, physical disabilities, autism and/or health/mental health challenges.

2. Contextual in terms of what is happening *around* the young person and could impact the possibility of them engaging with career activities – For example young carers, those eligible at school for pupil premium and/or free school meals, a 'child in need' as described by a local authority as requiring their intervention to flourish, or be a member of the Traveller community perhaps.

3. Personal – what is happening or has happened to the young person in the past and has interrupted their neurological, academic and social development and progress. These students will be educated in all settings – mainstream, specialist, SEMH, PRUs or AP, and may be 'looked after children'/'care experienced'. **The model used to better understand this group is called ACEs,** which stands for adverse childhood experiences.

Adverse childhood experiences

The original ACE study by Felitti was in 2002 when he was working with a group of individuals suffering from obesity. Felitti found that those who were most likely to lose weight were also those most likely to drop out of the programme. He dug deeper into their pasts and discovered that child abuse was 'extraordinarily commonplace' in this group and that the abuse preceded the development of obesity. He realised obesity was not the problem but that on the program, participants were using obesity as a remedy for managing more adverse events and injuries that had lain hidden sometimes for many years (trauma). These traumatic life experiences continued to heavily impact their lives as adults and in this example, obesity would protect them in their eyes as they would be unattractive to a potential abuser or people would be intimidated by them because of their size. This behaviour is called 'behavioural allostasis'. He discovered this when interviewing a woman who described being sexually active at the weight of 40 pounds when she was four years old, which was when her father started abusing her sexually.

What Felitti discovered was that ACEs have a strong correlation to risky health behaviours (drugs and alcohol abuse, smoking, and sexually risky behaviours) and chronic health conditions like heart disease, and low life potential (depression, suicide and work absenteeism).

Other doctors and institutions joined the original study and expanded their research in 2014. About 26,000 adults were asked to take part in research which sought to understand the impact of childhood events might affect adult health and 68% agreed, the vast majority of whom were middle-class, white Americans. Eight categories of adverse childhood experiences were included involving abuse and family dysfunction and categories of neglect were included in the original survey resulting in 10 categories now. Each category scores 1 so the maximum score is 10 even if the experience happens multiple times.

About 50% of young people score at least 1 and 8% of young people score 4 or more. The 10 items are personal/physical abuse, verbal/emotional abuse, sexual abuse, neglect and emotional neglect, family/parent with addiction issues, victims of domestic violence in the family, family member is in custody, family member has mental health illness, parent has disappeared (divorce, death, abandonment). As a careers leader/careers adviser or a member of staff working with young people in careers lessons, you probably won't know if a young person is or has experienced an adverse childhood experience, but you can see the extent to which they are engaged or not. Finding ways to engage even if for a short while helps; finding ways to build confidence and self-esteem, offering opportunities in short bursts that don't require huge amounts of concentration thus building interest; and most of all looking beyond the behaviours, beyond the surface. The focus of career conversations for both groups should be on positive career outcomes and the pathways towards achieving them, rather than emphasising disabilities or limitations.

> ♥ It is incredible how many careers professionals have not heard of ACEs and the devastating impact they can have on engagement with poor career outcomes. Please talk about ACEs with colleagues and in particular employers.

Intersectionality between Career SEND Groups One and Two

Whenever I talk about the two models someone always says 'ah but', so let's address the 'ah but' in the room. Come at this from the destination and start with the outcome in mind when planning career pathways. Whenever there is a model which is polarised, there is always a healthy debate about what sits in between the two points of view. With the Career SEND Groups, I am very aware that there will be young people who will inhabit the space in between. The differentiator between the two groups is whether a young person can successfully take and pass a GCSE/Level 2 at the grade level which gives them entry to a discreet set of career outcomes. This grade is often 4 or higher and is the entry criteria to sixth forms, FE colleges and apprenticeships.

GCSEs can be gained at lower grades 3–1 and are classed as Level 1 qualifications. It may be that a higher grade could be achieved in the future, but at the point of taking it, destinations for Career SEND Group Two would be denied that young person as the entry criteria are set at a higher level. The reason for the division between the two groups is to ensure the discussion is on the potential career destination and there are two sets of optimal career outcomes for each of the two Career SEND Groups. The wording that defines Career SEND Group Two is also quite deliberate, 'will or could', which reflect the fact that some young people are not ready to sit for GCSEs in Year 11 and may do them later. The capability is there but for whatever reason they are not quite ready. However, for someone in Career SEND Group One, it is not about a state of readiness. Intellectually they will never study at that level, and it is OK to say that if the focus of the discussion is on what outcomes and destinations *are* possible.

So, if a young person achieves a Level 1 GCSE and has an EHC Plan, they would be able to apply for a supported internship or an accessible apprenticeship or an FE college place if there is a suitable course. They may also be able to re-take GCSEs at a later stage and secure a higher grade, which then gives them entry to opportunities open to young people in Career SEND Group Two. Our Pathways poster is helpful at explaining the different routes (see page 124).

Where do vulnerable and disadvantaged young people meet SEND?

There are young people who are not formally diagnosed who may or may not have a SEND need, who may be vulnerable or disadvantaged. There are young people diagnosed with a SEND need who will not be vulnerable or disadvantaged by any other factor other than their diagnosed need. Vulnerability and disadvantage can come from lots of sources, including family circumstances; the local economy; where they live (e.g. rural versus inner city); the demands placed upon them (e.g.

young carer); the impact of insecure housing and homelessness and food poverty; mental health and anxiety; waiting for treatment services; and adverse childhood experiences, which are 'hidden'.

The Child Poverty Action Group in January 2024 identified that 3 million children live with food insecurity and in June 2024 that 4.3 million children lived in housing insecurity with over 140,000 actually homeless. That translates as 9 children in every class of 30. Nearly 1 million children miss out on free school meals. Child poverty is higher where there is a disabled person living in a household.

> ♥ It is highly unlikely that all the needs of every child or young person can be truly 'visible', and it is incumbent upon all of us to ensure the optimum career development can be experienced for *all* young people and ensure their voices are heard and aspirations are raised. Stakeholders should understand more about the broadest range of young people and collectively strive for the optimum career outcomes. It makes sense from an ethical and economic perspective.

Summary of key points

- **The SEND Code of Practice** – Use it to gain a clearer understanding of young people with additional needs, but try to avoid defining their potential career destinations around what they can't do; focus on what they can do.
- **Education, Health and Care Plans** – Remember that 27% of young people with SEND have one and 73% have an individual support plan. Treat all your learners' career development equally even though they will achieve a wide range of outcomes after school. Use the EHC Plan to raise aspirations and give clarity on career pathways.
- **The two Career SEND Groups: Career SEND Group One and Career SEND Group Two** – Use this model with all stakeholders. Remember, Career SEND Group One will typically be working below GSCE/Level 2 academically and Career SEND Group Two will or could be working at GCSE/Level 2 and above.
- **Scale of the challenge for young people with SEND achieving optimum career outcomes** – Both Career SEND Groups can experience major barriers to achieving their optimum career outcomes. For Group One it is predominantly a supply and demand issue; there are not enough supported training and employment opportunities. For Career SEND Group Two, the membership of this group is very complex; many will be in mainstream where their needs may not be diagnosed or understood or be being met and so the starting point for their career development can be much further back.

- **Employers' anxiety** – They can be anxious too and worried about not engaging appropriately.
- **Short description of the characteristics of the members of each of the Career SEND Groups** – This is important, but in conjunction with raising aspirations, identifying career possibilities and goals and how they can be achieved – remember can do, not can't do!
- **Vulnerable and disadvantaged young people who sit outside the SEND Code of Practice** – There are millions of young people who are at a disadvantage, for example young carers, care experienced children and young people, those in food poverty, and those in insecure housing. Many will not be diagnosed with a special need but will have additional needs that need to be factored into their early career development. Don't forget these young people when planning, as many will deliberately stay under the radar so as not to be noticed.
- **Optimum career outcomes for each of the two Career SEND Groups: Career SEND Group One and Career SEND Group Two** – There are two sets of optimum career outcomes, one for each group. Currently, those with EHC Plans can benefit from a supported internship and can come from either career group.

Resources

Career SEND Group One – Catcote Academy in Hartlepool is an outstanding example of a special school with the 'can do' philosophy at the heart of everything it does with its immortal strap-line – 'focus on what I can do not what I can't'. Watch this video to find out more! www.facebook.com/CatcoteAcademy/videos/catcote-academy-aspire/1783025801713079/

Career SEND Group One – Brookfields Special School in Reading is four-time Ofsted Outstanding school and has an excellent destination record when it comes to leavers going on to employer-related training and employment opportunities. This film was made a few years ago, but many of the messages still hold true. https://vimeo.com/163406325

Career SEND Group Two – Meet Billy video link: www.youtube.com/watch?v=3rod1B7EQMo

Suggestion – big cuppa and plentiful supply of your favourite biscuits at this point!

GUEST CONTRIBUTOR – DANIEL PIKETT, FOUNDER OF SPATIAL CAREERS

Daniel Pikett is a charismatic, Level 7-trained Careers Adviser, Careers Leader and neurodivergent. He is a powerful advocate for young people with the widest range of additional needs, particularly those who are neurodiverse. With his unique style, he enables all of us to better understand what is possible. Thanks, Dan.

In the vast cosmos of human cognition and experience, neurodiversity is a constellation of unique cognitive profiles, sensory perceptions and communication styles. Within this rich tapestry lies the journey of young individuals navigating their career paths amid societal expectations and personal aspirations. As I embark on this transformative exploration, I delve into the multifaceted landscape of neurodiversity, navigating the challenges, celebrating the strengths and paving pathways towards fulfilling careers for the next generation.

At the core of neurodiversity lies the recognition that everyone possesses a distinct set of talents, perspectives and contributions. Just as planets interact within a cosmic ecosystem, neurodiverse individuals interact within society, enriching the fabric of our collective existence. By embracing this diversity, I foster innovation, creativity, and resilience in the workforce, shaping a future where every young person can thrive.

As advocates for neurodivergent youth, our mission revolves around challenging stereotypes and empowering individuals to reach their full potential. Through developing self-awareness and decision-making skills, I nurture self-determination, enabling young people to chart their course in the world of work. A person-centred approach forms the cornerstone of this journey, encouraging clients to communicate their visions and aspirations for their future careers.

Transitioning through educational settings and into the workforce can be a daunting prospect for neurodivergent youth. Each transition presents unique challenges and opportunities, demanding thoughtful planning and robust support systems. Collaboration with parents, educators and other professionals becomes essential to mitigate anxiety and ensure a seamless progression. From early years through primary and secondary education, career development professionals play a pivotal role in preparing neurodivergent individuals for adulthood, fostering independence and addressing health needs.

Inclusive practices are paramount in creating environments where neurodivergent young people can thrive. This includes providing tailored support, accommodating diverse learning styles, and fostering a culture of acceptance and understanding. The #sameanddifferent model serves as a beacon of hope for promoting diversity, empathy, and inclusion in both educational and workplace settings. By prioritising autonomy and self-determination, I empower neurodivergent youth to navigate their career paths confidently and resiliently.

Understanding the intersection of legal mandates with social realities is crucial in supporting the career development of neurodivergent youth. Legislative frameworks, such as the SEND Code of Practice, guide inclusive education and employment pathways. By navigating these frameworks, career development professionals can advocate for equitable access to opportunities and resources, ensuring no young person is left behind.

Employers play a vital role in fostering inclusive workplaces that celebrate and embrace neurodiversity. By implementing inclusive hiring practices, providing support and accommodating diverse needs, organisations can unlock the full potential of their workforce. Celebrating neurodiversity not only enriches the workplace culture but also brings endless possibilities for personal growth and career development.

Supporting parents and caregivers in understanding neurodiversity is essential for guiding young people towards fulfilling careers. By providing resources, advocating for appropriate support and offering career guidance, parents can play a crucial role in preparing their children for the transition into the workforce. Collaboration between parents, educators and career development professionals ensures that young individuals receive the comprehensive support they need to succeed.

In empowering young neurodivergent individuals in their career development, inclusivity, understanding and empowerment are paramount. By challenging stereotypes, fostering self-determination, and navigating transitions with care and support, I pave the way for a future where every young person can thrive in their chosen career paths. Through collaboration, advocacy and celebration of neurodiversity, I create a world where diversity is embraced and inclusivity prevails, shaping a brighter future for future generations. This chapter sets the stage for an in-depth exploration of neurodiversity in the context of career development, guiding readers on a transformative journey towards understanding, acceptance and empowerment.

My little checklist – Top tips to improve your understanding of who young people with SEND are

Who are young people with SEND?	Top tips to improve your SEND careers practice	Planned action	Tick action completed
What do I understand about the term SEND and the SEND Code of Practice?	Don't get hung up on the diagnosis. Your focus in the first instance is understanding potential career outcomes – focus on 'can do' not 'can't do'.		
Who are my SEND learners?	Use both Career SEND Groups One and Two, and if you have learners that appear to fall between the groups consider their individual potential career outcome possibilities.		
Which Career SEND Group(s) are my learners in?	Appreciate you may have learners in both groups and will need to create a careers strategy that reflects this.		
Currently, what are the optimum career outcomes for my learners?	Use your destinations data to establish what the optimum outcomes are for learners *now*.		
What *could* the optimum career outcomes be for my learners in the future?	Use the list on page 33 to correlate what your learners *could* access in terms of other career outcome possibilities. At this stage don't think about local supply and demand issues.		
Can I articulate the key barriers to achieving optimum career outcomes?	Talk to your key stakeholder groups – SENCO, parents, carers and families, staff, employers, careers advisers, careers leaders, FE – and establish a shortlist.		
How can I use the PALs activities to raise the aspirations of my learners?	Be strategic and triangulate data from EHC Plans, young people directly, the careers team, potential career outcomes on offer locally, local employers and FE, and be more targeted about organising PALs related activities.		
How can I use #sameandifferent to enhance the delivery of careers?	Remember the three tenants – aspects that are the same as anyone else without SEND leaving school, same and different aspects which are the same but need to be delivered differently, and different aspects. You can use aspects of your own too.		
What ideas can I take from the case study and integrate into my practice?	The resources in this chapter are videos which you could use with employers and other stakeholders to generate discussion around diversity.		
What do I need to think about in terms of my practice when considering the 'achieving change/future focus' commentary?	Try to keep in front, use social media more, follow careers leaders and Careers Hubs on LinkedIn, check the DfE website for updates, use the Resource Directory on the CEC website. Create a timetable of upcoming changes.		

Chapter 3
The organisation of career development for young people with SEND – the people

- Appreciating the influences and influencers on career decisions, positive and negative
- A short history of career development and SEND
- The Careers and Enterprise Company
- Careers leaders
- Careers advisers

Appreciating the influences and influencers on career decisions, positive and negative

It is important to establish early on what young people's ideas are on their career possibilities which can appear early and can be entrenched and sometimes lack aspiration. Career influences can be overt or more insidious, positive or negative or neutral.

The ideas can come from external sources – family, what parents do (or don't do), teachers' influences, careers advisers' suggestions and influences, trends happening around them, friends, part-time jobs, social media, timing, available opportunities, the local area (e.g. is it rural?), transport availability and costs, social networks offline and online, other people's expectations, and role models (positive and negative).

Treating career development as a process and showing the link between career influences and career aspiration and academic level, is there an alignment between the aspects? This is an exercise worth doing early on; potentially with Year 7 in the summer term. You can learn a lot by enabling young people to express their career influences in safety, i.e. not having to share them openly. I remember doing this exercise with a group of Year 8s and one boy wrote saying he wanted a job where people didn't get hurt. I let the tutor know and she told me his family were dealers and he saw substance users in his home regularly.

Remember, when young people with additional needs or are vulnerable/disadvantaged express a career ambition, it is what they want and is not the result of other influences.

A short history of career development and SEND

Since 2012, the way that early career development is organised, funded and delivered in England has changed beyond recognition for most educational settings. Prior to the seismic changes in 2012, careers advisers formed the largest component of the early career development journey of young people with SEND, funded by the government with services delivered locally via Connexions which cost £486 million annually. Today, £453 million from the public purse is spent on the early career development of young people; the annual grant to the Careers and Enterprise Company (CEC) represents around 8% as at March 2024 of the total spending.

In 2012, careers advisers, including those skilled in SEND, ceased to be funded by the government and that money was put into the all-ages National Careers Services, which was predominantly online and not geared to the career needs of young people, especially those with SEND. Young people with special needs having access to careers advisers who understood them and knew their families and their needs was a lottery unless a local authority or school was prepared to pay the bill. Many careers advisers also retired at that time and there is still a shortage today.

In 2015, the Gatsby Benchmark Project based in schools the northeast commenced. There was a working group which included Talentino and several local special schools and charities, notably Catcote Academy and the Percy Headley Foundation, which examined the necessity of a 'SEND' set of Gatsby Benchmarks. It became evident quite quickly that this was not necessary, and it was the interpretation of the Gatsby Benchmarks which would lend itself more readily on behalf of the career development of young people with SEND. A joint statement was put out to this effect from Sir John Holman, the CEC and Disability Rights UK.

The National Careers Strategy was published in December 2017 with guidance on SEND. The Statutory Guidance was published in January 2018 and SEND was included too.

Key Points National Careers Strategy and Statutory Guidance 2018
from Talentino Career Development Company

GOVERNMENT WILL
* Review the Guidance annually
* Publish destinations data at KS4 and KS5

SCHOOLS NEED TO:
* Be responsible for the continuous quality improvement of careers
* A trained Careers Leader must be appointed who runs the Careers Programme and backed by SLT by September 2018
* Publish the careers programme on the website for pupils parents staff and Governors
* Identify a named Governor for Careers
* Keep systematic records of careers activities and decisions for each child
* Have their own dedicated enterprise Adviser to broker employers
* Careers Activities should be purchased from organisations with the Matrix Quality award
* Find out if the local Job Centre Plus offers the 'Support for Schools' programme
* Look out for the 20 new Careers Hubs around the country funded by Government / and funding for Careers Leader training in 500 schools

ADVICE AND GUIDANCE
* Careers Guidance is defined as 'the full range of activities under the 8 Gatsby benchmarks'
* Must secure independent careers guidance which is external to the school - this guidance is defined as careers activities including employer encounters, websites, Apps, phonelines, National Careers Service
* Personal Guidance can be given by trained staff from and in school but must be backed up by external sources
* All pupils should have opportunities for personal guidance interviews with a qualified careers advisor prior to key decisions at 16 and 18. This can be delivered by an internal suitably qualified careers adviser e.g. Level 6 QCG or the newer QCD and will be registered with the CDI on their professional register

SEND
* Consider the widest range of options
* Raise aspirations
* Help parents/families engage more
* Increase authentic employer encounters
* Differentiate as appropriate
* Improved career development for Looked After Children/PRUs/AP
* Multi agency approach
* Use best practice from Transitions Review
* Two free resources available from Education and Training Foundation website
* Use 16-19 Bursaries / 19+ if has EHC plan
* Use Access to work funding job coaches
* Careers guidance differentiated, person centred
* Staff work from the presumption of paid work
* Career decisions based on students' aspirations and abilities and needs
* Careers Adviser's skills to coach SEND pupils will be developed through more CPD available
* Named Careers Advisers encouraged to build longer term relationships with students and use EHC Plans or PEPs to support them

LEGAL REQUIREMENTS FOR SCHOOLS
* Anything saying 'must' is a legal requirement of the school
* Continued - provide external careers advice from qualified adviser
* New - provide access to providers of Apprenticeships and other Education providers
* New - Publish a Provider Access Policy
* Not doing this will result in a school showing unacceptable behaviour and Dept. Ed could write to the school
* Special Schools have been included in the guidance for Mainstream schools and guidance focused on different SEND groups

YOUNG PEOPLE CAN EXPECT A CAREER DEVELOPMENT JOURNEY TO INCLUDE:
* Finding information about their careers programme on the school website which starts in Year 8/earlier
* By the age of 14 have accessed careers information (LMI) to support their study decisions including local LMI
* Information about how important Maths and Science are leading to different rewarding STEM Careers
* Girls will have additional input into developing STEM careers
* By 16 have had 2 meaningful encounters with FE College Sixth form Apprenticeship providers
* Two Careers Guidance interviews before career decisions are made at 16 and 18
* 7 Employer encounters one per years 7 to 13
* 2 work experiences before 16 and before 18
* By 18 2 University visits if Uni is their goal
* Invited to join the school's Alumni network
* Able to access their individual Careers records

GATSBY BENCHMARKS
* All schools must meet all 8 by end of 2020
* All pupils all benchmarks Schools encouraged to use the Compass tool to evaluate progress against benchmarks - confidential to school
* Enterprise Advisers can use Tracker to help schools create a Careers Strategy
* Schools encouraged to take the Quality Standards award which will be more closely tied to the benchmarks

TALENTINO
www.talentinocareers.co.uk

The organisation of career development – the people

In 2018 the opportunity areas and cold spots were a new focus for the CEC. A new fund – CEF 18, which focused on disadvantaged young people – was launched. The first 20 Careers Hubs and a small number of SEND enterprise coordinators (ECs) were created with still no mention of SEND in the key performance indicators in the Grant Funding Agreement (GFA).

In 2019 the first Careers Leader Training took place. The first EC SEND Masterclasses ran virtually during the Covid pandemic in July 2020 and over 300 enterprise coordinators have received the training since then. The first SEND Community of Practice was created across the now 40-plus Careers Hubs. The second SEND Gatsby Toolkit was written by Talentino and produced by the CEC in 2020 and will be developed further in 2024/25.

The Big Inclusive SEND Careers Handbook

The Careers and Enterprise Company

- The improvements in career development and SEND made by the CEC since 2016
- How the Careers and Enterprise Company can support you:
  - Careers Hubs
  - Enterprise coordinators
  - Enterprise advisers
  - Compass+ – measuring the Gatsby Benchmarks
  - Evaluation – Future Skills Questionnaire
  - Resources Directory
- The impact of the Careers and Enterprise Company
- Guest contributor – John Yarham, Deputy CEO of the Careers and Enterprise Company

Introduction

The Careers and Enterprise Company (CEC) is the wholly funded *national body for careers education in England*, delivering support to schools and colleges to deliver modern, 21st-century careers education. It was created in 2016 when the CEC and The Gatsby Foundation published a joint statement with Disability Rights UK. Until 2018, the Careers and Enterprise Company was not mandated through its grant funding agreement to work with SEND or special schools. Talentino was appointed as the strategic partner for SEND for the CEC in December 2018, and along with a small number of key head office staff started generating some significant pieces of work including the first SEND Gatsby Toolkit and a second set of questions for Compass for Career SEND Group One/special schools in 2019. Gatsby also published *Perspectives*, a collection of essays about SEND in 2019.

Since 2019, the Careers and Enterprise Company supported by the earnest efforts of Careers Hubs, enterprise coordinators, enterprise advisers, and the partnership with Talentino has become the leading careers organisation in England for young people with SEND in terms of:

- strategic priorities identifying disadvantaged /vulnerable young people at the heart of its work
- operationalising the delivery of the strategic priorities locally by all Careers Hubs and therefore *all* educational settings

The organisation of career development – the people

- locating SEND/inclusion work in a knowledgeable and skilled education team
- supporting special schools with enterprise coordinators and enterprise advisers
- providing SEND Masterclass training to all enterprise coordinators, over 300 to date
- facilitating training for all careers leaders funded by 100% bursaries from the DfE
- allocating funding to SEND-specific projects that represent a significant percentage of the annual grant allocation
- offering free SEND-specific careers resources with exceptional take up
- surfacing best practices through the inclusion (previously SEND), now Improvement, Community of Practice (COP)
- engaging with the leading SEND organisations – Disability Rights UK, NASEN, Whole School SEND, BASE, DFN Project Search, NDTI, Ambitious about Autism, Thomas Pocklington Trust, and the National Young Deaf Association among others.

A pilot – CEF 18B – ran to support SEND, disadvantaged and vulnerable young people. Strand one of CEF 18B was to reach 1,000 SEND young people and strand two to reach 200 looked after children, 100 gypsy Roma/Traveller young people generating 400 career plans. For the first time, SEND was mentioned in the key performance indicators section of the GFA. Also, 564 special schools (35% of all special schools) joined the SEND COP. Termly events were held which included SENCOs in mainstream; SEND training was delivered for enterprise advisers; SEND EC Masterclasses continued and had the highest evaluation marks of all training ran during the pandemic lockdown.

In 2021/2022 the CEC 'rebranded' SEND as inclusion with a focus on reviewing barriers, and the first mention was made of using free school meals as a determinant of need. There were more SEND resources offered through the Resources Directory. The GFA stood at £27.7 million.

In 2022/23 the network deployed a tailored activation phase of SEND schools, a new set of employer standards was created, and a new inclusion COP was in place for March 2023. The function of inclusion was identified in the GFA (annual sum £29 million) as delivering a programme of sector-led coordinated activity across inclusion (SEND and AP), FE and Independent Training Providers and targeting developing sector resources to remove barriers to accessible careers education.

In 2023/24 the GFA budget stood at £29.7 million. The mandate was to roll out additional Careers Hubs to cover the country and all educational settings, work more closely with the National Careers Service, train careers leaders, and capture best practices; with five priorities capturing targeting economically disadvantaged young people indicated by free school meals via Careers Hubs and careers leaders by offering more programmes and more effective Cornerstone support as well as reducing the possibility of becoming NEET.

What this journey shows is that when the Careers and Enterprise Company was first created there was no obvious mandate from the funders to support the early career development of young people with SEND. Groups of young people described as disadvantaged or vulnerable, however, have always been mandated and it is well known that within these groups there will be significant proportions of young people with SEND. Special schools, however, were not mentioned until the creation of the Compass set of questions for special schools.

> ♥ The Careers and Enterprise Company is in a very potent situation working directly with most educational settings in England and by virtue of this fact most of the 1.51 million young people with SEND and the millions more disadvantaged/vulnerable young people. Connect with as many employers as you can through the Career Hubs, enterprise advisers and Cornerstones and get the message out about improving outcomes!

Improvements in career development and SEND made by the CEC since 2016

In 2023, Talentino was asked to write a report on the impact of the CEC in terms of the improvement of career development for young people with SEND since its inception in 2016. Part of the research was a survey which more than 70 special schools responded to. The following is a summary of their feedback. The survey that was carried out in June and July 2023 by 133 respondents bore this out. The key points are as follows.

Respondents were asked to identify the level of support for young people with SEND when they first started working with them and what they felt now in 2023. Thirty-six per cent of respondents said the level of support for SEND and career development when they started was poor, and only 23% said it was very good or good. The level of support identified now (in 2023) as poor was only 5% and very good/good was nearly 70%.

Respondents were asked to identify all the sources they would go to for support. The CEC came out on top with 80% and that result stayed the same from the start to the close of the survey with 133 respondents; only 8% of respondents came from the CEC so it was educational settings. Coming in second was employers (57%), and tied for third were Talentino, ECs and careers leaders (52%).

The final survey questions asked respondents to identify in their own words what three barriers they saw; there were nearly 400 responses. The top four categories by a long way were a lack of employer-led training and employment opportunities; a lack of readiness and inclination of employers to get engaged; insufficient FE provision that did not lead to employment; and the complexities around parents' aspirations for their child resulting in poor outcomes.

This data has been correlated with the Compass data from 2019 to 2023 from special schools and APs concerning the survey questions that cited multiple barriers and the survey questions which identified what had improved. For example, employer engagement had improved (43%), but in the survey, 45% of respondents said employers continued to be reticent to engage.

There are changes in the offing with the SEND reforms where more young people with SEND will be educated in mainstream; the recent recommendations of the Education Select Committee; the DfE Careers Education paper including a response to the Education Select Committee recommendations; a potential 2023 summer publication; the output of the Ofsted Thematic Careers Review which will include a SEND appendix (summer 2023); the publication of the Careers Guidance Guarantee in July 2023; and finally the output of the Gatsby 10-year paper at the end of 2024 for implementation in September 2025 (www.careersandenterprise.co.uk/our-evidence/evidence-and-reports/careers-education-2022-23-now-next/).

How the Careers and Enterprise Company can support you

The core strategic priorities of the Careers and Enterprise Company in 2024 are to:

1. Raise the quality of careers provision in schools, special schools, and colleges against the Gatsby Benchmarks through training for the education workforce, targeted support, and quality assurance
2. Drive more high-quality experiences with employers for students and teachers – with a focus on current 'cold spots'

3. Amplify apprenticeships, technical and vocational routes – including by supporting the implementation of the Provider Access Legislation (PAL)
4. Focus on interventions for economically disadvantaged young people (FSM) and those who face most barriers – through identifying and addressing the needs of specific cohorts
5. Connect careers provision in schools and colleges to the needs of local economies – as articulated through Local Skills Improvement Plans (LSIPs).

They do this through facilitating Careers Hubs, enterprise coordinators, enterprise advisers, measuring the Gatsby Benchmarks and measuring the impact of career development in school. *All services are free at the point of delivery.*

Careers Hubs are locally based across all areas in England, and offer support to careers leaders, schools and SLT teams to deliver their careers programmes in line with the Gatsby Benchmarks for good careers guidance. Specifically they offer fully funded careers leader training; connecting employers and training providers with schools, special schools and colleges; and sharing digital tools like Compass and the Resource Directory. Find yours at www.careersandenterprise.co.uk/careers-hubs/.

Enterprise coordinators work directly with schools, special schools and colleges to enhance the delivery of their career development through the Gatsby Benchmarks. Enterprise coordinators work via the Careers Hubs; again if you want to find yours use the link above.

Enterprise advisers are volunteers from business and there are over 4,000 working across all types of schools and colleges. They bring their individual knowledge, skills and networks to enhance the careers offerings to learners. They are always in demand, so if you know of someone who would like to volunteer apply at www.careersandenterprise.co.uk/employers/contact-us-about-becoming-an-enterprise-adviser/ or via email ea@careersandenterprise.co.uk.

The tool that you can use to help you measure the Gatsby Benchmarks is Compass/Compass+. It is free to all schools, special schools and colleges that complete it termly. It pulls data from school MIS systems to support individual career development, and schools control the data that is shared. It can help you to:

- assess your school's careers provision against the Gatsby Benchmarks
- track individual students' careers interests and intended destinations (what they plan to do after leaving school)

- track individual students' actual destinations (what they do for three years after leaving the school)
- plan and track careers activities for individual students
- input and store details of third-party organisations and contacts that can support your school with careers provision
- download key information into reports, for the following purposes:
  - analysis and reporting within your school
  - *t*o provide data to local authorities to support them in their statutory duty to record the intended destinations of 16-year-olds
  - to provide systematic records to each student of the individual advice given to them as recommended in the Gatsby Benchmarks.

Careers leader training is fully funded by the DfE and worth over £1000, Level 6. There is a new top-up course too. Find out more at www.careersandenterprise.co.uk/careers-leaders/careers-leader-training/.

The **Resources Directory** is a free resource for all types of schools including those in the independent sector. There are multiple SEND-related careers resources and the majority are free too. New resources get added weekly and there are thousands of users monthly from across the world. Resources are quality checked before being added. See the link https://resources.careersandenterprise.co.uk/.

Summary of key points

The Careers and Enterprise Company has matured into the most significant careers organisation in terms of its potential to improve outcomes for young people with SEND or who are vulnerable or disadvantaged. I would like to see its reach extended on the transition from school to the first destination after school to avoid losing 'talent in transition'. We are getting career development right in schools, but NEETs are rising and employment rates for SEND groups remain stubbornly low, so extending that mandate could be key. All the Careers Hubs have moved from local enterprise partnerships under the auspices of local government, in the future there may be a risk if funding is not ringfenced. It makes for strong connectivity between the Careers Hubs and local authorities that have statutory responsibilities for many of these young people.

GUEST CONTRIBUTOR – JOHN YARHAM, DEPUTY CEO OF THE CAREERS AND ENTERPRISE COMPANY

What I love about John is his consistency, his deep expert experience of early career development and his total devotion to the cause. He is the professional's professional. In his contribution you can feel his passion mirrored in his words. John has deeply ingrained integrity and he doesn't just reside at the 'brand level'; better outcomes really matter to him.

Thinking about how to introduce the role of the Careers and Enterprise Company reminds me of reading Michael Rosen's famous book *Going on a Bear Hunt* to my daughters when they were young. The line from that book that sticks in my mind – possibly because it was conducive to extra accentuation – was: 'Can't go over it, can't go under it, can't go around it, got to go through it!'

We must go *through* schools – in all their guises – and colleges to achieve the greatest impact for young people in their career development. Working directly with the people that hold the knowledge and influence to make the greatest difference to young people's lives is critical. Attempting to go around the system is not sustainable or as impactful.

With that principle established as a key tenet of the Careers and Enterprise Company's operating model, it prompted me to reflect further on the other aspects of a national body for careers education that are important to achieve impact in helping every young person to find their best next step.

When I think of educators generally, and particularly those working with children and young people with special needs, their universal passion to make a difference is what first springs to mind. It's vital, therefore, that a national body aiming to work through the system in the way that I have outlined – a model highly reliant on trust – attempts to match that passion.

This is potentially more difficult to achieve in organisations that are not directly serving young people and not facing the same day-to-day pressures as those on the front line. It creates a dependency on careful recruitment and an emphasis on strong underpinning values that display the same unswerving belief in the potential of young people as held by educators. The importance of values (particularly integrity) is also a useful opportunity to remind ourselves of the enduring relevance of the Nolan Principles, almost 30 years on from their creation, which I believe should remain as a guiding star for any organisation serving the public.

The importance of that passion extends to the partner organisations that I work with – none better represented than by the author of this book, Jenny Connick, and her organisation, Talentino.

Explicitly matching the passion of educators to make a difference is therefore a given, but a national body must also add clear value through the expertise that it brings. The comfort of not facing the type of day-to-day pressures experienced by those on the front line affords the opportunity to invest energy into understanding best practices and creating approaches that propagate these, such as the Careers Impact System. This doesn't mean retrospective nasal gazing but active participation in approaches that lead to quality improvement. The collection of data and ongoing evidence is an important facet of this, alongside more qualitative approaches including training and development.

Additionality also comes in the form of cross-institutional approaches. These often require some form of deliberate prompting to become established. Linking employers and educators, special schools and mainstream schools, and schools and colleges are all highly valuable. Creating structures that foster those types of collaborations and focus on supporting the successful transition of young people – such as Careers Hubs and communities of practice – is critical.

Finally, a national body needs to be reflective. Reflective of where it is and isn't making impact. How it can improve and adapt. Active in seeking meaningful innovation. Porous to feedback and ideas.

And with that, I welcome your feedback on what you find in this chapter, and the principles that I have set out in this section.

My little checklist – Top tips to improve your inclusive careers practice

How the CEC can help me improve outcomes	Top tips to improve my understanding of how the CEC can help me improve outcomes	Planned action	Tick action completed
Have you connected with your local Careers Hub?	*This is a free resource and enables you to more easily connect with other Careers Leaders and potentially employers*		
Have you got an enterprise coordinator?	*The EC will have a dedicated group of schools local to you enabling you to connect*		
Have you been provided with an enterprise adviser?	*EAs provide different types of support and their skillset is aligned to your challenge*		
Do you know someone who would like to volunteer as an enterprise adviser?	*Usually employed or self-employed or recently retired*		
Have you made an application for or received your careers leader training and bursary?	*Excellent training which you can get 100% bursary for worth £1000*		
Are using Compass+?	*Access via your EC*		
Are you using the FSQ?	*Access via the FSQ*		
Do you have enough employers to deliver against GBM 5 and 6?	*Talk to your EC around how to increase the number and supply*		
Do you use the Employer Standards with your employers?	*Increases the standard of employers' contribution*		
Have you used the Resource Directory lately?	*Lots of resources organised into different categories including SEND*		
Have you accessed the Improvement or Independent Special Schools COP?	*Easy way to find out what others are doing to improve their inclusive careers offer, access via EC*		
Have you signed up for the latest annual Talentino CPD SEND Careers Conference?	*Usually run in November each year, CPD certified by the CDI*		

Careers leaders

- The careers leader role
- #sameandifferent – a career delivery model for SEND and inclusion
- Strategic careers health check for SEND
- Guest contributor – Kelly Dillon, Head of Removing Barriers at the Careers and Enterprise Company

Introduction

The top-selling careers book from Trotman Publishing in 2023 was *The Careers Leader Handbook* by David Andrews and Tristram Hooley, who covered among other things the role of a careers leader, continuous improvement and delivering an outstanding careers programme through the Gatsby Benchmarks.

So, it made me think: what can I offer you outside of what you may have read in their book? Well, dear chum, I am offering a model through which to view the career development of young people with SEND – #sameandifferent and a strategic careers health check process which will help you to organise and facilitate an impactful careers programme for your SEND students, improving the possibility and probability of optimal career outcomes.

The careers leader is a relatively new role, with the first training only being carried out in 2019, and there is still some confusion about the difference between a careers leader and careers adviser. Simply put, the careers leader will facilitate a career development programme through the Gatsby Benchmark Framework, including the strategy, planning, delivery, transition of students, evaluation and destinations.

The careers adviser, in an educational context, will be a Level 6 qualified professional who delivers personal careers guidance as described in Gatsby Benchmark 8. A careers leader can be a careers adviser as well; however, that makes for a *very* busy work life! A careers leader qualification does not qualify you to deliver personal guidance. Careers advisers can be internal (i.e. employed by the school, special school or college) or external (i.e. independent or belonging to a careers organisation or the local authority). Previously, the deployment of an internal careers adviser was not seen as impartial, one of the requirements for the role; however, the National Careers Strategy in 2017 addressed this by stating that the qualification itself indicated impartiality would be taken as a given.

The careers leader role

The careers leader role is not for the faint-hearted, particularly when working on behalf of young people with additional needs/SEND. However, it can be incredibly rewarding, and you can make a sustainable impact on young people's lives – and there are not many roles that do that!

It operates at a strategic level, and you need skills that include leadership, management, coordination and networking. You will either be in a senior position already or have significant relationships and be able to influence the senior team, including governors.

You will be responsible for the delivery of a school's careers programme so that it delivers against the Gatsby Benchmarks; ensure that careers are compliant and meet statutory requirements, for example what is published on the website; and meeting Provider Access Legislation and Year 7 Careers Guidance. You will track destinations for at least three years, if possible, and measure the impact of careers at an individual student level using the FSQ tool and at a school level using Compass in addition to your own annual evaluation.

Specifically, you will be engaged in planning, implementation, quality assurance, managing the delivery of careers guidance; partnering with external stakeholders like local authorities, virtual schools in the case of looked after children, supported employment providers and job coaches, and training providers; working with SENDCOs and the pastoral care team internally; as well as coordinating the efforts of other staff teaching careers in the curriculum. I am very tempted to say 'and then it's lunchtime' but that would seem too glib!

You will be responsible for your own continuous professional development (CPD) starting with the Careers Leader Training L6 qualification, which is funded by the DfE.

Driving a positive and plentiful employer network that delivers employer engagement activities and work experiences is paramount.

> ❤ Your role is vital to increasing the probability and possibility of young people with SEND achieving optimal career outcomes from school, and every element described here will contribute towards that. There is plenty of support, groups on social media, the Resource Directory, and other schools local to you as well as the inclusion COP. In addition, it will be helpful if you have a strong relationship with your Careers Hub, enterprise coordinator and enterprise adviser.

#sameandifferent – a career delivery model for SEND and inclusion

The #sameandifferent model, which I developed a few years ago, seeks to reduce employer anxiety. It explores the various aspects of early career development for young people with SEND and those who don't have SEND but who are on the cusp of leaving school. It helps all career stakeholders – including parents, carers and families; careers leaders and careers advisers; and employers – to identify aspects which are the:

1. **Same** – Aspects falling under this category have the **same value** for young people with SEND as they do for those without SEND. These aspects are universally relevant and apply equally to both groups.

2. **Same and different** – These aspects also hold value for young people with SEND, but they need to be delivered differently. The approach may vary due to individual needs, but the underlying value remains consistent.

3. **Different** – Aspects categorised as 'different" are specifically relevant to young people with SEND. They might not apply to their peers without SEND. These aspects address unique requirements and considerations.

The value of this model, and what I have found with both careers practitioners and employers alike, is it reduces the anxiety around diversity and increases understanding of all stakeholders to improve their contribution to aspirations being raised and met. There are two versions of this model, tailored to different SEND career groups:

- **Version 1** – Designed for SEND Career Group One students with communication/interaction or cognition and learning difficulties who typically won't take GCSEs or Level 2 qualifications. Note that this model may not fully apply to students with highly complex needs, such as profound and multiple learning difficulties (PMLD).

- **Version 2** – Intended for SEND Career Group Two students with SEND; social, emotional and mental health difficulties (SEMH); and behavioural, sensory and/or physical needs and who would or could take Level 2 qualifications and higher.

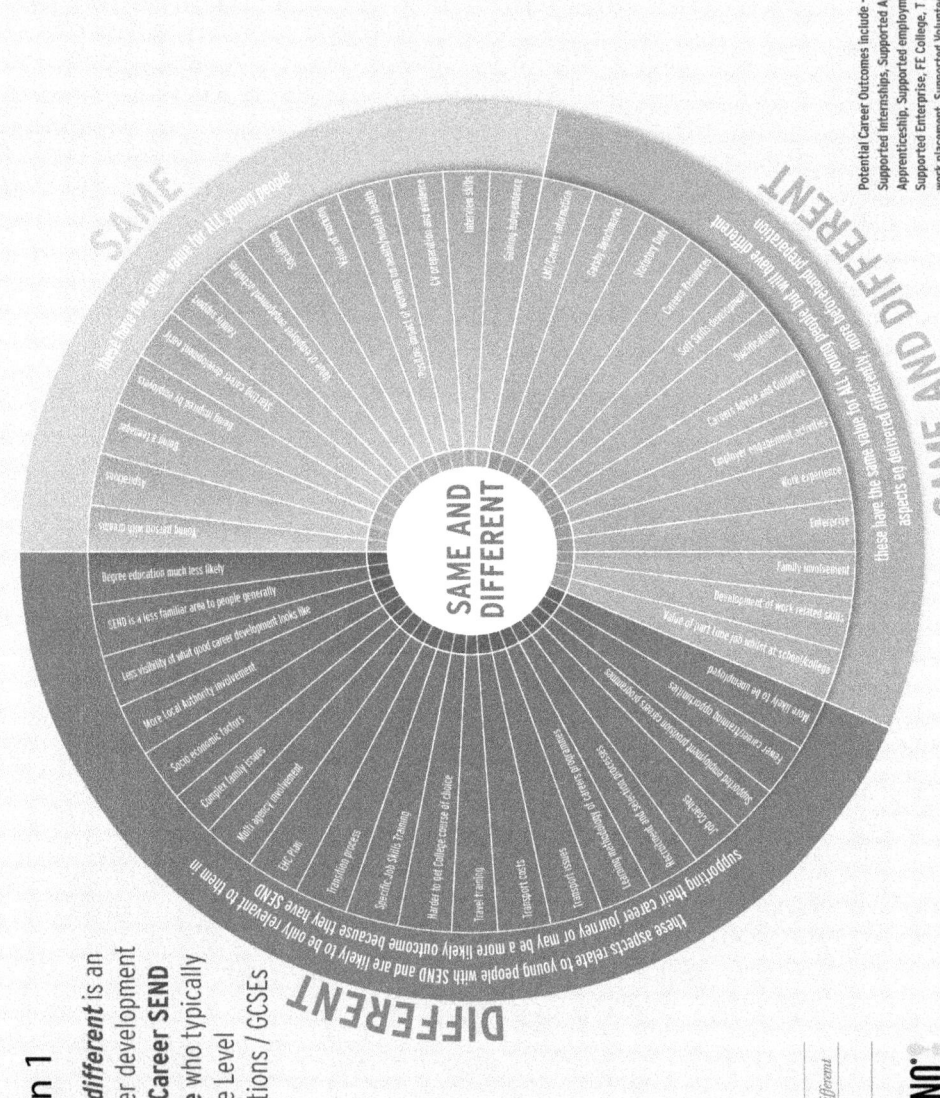

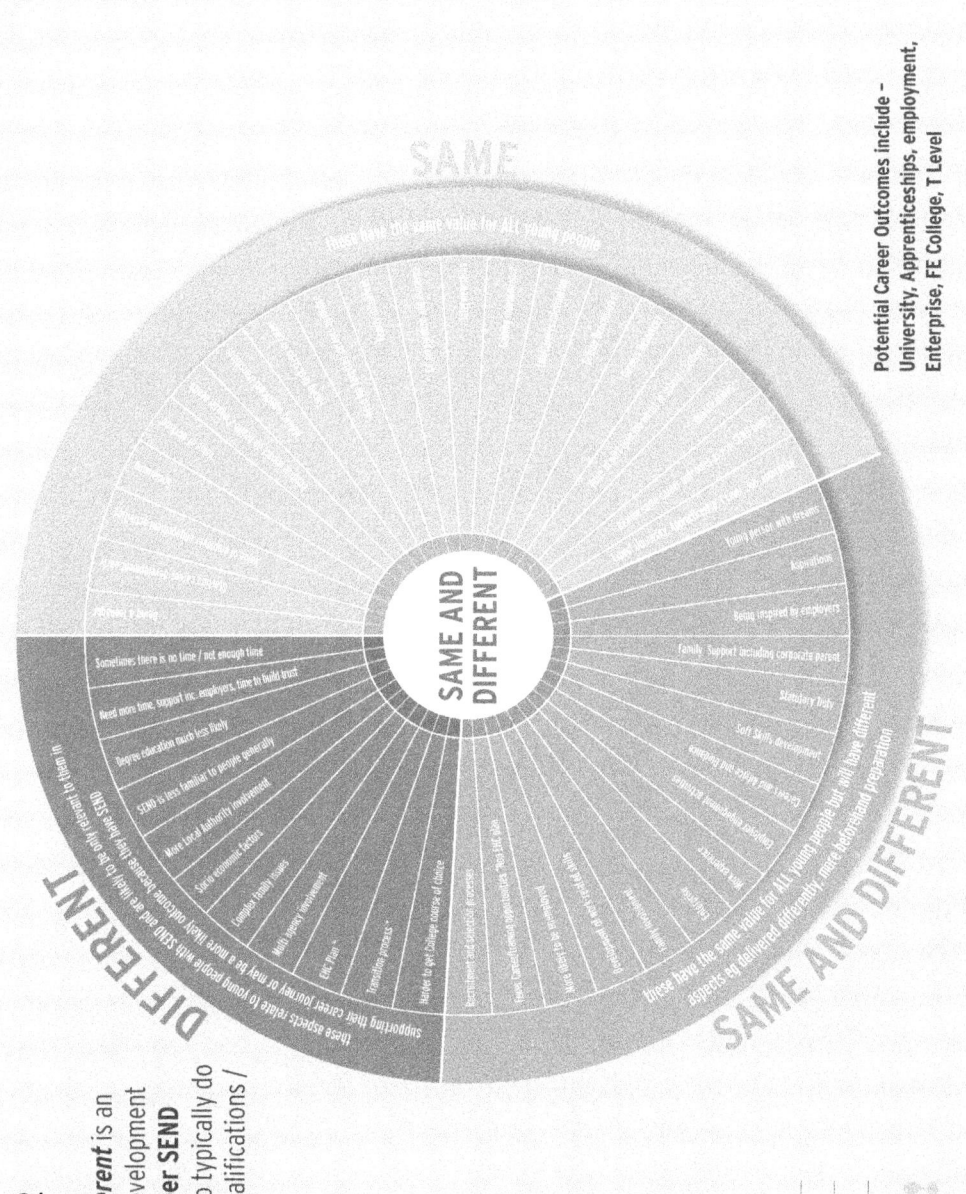

Version 2

#Sameanddifferent is an early career development model for **Career SEND**

Group Two who typically do take Level 2 qualifications / GCSEs

Potential Career Outcomes include – University, Apprenticeships, employment, Enterprise, FE College, T Level

- Some
- Same and Different
- Different

TALENTINO

What is interesting when comparing the two models is that for Career SEND Group One, there are significantly more aspects which are different and need to be delivered differently than for Career SEND Group Two or for young people with no additional needs.

For Career SEND Group Two, there are significantly more aspects which are the same as for young people with no additional needs and significantly fewer aspects that are different or need to be delivered differently than for Career SEND Group One. It is possible that the aspects which are the same but different for this group need greater attention to detail in terms of *how* they are delivered given the wide range of needs exemplified by the different membership groups in Career SEND Group Two.

Use the #sameanddifferent model with employers as it lowers their anxieties about diversity and difference and raises their game in terms of approaching employer engagement activities from a can-do perspective. In education, it makes sense to plan career activities starting with the potential career destination after school and working backwards from that point to enable the young person to have the maximum possibility to achieve an optimum career outcome whatever that is.

Summary of key points
The role of the careers leader can make all the difference. It can be tough but *so* rewarding. Take up the professional training opportunity, approach the career development of young people with additional needs as a privilege and take enjoyment from the advances they and you will make. Use all the tools at your disposal, and don't forget about your own continuous CPD, there are lots of free opportunities. Enjoy it!

Resources
www.careersandenterprise.co.uk/media/uhtkww5h/understanding-careers-leader-role-careers-enterprise.pdf

www.careersandenterprise.co.uk/careers-leaders/

https://resources.careersandenterprise.co.uk/sites/default/files/2021-07/careers_leaders_in_colleges_0.pdf

GUEST CONTRIBUTOR – KELLY DILLON, HEAD OF REMOVING BARRIERS AT THE CAREERS AND ENTERPRISE COMPANY

Kelly is quite simply the Batman to my Robin with regard to inclusion and SEND, a powerhouse of change and influence, never standing still. Her perspective on careers leaders is, as expected, to the point and pragmatic. Thanks, Kelly.

Careers leaders play such an important role in ensuring we are able to support every young person to take their best next step. When we think about our young people with additional needs this becomes an even more important role. The careers leader is the driver for bringing together all of the elements needed to ensure young people with additional needs receive an equitable offer that is tailored to meet their needs and therefore enabling that cross-department working with SENCO, SEND team, careers adviser, pastoral and all the other actors who support the young person to enable positive career outcomes to take place.

When it comes to a young person with additional needs it's like piecing together a huge jigsaw full of skills and knowledge with the young person at the centre and the careers leader as the organiser. Where this is done well, evidence shows this can have a monumental impact for the young person and their families, but it's no easy task!

When we look across different types of educational institutions, we can see many different models of careers leaders and career leadership. Where we see best practice is where there is distributed career leadership across the institution from senior leadership to pastoral and everything in between and around. Recognising that everyone in the institution, and the wider community such as speech and language and other professionals and of course family and friends, can play a part in ensuring positive outcomes for young people with additional needs (and for all young people) is essential. The careers leaders' role is to bring all of this together in a cohesive plan, which is written with intent and aims to deliver real impact not just when they leave that institution but for life.

Harnessing the skills and knowledge of everyone around the young person and their life experiences alongside the relationship they have with the young person is the key to delivering a positive outcome for all that is aspirational and ultimately supports that young person to be the best version of themselves and be equipped with the knowledge, skills and behaviours needed to enable that to happen.

The Big Inclusive SEND Careers Handbook

Inclusive SEND careers health check checklist

Name of Interviewer	
Name of Interviewee	
School Name	
School/College Type (e.g. special, SEMH, PRU, AP, mainstream)	
Number of pupils and structure (e.g. age range, post-16, 19-25, etc.)	
Pupil profile (e.g. SEND, MLD, PMLD, ASD, SEMH, etc.)	
Number of leavers in current academic year	
Range of destinations of leavers in the last two years	

Section One – Careers Leadership	Action needed	Evidence	Review	Action completed
A careers leader has been appointed and is a member of the SLT or is working closely with the SLT in a meaningful way.				
The careers leader has applied for training and a bursary.				
The careers leader is undergoing training.				
The careers leader has completed the training course successfully.				
The school has appointed a named governor for careers.				
The school is considering taking the Quality Standards in Careers Award or has already achieved the award.				

The organisation of career development – the people

Inclusive SEND careers health checklist

Despite career development improving in schools, special schools and colleges, complacency mustn't creep in. I have created a strategic careers health check which you could carry out as a new careers leader, or if you are a careers leader new to a school or as the basis of an annual improvement plan. I have condensed it into the 'My little checklist' in this chapter, but you can find it at the following website to download it as a PDF or Word document: https://resources.careersandenterprise.co.uk/resources/send-careers-health-checklist

Section Two - Strategic Careers Plan	Action needed	Evidence	Review	Action completed
The Strategic Careers Plan has been created and is linked to the whole school development/improvement plan.				
The school has registered with the Careers and Enterprise Company.				
The school has been contacted by and is working with an enterprise coordinator.				
The school has been allocated and is working with an enterprise adviser.				
The school belongs to the local Careers Hub.				
The school belongs to the local Improvement Community of Practice.				
A Careers Programme has been created which is progressive and incorporates the needs of each and every student.				
The school uses Compass+ and questions for special schools to assess progress against the Gatsby Benchmarks.				
The Careers Programme is published and available on the website.				
The Careers Programme is published and available on the website with accessible and relevant information for parents/carers.				
The Careers Programme is published and available on the website with accessible and relevant information for students.				
The Provider Access Policy is published on the school website in the approved format.				
The school can provide evidence of enabling post-16 providers to provide students and their families with information.				

	Action needed	Evidence	Review	Action completed
The school can demonstrate an approach of continuous improvement through an annual evaluation and regular reviews of the careers offering.				
Careers activities are purchased from organisations with the matrix quality award for careers.				
The school works with the local job Centre and the Support for Schools Programme.				

Section Three – Gatsby Benchmarks	Action needed	Evidence	Review	Action completed
A Compass+ report is completed termly to measure progress against all eight Gatsby Benchmarks.				

Section Four – personal guidance	Action needed	Evidence	Review	Action completed
The school can demonstrate how it evaluates the contribution of the careers adviser.				
The careers adviser is highly competent at advising young people with additional needs.				
The careers adviser engages with parents, carers and families providing information and guidance.				
Provision of Personal Guidance is offered from an L6-qualified careers adviser – one guidance meeting by age 16.				
Personal guidance is offered from an L6-qualified careers adviser – one guidance meeting by age 18.				
Exploratory discussions have taken place to scope how careers guidance could be offered to younger students from Year 7.				
Personal guidance is offered to all students from Year 7.				

The organisation of career development – the people

Section Five – Young person's careers experience at school/college	Action needed	Evidence	Review	Action completed
By 14, students have accessed/been supported to access LMI careers information to inform careers decisions.				
Information has been provided on the importance of maths and science that leads to STEM careers where appropriate.				
Girls have had additional input in developing STEM-related careers where appropriate.				
By age 16, students have had a meaningful encounter with a range of sixth-form providers (e.g. FE college, apprenticeship provider).				
Schools can demonstrate how they engage parents, carers and families early in the transition process.				
All students have experienced a meaningful employer encounter annually between Years 7 and 13.				
All students have experienced two work experiences, one by 16, one by 18, externally or internally.				
All students have visited a minimum of two universities or FE colleges by age 18 if university is the preferred career destination.				
All school leavers are invited to join the school's alumni network on leaving.				
Supported internships and accessible apprenticeships are actively promoted from Year 7.				
Vocational profiles are being used where appropriate.				

The Big Inclusive SEND Careers Handbook

Section Six – Exploring the following aspects of career development for students with SEND	Action needed	Evidence	Review	Action completed
The widest possible range of destinations is being explored.				
Activities are in place to raise aspirations.				
Initiatives are in place to support and increase engagement with families.				
A dedicated team member is taking action to increase authentic employer encounters.				
Your careers offering is differentiated as appropriate for your students.				
Looked after children and children in APs and PRUs receive tailored career development.				
16–19/25 bursaries are utilised if applicable.				
Access to Work funding for trained job coaches is utilised.				
Career decisions are based on students' aspirations.				
Staff are working from the presumption of paid work.				
Effective use of EHC Plans and transition planning processes is in place where applicable.				
The school has looked at the free SEND careers resources on the Careers and Enterprise Company website, NDTI and Barclays LifeSkills for further support.				
Learners are benefiting from employer relationships.				

Careers advisers – creating an inclusive careers guidance space

- The careers adviser's impact on improving career/life outcomes
- Working as part of the Careers Team
- Creating and inclusive careers guidance environment
- Trauma-informed careers guidance and ACEs (adverse childhood experiences)
- Guest contributor – David Morgan, CEO of Career Development Institute (CDI)

Introduction

You may be a qualified careers adviser reading this, you may be a student careers adviser, you may have no knowledge of SEND, or you may be that rare breed that is comfortable, confident and competent around working with the most diverse young people. I have used the term Careers Adviser; this is most commonly used by educational settings although I appreciate the CDI uses the term Careers Guidance Practitioner. There is a statutory requirement to meet for personal careers guidance and young people, and it is the same for young people with SEND.

♥ As there continues to be confusion in some people's minds, I need to spell out the definition of the term 'careers guidance'. According to the National Careers Strategy, careers guidance covers activities which deliver any of the eight Gatsby Benchmarks. The term 'personal careers guidance' applies to the work that a careers adviser does. To qualify for scoring against Gatsby Benchmark 8, the careers adviser must be qualified at Level 6 or above in the relevant professional qualification.

There is no doubt there is a shortage of qualified careers advisers at Level 6, and numbers according to research, are diminishing. The statutory duty to deliver the number of personal guidance sessions cannot be met with the current numbers. The Labour Party has said it will strengthen careers advisers.

I think, if I can be bold, that current careers advisers should increase their knowledge and skills around young people/adults with additional needs to increase the possibility of these young people successfully navigating career paths that lead to better career outcomes. Life is getting more complex for many and we need to be skilled and able.

The careers adviser's impact on improving career/life outcomes

The National Careers Strategy states that young people with SEND should have a long-term relationship with a named careers adviser who would get to know them and their family. This is sadly not the norm and probably hasn't been since 2012 when Connexions, the nationally funded careers adviser organisation, lost its funding to the online National Careers Service.

A professional, knowledgeable careers adviser can add a lot of value to the career experience of a young person with additional needs and ultimately to their career destination after school. However, too often the soft option of the nearest FE college is highlighted rather than being more challenging and creative. The recent Ofsted Thematic Review of Careers said that careers advisers should be talking about skills and work experience, which is interesting.

Note to self if you are a careers adviser: thoroughly research the potential options for the young people you work with and think about what comes after the first destination after school. For example, the employment rate of students who do a supported internship or accessible apprenticeship is 65%–100%. Anecdotally, the employment rate after FE college is 27%. For people with learning disabilities, it is 4.7% but 86% want a paid job. Careers education is getting better for SEND students in school, but the supply of destinations needs to follow suit.

Working as part of the Careers Team

You may find yourself working with other professionals when it comes to advising a young person with SEND, and it is helpful to think of yourself as part of that team which could include: the careers leader, SENDCO, parents/carers/family, local authority, adult/social care team, medical staff, pastoral care team, looked after children team, employers, training providers and job coaches. They will all have knowledge and expertise as you do; it is about collaborating to achieve the optimal career outcome for the young person.

Creating an inclusive careers guidance environment

There are courses which can help you learn more about inclusive personal careers guidance, but I felt this little section would give you a good taste of what you need to think about and do at a practical level. Inclusive careers guidance spaces need to be thought through on a macro and micro level. When planning, think about it as providing tweaks and adaptations; that it needs to be person-centred, whole child. Avoid labelling/labels and think about strengths and advantages.

The fundamentals are important including recognising relationships are key; you cannot operate in an emotional vacuum. Now, I'm not suggesting this is for everyone, but I was talking to the head teacher of a PRU recently and he said you have to put a piece of yourself into the relationship, love even. I know what he means as I personally cannot go into career coaching situations with vulnerable young people in an emotional vacuum. Not to the exclusion of losing yourself but even so. Another teacher in a special school when I was visiting gave a student a big hug and I asked afterwards, what about safeguarding? They said the hug was probably the only one that young person would have had all week. I'm not advocating a love-in but the best relationships are trusting, warm and authentic.

The impact of using visuals and other prompts can be really helpful. Some will struggle as readers and need your support. What has happened immediately prior to your session could or will have an impact on the session so take that on board. Don't take skills for granted, for example note-taking. Avoiding being critical and think about praise; but that may not work for everyone. I remember running a session in a PRU and when I congratulated a student on a piece of work, they said please don't say that, I don't know what to do with it and it makes me anxious. If you are working with diverse young people, they may not recognise what is happening, metacognition, they will need your help.

To effectively differentiate our careers guidance space think about the eight Rs:

- **Room**, the space – is it uncluttered, will you be disturbed, is there anyone else using it, does the young person know where it is?
- **Relationship**, know the young person – have you had information in advance, is there a possibility to meet beforehand, can they have information about you and what is going to happen during the session?
- **Resources**, simple enabling access to participation – think about symbols, visuals, fidget toys, small whiteboards, and pens/rubbers to take notes.
- **Response** of the adult to and by the young person – check your own emotional state and how you are behaving towards the young person; notice their cues or lack of.
- **Relevance** to the young person and their interests – find an area of interest and make a connection; look through their lens, not yours.
- **Resilience**, making errors and feeling that is OK and trying again – yours and theirs.
- **Retention**, about the level of independence and prompts – working with Career SEND Group One means a young person will not retain

information so write everything down, take short notes during a write-up afterwards.
- **Recall**, related to retention – ask the young person to paraphrase agreed courses of action or other important information.

The five phases of a careers guidance session
For things to have the best chance of going well, you need to consider what you could do at each of the five stages of the careers guidance session, namely:
- **transition** – entering the room
- **delivery 'instructions'** – starting the session
- **delivering the session** and engaging the student in 'work'
- **how is the young person fitting into** the session/sensory needs met
- **the last 5 minutes**.

Transition – first phase
- Find out what room you are in, if there are lots of displays, if you are likely to get interrupted, who else will be there, 'do not disturb' notice.
- Arrive early, prepare the room beforehand – reduce mess, organise seating, clear the desk/table; Can a chair user enter easily, use the room? Manage everyone's personal space.
- Meet and greet – stand by the open door and smile, ask how they are (you may or may not get a response).
- Provide a settling task – unpack a card set?
- Use visual prompts to indicate the session is starting, perhaps a card set including an oops card for unplanned events/changes.
- Make fidget toys available on the table, provide a small whiteboard/pen/rubber, stick a piece of Velcro under the table.

Delivery 'instructions' – starting the session
- Ensure everyone is settled.
- If you have parents/carers/family in the room explain you will be talking directly to the young person and will ask for their involvement.
- Focus on the aspect of the career development process planned, stick to the script and explain what the focus of the session is.
- Be realistic – is this one session only and how can the young person benefit?
- Don't give lots of directions at once, one thing at a time, stick to the script.

The organisation of career development – the people

- Support instructions with gestures and facial expressions.
- Avoid 'chat'.
- Use 'dial' thumbs.

Delivering the session and engaging the student in 'work'

- Sometimes it's hard to get started. Using IT, a tablet or laptop, or individual whiteboard might help.
- No right or wrong answers.
- Exploration, option possibilities.
- Identify personal strengths, preferences, skills, and qualities.
- Provide ideas for study, training and working.
- Commence a CV/vocational profile.
- Transition (see page 72).
- Use the EHC Plan.
- Add value to their early career development.
- Output – idea generation, actions by who, recording afterwards.

Ending the session

- Signal 5 minutes before the end.
- Finish punctually.
- Finish calmly.
- Avoid 'chat', finished means finished.

> ♥ To improve the possibility of an inclusive career's guidance session, it may seem a lot to take on board, but it will soon become second nature and other young people who do not have additional needs may also benefit from your revised approach. Good luck!

Trauma-informed therapeutic personal careers guidance and ACEs (adverse childhood experiences)

I have included this relatively new field within personal guidance coaching. Trauma-informed counselling has been around since the early 1970s when Vietnam veterans showed signs of PTSD and therapists recognised this for the first time and began to use trauma-informed counselling to treat them. Trauma is an inherent part of many vulnerable and disadvantaged groups including those who have experienced adverse childhood experiences.

For young people who have or are experiencing trauma or ACEs, it may be appropriate to consider approaching their personal guidance through a trauma-informed approach which recognises the impact of trauma on the young person and the services they need which may differ in nature from other young people. Trauma is individual as is the impact of trauma and can have lasting effects neurologically, emotionally and developmentally, especially if the trauma happened as a child.

First, you need to think about yourself. If you already know what the nature of the trauma is before you start the interview, you will need to be honest with yourself and decide if there are any triggers which might remind you of your own personal trauma if relevant.

Second, using the theory of unconditional positive regard/Roger's therapeutic conditions, are you able to enter into what is essentially a therapeutic environment fully accepting of what an individual may have faced or done without imposing any of your own feelings so you can generate a safe, non-judgemental environment? It is about asking yourself if you can be truly authentic, accepting and relating in a positively emotional way with your client.

Key aspects of the trauma-informed careers guidance session or the conditions are to:

- create a safe space and safety
- recognise the signs/symptoms of trauma
- generate trust
- avoid re-traumatisation
- provide choice
- empower the client
- work together, collaborate
- be transparent
- think about peer support for you.

With the ever-increasing numbers of disadvantaged and vulnerable young people, there is a need to factor this type of personal careers guidance in our practice but being skilled and authentic to help make a difference.

This is a useful resource for trauma-informed practice and aspects to think about: www.gov.uk/government/publications/working-definition-of-trauma-informed-practice/working-definition-of-trauma-informed-practice

♥ There is no doubt that many careers stakeholders do not fully appreciate the impact of adverse childhood experiences on the possibility of a young person engaging in early career development. If your focus is survival, careers seem irrelevant. You have learnt about, or maybe you already know about ACEs and the impact trauma-informed careers coaching can have. Please talk to other colleagues and employers about this important area so these young people can be supported in the right way. They won't say but they need you to do this.

Summary of key points

The careers adviser has huge potential to impact career/life outcomes, both positively and negatively. Working with multiple professionals and collaborating is key. When it comes to your individual practice, creating an inclusive careers guidance space takes a bit of time to get used to, but your client will reap the benefits and you will enjoy it more knowing you have done your best to deliver authentic engagement. Finally, for young people (and adults), approaching the ideas around trauma-informed careers guidance can improve your inclusive careers practice for young people who have experienced adverse childhood experiences and need specialised support.

References

- *Unconditional Positive Regard*, Volume 3, edited by Jerold Bozarth and Paul Wilkins
- *Stop F*cking Nodding and Other Things 16-Year-Olds Say in Therapy* by Jeannine Connor
- www.gov.scot/publications/trauma-informed-practice-toolkit-scotland/
- www.careersandenterprise.co.uk/media/ftbnck0i/1492_pgf-final-report.pdf

Resources

CDI course: www.thecdi.net/training-and-events/edi-lunchtime-sessions-trauma-based-career-counselling and contact edi.associate@thecdi.net

GUEST CONTRIBUTOR – DAVID MORGAN, CEO OF CDI

David is like a really good bottle of Italian red wine; he has layers upon layers. On the surface, he is one of the nice guys: relaxed and professional. He is a staunch environmentalist. Then you go a bit deeper, and you see he wants change but won't trample on people to achieve it. Here David describes why change is important for young people with special needs and the impact careers advisers can have beyond the statutory duties and influences at all levels to achieve this. Thank you, David.

High-quality careers guidance is important for all young people, but it is critical for young people with special educational needs and disabilities (SEND) who may have a greater need for impartial and informed support. *Careers education* can widen perspectives, help young people gain experience of work and build their career management skills. *Personal career guidance* helps them define their career aspirations, strengths, barriers and networks, and *careers information and advice* are vital for them to choose the best pathway and move on to the next stage of education or work.

Schools and colleges should incorporate all these areas into a comprehensive and coordinated careers programme. The careers leader training offered in England does not qualify someone to offer information, advice and guidance but does equip people to develop a careers strategy and implement a whole-school careers education programme.

Careers professionals who provide information and advice should be qualified to level 4 (SCQF level 7–9), and those providing personal careers guidance should hold a level 6 or level 7 (SCQF level 11) career development qualification. The UK Statutory Guidance for schools also states the level 6/7 requirement. This ensures the careers adviser has studied the theory behind career development and achieved a level of practical capability.

It is also recommended that schools, special schools and colleges look for careers advisers on the UK Register of Career Development Professionals, which ensures they are qualified, abide by the CDI Code of Ethics and undertake at least 25 hours of continuous professional development (CPD) each year.

The Careers and Enterprise Company reported that for 2022/23, 86% of mainstream schools said most students had at least one personal guidance meeting. This dropped to 71% in special schools, though the gap was reduced compared to 2021/22 (insight-briefing-gatsby-benchmark-results-2022-2023.pdf [careersandenterprise.co.uk]).

This shows there is more to be done to support young people in special schools, though we also need to be aware of the experience of young people with SEND in mainstream schools and other educational settings. One of the challenges is ensuring they are receiving support from a careers adviser who has had training or experience in working with SEND young people.

SEND support is covered in the key career development qualifications and can be enhanced through CPD. There are many organisations, including Talentino and the CDI, which offer free or paid webinars, events and courses that allow careers advisers to gain insight into supporting young people with specific disabilities or educational needs. It is crucial that schools and colleges allow their careers advisers time to gain and maintain the skills and knowledge that enables them to support all young people in their setting.

This is important as young people with SEND may require additional careers support, whether they are in a mainstream school or college, a special school, a pupil referral unit or other specialist educational institution. There may be additional considerations the careers programme needs to consider, such as different approaches to experiences in the workplace – including such considerations as building confidence travelling unaccompanied to a workplace.

The role of the careers adviser is also important in the context of the educational setting and the student's needs. Statutory Guidance states the CDI's recommendation that personal careers guidance meetings should be a minimum of 45 minutes. But some young people may need more time to become comfortable talking with a new person, or it can take longer to express themselves if they use alternative communication methods.

This is where it is beneficial for the careers adviser to be embedded in the organisation's careers team, so they can build a rapport with students, have insight into any additional support they may need, and understand the potential barriers they may face in their career. This allows them to maximise the support they can offer before, during and after the personal careers guidance meeting.

While the way career development is organised doesn't always lend itself well to the continuity of service, for some young people with SEND it would be advantageous to build a relationship with a careers adviser that continues throughout their education, training and employment. This, along with capturing careers notes on the Education, Health, and Care (EHC) Plan, is something the CDI and colleagues championed at the 2024 House of Lords inquiry into the transition from education to work for disabled young people.

My little checklist – Top tips to improve your inclusive personal guidance

My little checklist – Careers Adviser	Top tips to improve my understanding of how to deliver Inclusive Careers Advice and Guidance	Planned action	Tick action completed
Are you trained to Level 6 if you are working in education?	This is key to deliver against Gatsby Benchmark 8 for your client		
Do you fully appreciate the impact you could have on life outcomes?	Many families will look to you for advice and trust your advice making critical decisions		
Do you work as part of a Careers Team?	Even if you are an external Careers Adviser seek out other virtual team members		
Can you articulate the difference between the two Career SEND Groups, one and two?	Anxiety is a key barrier and this model reduces anxiety focusing on potential outcomes not the special needs initially		
How do you create a more inclusive careers guidance space?	Remember the 8 R's and the 5 phases and adapt your practice to implement		
What is your level of understanding of ACEs and their impact on young people?	Do your own research around Adverse Childhood Experiences particularly if you work in PRUs, AP, SEMH schools		
Have you considered learning more about Trauma Informed Careers Advice and Guidance?	If young people who have experienced an 'ACE' this could be worth considering		
What is your understanding of Unconditional Positive Regard?	Research this and quietly assess your own practice against this model, not easy		
Do you understand the careers model #sameandifferent?	This will help you to differentiate your practice and better understand what authentic guidance looks like		
Do you always make sure you understand the full range of opportunities locally including the local offer?	Including Accessible Apprenticeships and Supported Internships		
Are you aware of the different levels of support?	For example, how Access to Work, PIP, EHC plans		

Chapter 4
The organisation of career development and young people with SEND – the process

Gatsby Benchmarks

- The eight Gatsby Benchmarks
- Looking at the eight Gatsby Benchmarks from a SEND perspective
- SEND Gatsby Toolkit 1–8 – what good looks like for Career SEND Groups One and Two
- Guest Contributor - Ryan Gibson, Gatsby Foundation

Introduction

The Gatsby Benchmarks were piloted in 2015, led by our guest in this chapter, Ryan Gibson, under the guidance of Sir John Holman. Most schools, special schools and colleges use them to guide the planning, delivery and evaluation of their careers programme. The tool – Compass – is usually used termly to monitor progress, and 'scores' can go up and down, so it isn't an escalator for performance, score 100% and that's it.

When it comes to SEND, there was initially a lot of discussion in terms of whether there needed to be a different or alternative set of benchmarks for SEND students. After discussions with various special schools and experts, it was agreed that a different set was not necessary, but the value of the Gatsby Benchmarks in SEND settings or for students with additional needs would be in the translation of the benchmarks so they made sense in their careers' context and experience.

Interestingly, I had a discussion with a school that challenged this concept, saying other schools would split off different groups and not include them in the group that they were reporting through the Compass evaluation as there would be needs that could not be co-expressed with other students. So, the 'score' did not reflect the whole cohort. Others said students were effectively 'off rolled' and not included in the assessment. There was even a suggestion someone was going to write their own!

Interestingly, the benchmark which seems to cause the most challenge is Gatsby Benchmark 1, Careers Strategy, but for me, this is the most powerful one in terms of setting the scene for your whole cohort of students, whatever their pathway. Career SEND Group One students will follow one of three pathways – employment, supported employment/supported independent living/supported living, or community and leisure. These are blunt terms, but they indicate the different types of pathways. For Career SEND Group Two, the destinations are the same as their peers, but it is the career development journey that needs to be different (see the #sameandifferent model in Chapter 6). Gatsby Benchmark 1 provides the planning space to identify different pathways and destinations and the career programmes that need to underpin them. On that basis, certainly from a planning perspective, no student needs to be excluded. You may reflect the majority group using Compass but then you pull off the Compass questions and do a desk-based assessment of the other cohorts in your school so you still get that overall view and can apply the same/similar evaluation processes.

The eight Gatsby Benchmarks

1. **A stable careers programme** – Every school and college should have an embedded programme of career education and guidance that is known and understood by students, parents, teachers, governors and employers.
2. **Learning from career and labour market information** – Every student should have access to good quality information about future study options and labour market opportunities. They will need the support of an informed adviser to make the best use of available information.
3. **Addressing the needs of each student** – Students have different career guidance needs at different stages. Opportunities for advice

and support need to be tailored to each student. A careers programme should embed equality and diversity considerations throughout.

4. **Linking curriculum learning to careers** – All teachers should link curriculum learning with careers. STEM subject teachers should highlight the relevance of STEM subjects for a wide range of future career paths.
5. **Encounters with employers and employees** – Every student should have multiple opportunities to learn from employers about work, employment and the skills that are valued in the workplace. This can be through a range of enrichment activities including visiting speakers, mentoring and enterprise schemes.
6. **Experiences of workplaces** – Every student should have first-hand experiences of the workplace through work visits, work shadowing and/or work experience to help their exploration of career opportunities and expand their networks.
7. **Encounters with further and higher education** – All students should understand the full range of learning opportunities that are available to them. This includes academic and vocational routes and learning in schools, colleges, universities and the workplace.
8. **Personal guidance** – Every student should have opportunities for guidance interviews with a careers adviser who could be internal (employed by the school/college) or external, provided they are trained to an appropriate level (L6). These should be made available whenever significant study or career choices are being made.

Looking at the eight Gatsby Benchmarks from a SEND perspective

I was commissioned to write both editions of the SEND Gatsby Toolkits in 2018 and 2020 (https://resources.careersandenterprise.co.uk/resources/gatsby-benchmark-toolkit-send) which introduced the concept of the two Career SEND Groups (see Chapter 3 for a reminder). In this chapter I have reflected the key points for each of the Gatsby Benchmarks from the toolkit rather than create a new narrative. I have seen people use the first edition with the blue cover; you need the second one with the orange cover. I understand it will be updated in the near future.

Think about the definitions of the two Career SEND Groups and the three pathways within Career SEND Group One and the membership groups in Career SEND Group Two, and look at the benchmarks through those collective lenses and think about what should be included to deliver what is relevant to the different cohorts.

The aims of careers provision are the same for all young people: independent living and working, choice, hope and optimism, adaptability and resilience, access to and engagement in decent work in all its forms (personal, gift and paid work), opportunities to learn and make progress, and the pursuit of wellbeing and happiness. Where the differences lie for young people with SEND is in how they need to learn, their priorities within that learning, how far they can get, at what rate they can progress and the willingness of the businesses and people around them to accommodate their needs.

SEND Gatsby Toolkit – what good looks like for Career SEND Groups One and Two

Gatsby Benchmark 1 – a stable careers programme

Career SEND Group One – Pathway One: formal and Pathway Two: semi-formal; and Career SEND Group Two – key pointers

A whole-school careers programme typically involves an overarching strategy with details of how activities can help students make better decisions about their futures. An effective programme includes:

- opportunities across the curriculum to develop transferable life and social skills that support careers, employability and enterprise
- development of students' self-advocacy, negotiation, decision-making and transition skills
- purposeful interactions with a range of trusted and familiar adults, including school staff and visitors
- partnership with parents and carers
- recognition of the learner voice and the active involvement of young people in decisions that affect their future, both individually and collectively
- information, advice and guidance.

The curriculum and the way it is delivered needs to be flexibly tailored for each student. Special schools need to develop a programme that is relevant to their students, whilst mainstream schools should ensure that their programmes are suitable for all their learners including those with SEND.

To comply with the SEND Code of Practice 2015, a school's SEND information report must include information about 'arrangements for supporting children and young people in moving between phases of education and in preparing for adulthood. As young people prepare for adulthood outcomes should reflect their ambitions, which could include higher education, employment, independent living, and participation in society'.

Parents, carers and families need to be provided with opportunities to understand the careers programme and careers activities being offered to their child/ children. Information about your careers programme must be published on your website. However, not every family will have online access and there may well be barriers to information getting through so be creative about how to achieve this. Involve parents/carers in the preparation for career transitions, career decisions, work experience and employer encounters so their child can fully participate.

Identify the range of optimal outcomes and the pathways towards them (use Chapter 5 to help you). Create a careers programme that reflects the pathways to the potential destinations.

Career SEND Group One – Pathway Three: pre-formal/sensory

For students with the most complex needs/PMLD, a holistic careers programme must reflect the core themes of the Preparation for Adulthood (PFA) programme including health, independent living, education, housing options, relationships and community. Information about your careers programme must be published on your website. However, not every family will have online access and there may well be barriers to information getting through so be creative about how to achieve this. Parents/carers may need support to build their confidence and involve them in the preparation for career transitions, career decisions, and employer encounters so their child can fully participate in their own way.

Identify the range of potential optimal outcomes and the pathways towards them. Check out the local offer, talk to families, other agencies involved, check the local FE offer for PMLD learners, and find out funding requirements and application dates. Work with staff and families to establish authentic careers guidance activities.

Gatsby Benchmark 2 – learning from career and labour market information

Career SEND Group One – Pathway One: formal and Pathway Two: semi-formal; and Career SEND Group Two and Career SEND Group One – Pathway Three

The overall aim of this benchmark remains the same for both groups, but the content will reflect the relevant information that each cohort and their family needs. Ensure young people have access to high-quality and relevant LMI which is available in accessible formats tailored to students' needs. Suitable formats include Braille, symbol language, British Sign Language (BSL), Makaton, videos and audio formats.

Young people with SEND may develop socially, emotionally, cognitively or physically at different rates, and careful consideration needs to be given to help them process information. The SEND Code of Practice stresses the importance of high aspirations for successful transitioning with long-term goal planning starting well before Year 9. It also says, 'Schools should seek partnerships with employment services, businesses, housing agencies, disability organisations and arts and sports groups, to help children understand what is available to them as they get older, and what it is possible for them to achieve'.

Young people with SEND and their families need specific information about which support mechanisms are available to help them enter the workplace including disability rights, assistive technology and available benefit packages.

Young people with SEND and their families benefit from hearing about other young people's achievements and what employers are offering regionally. They can do these career talks via the school's alumni network. According to the SEND Code of Practice, 'It can be powerful to meet disabled adults who are successful in their work or who have made a significant contribution to their community'.

Careers information for a young person with SEND should focus on raising aspirations, building awareness and understanding personal possibilities as well as providing access to opportunities for developing work-based skills. The information needs to be engaging, with careful thought given to layout and content in a way that is appropriate for that young person.

Parents' evenings or EHCP (Education, Health and Care Plan) annual review meetings are a good way to involve families in labour market and pathway discussions. Involving a young person's family is key to a successful transition and is well established as best practice.

Think local. These young people will not travel long distances. Don't get hung up on the growth industries; opportunities are scarce. Generate 'home grown' opportunities from your employer network.

Gatsby Benchmark 3 – addressing the needs of each student; all groups

Ensure each student's individual needs are addressed, and extra support is provided at the right time to raise aspirations. Outstanding provision in SEND settings offers a person-centred approach, and students with complex needs will have an EHCP that considers all aspects of their lives.

Schools develop use of vocational profiles. The National Development Team for Inclusion (NDTi) and the British Association of Supported Employment (BASE) define a vocational profile as a form of assessment to understand an individual's experience, skills, abilities, interests, aspirations and needs in relation to employment. The aim is to understand the person in-depth and to allow for the best possible job match or work experience placement. It provides a picture of the ideal conditions needed in a workplace for the student to be successful. See page 33.

There are many potential career pathways and options for a young person with SEND. These opportunities are identified by addressing the individual needs of the student, for example, by looking at their healthcare needs, cognitive ability, capacity to regulate emotions or social awareness. See https://www.ndti.org.uk/resources/publication/vocational-profile. A creative approach is taken to the career outcome continuum: at one end, someone can travel independently to a paid job and at the other end, may need 24/7 care and support.

The school collects and maintains accurate data for each student around their education, training and employment destinations for at least three years after they leave. Schools ensure that students can access simple documentation such as a career journal or learning record to help them record their skills and experiences, building a compelling story for job applications and interviews. The National Careers Strategy identifies that all young people should have an individual career plan reiterated in the recent Ofsted Thematic Review of Careers. Schools and colleges maintain contact with past students to create an opportunity for an alumni network and inspiring role models for current students.

> ♥ We can identify the different Career SEND Groups, One and Two. We can establish what optimal career outcomes look like for each group. We can identify the three pathways in Career SEND Group One and the membership groups in Career SEND Group Two. When you use the Gatsby Benchmarks, think about all these elements and use your very best interpretation skills to ensure what you are planning aligns to the projected outcome to establish their personalised individual career development plan. Success or otherwise ultimately happens at the individual level.

Gatsby Benchmark 4 – linking curriculum learning to careers; all groups

Curriculum learning can be linked with careers and careers can be embedded in any subject and learning topic, in addition to co-curricular provisions such as clubs, celebration events and productions. Whole-school teaching and learning focuses on the relevance of subjects to everyday independent living, future learning and leisure, livelihood planning, and employability skills. Careers provision is integral to the whole curriculum and not relegated to the margins. Young people with SEND need a personalised careers curriculum, which is often the case in special schools but more of a challenge in mainstream.

Schools can benefit by using up-to-date, research-based evidence of what works in SEND teaching and learning when designing careers-related curriculum interventions. Linking curriculum learning to careers is also about using teaching approaches that develop transferable career skills. This includes working as autonomously as possible, organising thinking, meeting deadlines, persisting and being reliable.

Linking curriculum learning to careers involves harnessing the concepts, methods, perspectives and forms of explanation of the subjects taught in the school, for example maths for numeracy, time management and finance; science and technology for investigation, prediction and exploring the wide range of jobs in STEM from CSI to the space industry; English for self-presentation, telling your own story and writing occupational information; PSHCE (personal, social, health, and citizenship education) for self-care, building safe relationships, assertiveness, negotiation, managing stress and emotional intelligence; geography for independent travel, growth sectors of the economy, green living and working; history for how work has changed and the future of work; art for the design of work clothes, what to wear and the design of the work environment; music for influencing the mood of consumers, work songs and planning a performance; computing and digital technology for freeing students from the barriers of production such as handwriting difficulties or physically carrying books so that they can function at higher levels; and catering for producing food at home or in a catering environment.

The school or college recognises that the reach of subject teaching is far greater than what can be achieved through a few careers education sessions. Having careers as a cross-curricular subject in the school curriculum can give young people access to both work-related experiences and explicit skills, alongside ensuring the subject curriculum relates to the workplace.

For students with learning difficulties, the careers programme may also incorporate a broader curriculum of independent living skills, social skills and travel training delivered by regular staff at school or by employer volunteers or mentors. Students with SEND need to have a tailored approach that considers their own pace of learning and unique abilities.

Gatsby Benchmark 5 – encounters with employers and employees; all groups

This benchmark can be reframed as a two-way benefit for both young people with additional needs *and* employers. Build sustainable relationships with local employers and plan mentoring, careers talks, mock interviews, enterprise competitions and workplace visits in partnership. The encounters are well planned and help to increase students' enthusiasm and confidence. Employers are fully briefed to understand the needs of the students and there is strong partnership work. In the best examples, schools offer a progressive range of encounters considering the development needs of individual students and take account of the different effects for different kinds of activities, for example, sequencing of these activities to ensure they are age-appropriate and progressive. Also important for effective implementation is proper briefing and debriefing. Schools also ensure that there is a strategic and structured approach to the learning and a shared sense of purpose with key partners including families, employers, teachers and other agencies. Care is taken to ensure that students with social, emotional or behavioural needs benefit from a longer introduction and preparation for employer engagement activities.

Gatsby Benchmark 6 – experiences of workplaces; all groups

Meaningful experiences of workplaces are interactions with the world of work in a real work location. Schools are real workplaces too and can offer an appropriate balance of challenge and support for carefully identified students such as sheltered or internal work experience placements. It is important to create a range of possible workplace experiences such as visits, work shadowing, work experience and career-related volunteering and citizenship, and they can be internal work experience and enterprise. For young people with SEND, there may be a need to spend more time on planning and communication and agreeing expectations on both sides.

The school will hold pre-work sessions with the employer before the student arrives. The school and employer will agree on the level of support necessary for the student and employer. If necessary, schools can often provide training for the employer. After the encounter, there should be a full debriefing for the employer, school and student to help improve future workplace experiences. For students with the most severe learning difficulties, internal work experience can provide similar effects to external experiences and help them develop work-related skills, confidence and self-esteem.

Students with social, emotional, mental health (SEMH) or behavioural problems may benefit from employer engagement activities organised for them on an individual basis. These should be provided with as much pre-work and support during the activity as possible.

For students with moderate learning difficulties, a planned programme of graduated employer engagement from key stage four can build confidence and employability skills. As students develop more of a sense of the job fields they are interested in, job coaches can be integrated into the programme to help them build job-specific skills. Supported employment providers who have great employer connections can start to bring value to the individual student and can result in bringing the young person closer to employment.

Gatsby Benchmark 7 – encounters with further and higher education; all groups

This is covered by Provider Access Legislation requirements. Meaningful encounters can be with providers of apprenticeships, work-based training, and further and higher education, and providers of the local offer, facilitated both in school and through offsite visits. Young people can learn about post compulsory schooling options in a range of ways including through direct interactions with lecturers, current students or apprentices and alumni.

Careful early planning is essential to avoid young people dropping out or losing confidence and risking becoming NEET. Young people with SEMH or behavioural difficulties in special schools can find it helpful to be introduced early to the range of options they have after completing school. For example, moving on and transition fairs will invite all local colleges to allow students to find out about courses.

Students should be encouraged to explore the full range of routes available including their local college, apprenticeships, traineeships, vocational opportunities and higher education. Schools should understand that some students will continue to need transport to college. Families may prefer their child goes to college and this may need funding agreed on upfront.

Note: *For students with the most complex needs,* identify the range of optimal outcomes and the pathways towards them. Check out the local offer, talk to families and other agencies involved, check local FE offers for PMLD learners, and find out funding requirements and application dates. Work with staff and families to establish authentic careers guidance activities.

> ♥ Most young people with SEND go onto FE college. Courses vary in value and application processes can produce disappointment. With the new Local Skills Improvement Plans, employers should be a major driving force in the courses that FE colleges are offering. If you find roadblocks to your students being accepted, work with the college so it really understands the ramifications on the individual young person of being rejected or not providing courses which lead to employment instead of providing a merry-go-round of material students did whilst at school. It is a big hairy problem in some places and needs tackling. Have a go at it (politely and offering doughnuts too). One special school I worked with completely changed the tide, working proactively.

Gatsby Benchmark 8 – personal guidance; all groups

Students with SEND have access to continued guidance and support to help them explore opportunities and develop skills to make effective transitions. The personal guidance on offer fosters improved self-determination through developing self-awareness, practising decision-making skills and setting goals. The development of individualised and comprehensive plans which include student self-determination, advocacy and input in transition planning, and family or parent involvement.

In special schools, young people with SEND and those with EHCPs have annual transition reviews from Year 9. This is an opportunity to discuss their futures and put a system of support in place. This draws on support from a range of agencies. The EHCP will aim to support students achieving goals in relation to learning and future employment, home and independence, friends, relationships, community, and health and wellbeing.

Staff who work with students in schools and colleges are ideally placed to provide careers guidance activities. Vocational profiles are a useful tool used as part of the provision of information, advice and guidance services.

Family involvement will also ensure the best outcome. When parents are involved in the transition planning process, young people with moderate to severe SEND are more likely to earn higher wages, work more hours, remain in employment for longer, have better community adjustment outcomes and live more independently. Personal guidance must be delivered by an L6-qualified careers adviser who works with the school and family. They can be employed by the school or an external brought in.

Summary of key points

The Gatsby Benchmarks work for all young people, whether they have additional needs or not. It is our knowledge of our learners and optimal career destinations, local knowledge, skill in planning, creativity in identifying and sourcing opportunities, and sharing our ideas with careers leaders in other schools that makes them really come to life. I would be very happy to hear more about how you use them and make them work for your students.

The Gatsby Foundation is carrying out a 10-year review to establish what the Gatsby Benchmarks would need to look like in 10 years' time. It has consulted widely including around SEND, which has been very much part of the review. This is brilliant as opposed to being an afterthought as is often the case. The timeline is September 2024 for publication and September 2025 for implementation. The initial findings have been identified (see the following 'Guest contributor' section) and I can't help but feel there will be an enhanced focus on disadvantaged and vulnerable young people who will inevitably include our cohorts in different settings.

💻 Resources

https://resources.careersandenterprise.co.uk/resources/gatsby-benchmark-toolkit-send

www.gatsby.org.uk/education/programmes/good-career-guidance-the-next-ten-years#:~:text=In%20November%202023%20we%20issued,a%20report%20in%20late%202024

GUEST CONTRIBUTOR – RYAN GIBSON, GATSBY FOUNDATION

Ryan Gibson is an absolute legend and is synonymous with the Gatsby Benchmarks having led the original pilot in the northeast in 2015. He has been the keenest advocate from the start about inclusion and young people with SEND/additional needs. In less than 10 years, 90% of all types of educational settings have embedded them. We look forward to your next 10 years Ryan!

The Gatsby Benchmarks

The Gatsby Benchmarks are a framework designed for institutions to use to help them provide the very best career guidance for all young people. The eight benchmarks, developed by Professor Sir John Holman and published in the Gatsby Foundation's 'Good Career Guidance' Report in 2014, outline what needs to be in place.

The benchmarks are based on international evidence of what works and, as the world-class standard for good career guidance, they rightly set a high bar. They are challenging but achievable and have been enthusiastically embraced across education and business. Each benchmark has a title and is broken down into a summary statement with associated measurable criteria. Schools and colleges self-assess against the benchmarks and can use the Career and Enterprise Company's free digital tool, Compass, to record and measure their progress. In 2022/23 over 90% of schools and colleges completed assessments, with data showing a national average benchmark score of 5.5. Achievement in special schools is even higher, with an average of 6. Infrastructure has developed around the benchmarks too; career leaders can participate in career leader training, enhancing their ability to implement and achieve the benchmarks in their setting, and a national network of career hubs now exists, enabling resources and best practice to be shared locally as well as across the country.

Over the last decade the benchmarks have created a common language for careers and established a shared understanding of what good looks like across the sector. Since their inclusion in the Department for Education's careers strategy in 2017 they have been inspiring innovation in systems and structures as well as policies and practices. The careers legislative framework has also been strengthened in that time, with the careers duty recently extended to begin from Year 7, bringing it in line with the benchmarks.

Whilst the Gatsby Benchmark framework is for institutions, the ultimate beneficiaries are young people. Some young people have complex needs, others more moderate ones, and it can be common for a young person to have a combination of needs. Every young person is an individual and the benchmarks recognise this. Regardless of setting, they require those leading careers programmes to ensure their provision is 'tailored to the needs of each pupil' and that the programme is understood by young people and their parents and carers. Being clear about the intent of the careers programme, ensuring quality of delivery and focusing on the impact of provision is key. As one career leader put it 'the Benchmarks encourage us to think about the "why", before planning the "what"'.

During the original pilot of the benchmarks in the northeast of England, between 2015 and 2017, the Gatsby Foundation consulted with experts from special schools and colleges, together with SEND specialists from mainstream schools and experts from specialist organisations. The clear message then was the same as it is now – the high aspiration of the framework of the eight Gatsby Benchmarks makes a difference and the same framework of high expectations should be available to all young people.

Careers leaders, SENDCOs and other key staff are increasingly working more closely together to ensure there is equity of information, opportunities and experiences, and that career guidance is effective. The benchmarks frame what good looks like and encourage professionals to think about what is possible and appropriate for each young person in their setting and how their careers programme should be delivered to best meet the needs of each learner.

Whether a young person is Career SEND Group One or Career SEND Group Two, it is the professionals who work with young people with SEND every day who are the experts and who are best placed to adapt their career guidance activity to the different needs of their students. There are many excellent examples of impactful practices that have been implemented for young people with special educational needs and disabilities in settings up and down the country showing how the benchmarks can be achieved for learners with a range of different needs.

The benchmarks have helped to transform careers provision in England, but the work is not yet complete. The year 2024 marks 10 years since the publication of the Gatsby Benchmark Framework and over the last decade there have been innovations in careers guidance generated by schools, colleges and employers as well as significant changes in education and the labour market and advances in technology.

The Gatsby Foundation is reflecting on these changes, unpicking the challenges that persist and thinking about the next 10 years of good career guidance and if any refinements might be needed to the framework of the benchmarks. As part of an extensive research programme including literature reviews, roundtables and visits, Gatsby carried out a national consultation survey in 2023, completed by over 1,200 education and business stakeholders. It found:

- The Gatsby Benchmarks are universally supported – 94% see them as a valuable framework for career guidance.
- Every benchmark is highly valued as part of the overall framework. The value placed on each of the eight benchmarks individually ranges from 96% to 99%.
- The vast majority (88%) of secondary school and college leaders say that the benchmarks have had a positive impact on their students.

Gatsby has concluded that radical change is not needed and that stability is important. It is committed to only making changes to the benchmarks that will lead to even greater impact on outcomes for young people. A final report, including any refinements to the framework of the benchmarks and any wider recommendations, is planned to be published in late 2024.

As I look ahead to the next 10 years of good career guidance, a relentless focus on 'each' and 'every' young person and a belief that all young people should experience the very best careers provision will always be at the heart of the benchmarks. As Sir John Holman himself wrote 'career guidance is vital for social mobility. It is about showing young people – whatever their circumstances – the options open to them, and helping them to make the best choices for their future'.

My little checklist – Top tips to improve your understanding of GBMs and SEND/inclusion

Gatsby Benchmarks (GBMs) and SEND	Top tips to improve your use of the Gatsby Benchmarks	Action	Tick action completed
How are you currently assessing the GBM performance of your school using Compass/Compass+?	Are you able to group all students together, or do you 'de-select' groups to only report on one main group? Can you establish a way of creating a report against the GBMs of all groups (probably three maximum). Use the Compass+ desk-based scoring using the same questions.		
For top tips use the SEND Gatsby Toolkit and refer to the imminent Gatsby 10 Year Review report due Autumn 2024	Using the section on SEND and the GBMs, identify what improvements you could make in the design, planning, collaboration, delivery and evaluation of each GBM for each of your three mini Career SEND Groups.	Using the improvements you have identified, highlight the actions that need to be taken and by whom and when.	
GBM 1 – Does your careers strategy include all students, all pathways, all outcomes?			
GBM 2 – Does your approach to LMI extend beyond sector-based information to information on travel training, job coaches, vocational profiling, supported internships, accessible apprenticeships?			
GBM 3 – How does your careers strategy impact the individual level?			
GBM 4 – How inclusive is your careers curriculum? How is that expressed?			
GBM 5 – How do you ensure employers are engaging with your students?			
GBM 6 – How do you ensure employers are supporting your students beyond the school gate?			
GBM 7 – Is your relationship with your local FE college proactive and challenging so they add value to all your students who wish to attend?			
GBM 8 – What impact does the careers adviser have on outcomes of SEND young people?			

Career development process at schools, special schools and colleges

- Key stakeholders and perspectives
- The organisation of early career development at school
- Funding plays a part
- Quality and standards of career development
- Guest contributor – Nicola Hall, Director of Education at the Careers and Enterprise Company

Introduction

'Oh, so they *want* to work, do they'? The assumptions that are made about young people with the widest range of additional needs come from a place of misunderstanding around who these young people are and what they can do, in other words, what they 'can do'.

The organisation of early career development requires a complex network of key stakeholders, administration of burdensome processes, sporadic funding decisions, and the connectivity or otherwise of them and the processes they are involved with are key to facilitating the best outcomes.

Key stakeholders and perspectives

The **young person with additional needs** should be central to all key stakeholders' role in their early career development. Primary stakeholders include family, parents, or whoever is significant in that young person's life and could be related or not, for example foster carers.

In school, there should be a person who has responsibility for careers – the careers leader – and they should ensure that young people defined as having special needs and/or disabilities are able to access career development that will increase their chances of achieving optimal career outcomes on leaving school.

SENDCOs are senior appointments made in school who have special training and dedicated responsibilities for young people with additional needs.

♥ SENDCOs and careers leaders need to be best chums to increase the possibility and probability of better outcomes (and share muffins)

The senior leadership team will have statutory responsibilities towards the planning and reporting of this group of young people.

Every school should have a careers governor, and they will or should be made aware of the career development strategy for young people with additional needs.

You may have an external careers programme like Talentino's Careers at EVERY level or MORE when your staff are trained to run the programme with specialist SEND resources or other curriculums or create one of your own. Obviously, other programmes are available!

Staff at school should be involved in the delivery of careers curriculum lessons and may provide support for employer engagement opportunities.

If you have a dedicated skills programme like Skills Builder, they will provide training and resources for staff at school and opportunities for students. World Skills provides skills competitions nationally and globally.

The careers adviser (preferably L6) may be part of the school team or external to the school. Either way, the young person has the statutory right to a careers 'interview' by the age of 16 and one by the age of 18. This can be tricky to achieve as many careers advisers are not experienced in SEND and young people with additional needs, and there is a national shortage of careers advisers.

A young person might meet former students delivering SEND alumni sessions.

Supporting over 90% of schools, special schools and colleges in England is the national Careers and Enterprise Company. It delivers Careers Hubs around the country through a network of enterprise coordinators who work directly with careers leaders in schools and volunteer employer enterprise advisers who also work directly with schools in different ways and support their career development processes directly and indirectly with students. All Enterprise Coordinators are trained by Talentino in a one-day SEND Masterclass, so they learn more about young people and SEND and what the optimal career outcomes look like.

A young person may have an Education, Health and Care Plan which will involve the local authority and a social worker potentially. The local authority might have teams dedicated to different aspects of SEND, such as looked after children / care experienced and NEET prevention, and will be subject to local area SEND inspections which will cover the career development of these young people. Every local authority also has a Parent Carer Forum, and it might get involved.

Enterprise is an important part of the early career development of many young people with additional needs, so organisations like the Peter Jones Foundation, Young Enterprise and The Princes Trust may be involved.

National charities and charities operating locally might be involved, such as Disability Rights UK, Mencap, SCOPE and Ambitious about Autism.

Mental health, health and therapeutic professionals may play a regular part in the young person's life and need to be factored in. Social media plays a big part, with sites such as Special Needs Jungle providing parents with information.

The Job Centre and the disability employment adviser may also get involved proactively before a young person leaves school.

Job coaches who support the development of skills might start working with young people before they leave school via Access to Work funding.

Any potential destination that a young person may go to is also a key stakeholder before they leave school, including an FE college, a specialist college, an employer-led training or employment opportunity, training provider, university, and anyone providing additional support, for example UCAS and The Sutton Trust.

The National Careers Service also has a role with young people with SEND up to the age of 25 years. It can provide a chatbot for basic careers questions or a 'live' careers adviser.

In recent announcements, the National Careers Service and Job Centres will join together.

The local business community will comprise the network of employers you work with now and new employers that you have not yet connected with. They might include business representative organisations like chambers of commerce, Business in the Community and other local groups.

Local travel companies can be key. Some will offer discounts on travel which is great but not if you can't use the ticket until after work starts. Find out what is available locally.

The organisation of early career development at school

The organisation of career development at school should start as early as possible, in early years or primary. From Year 7, the careers programme is augmented via the Gatsby Benchmarks and should start in a systematic way. If there is an EHC Plan/IEP in place, annual reviews will occur with internal staff, the family, and professionals from the local Authority and potentially a careers adviser, particularly for the Year 9 Transition Review. Careers adviser 'interviews' should be offered to students in Year 7 and another opportunity by the end of Year 11 and Year 13/14 and is the student's statutory right. Work experience and employer encounters as well as LMI information being offered from Year 10 and ensuring a personal career development plan is in place are crucial. The school also has a statutory responsibility, PALS, to ensure that students meet training providers, and engage in visits to potential destinations such as FE colleges, residential settings, universities, or employer-provided training places.

Funding plays a part

Funding and early career development can impact on whether a student can access job coaching, a supported internship or accessible apprenticeship. There is a pilot currently for 200 students who do not have the usually required EHC Plan in place. It's probably fair to say that decisions on requests for Access to Work funding are not always universally applied. Local travel companies' funding support will differ; you need to find out what yours looks like. PIP (Personal Independence Payments) funding is being brought into question. The support in terms of funding and funded services will also look different everywhere.

> ♥ Look for funding from Access to Work, the local authority, local employer programmes, local charities and dedicated groups. Think about the National Lottery small grants. You may be able to fundraise through your own enterprises.

Quality and standards of career development

There are different ways to ensure the quality of career development for young people with additional needs including Ofsted inspections; the Gatsby Benchmarks measured by Compass; the qualification status of careers advisers at L6 as a minimum; careers leader L6 qualification training; the recommended requirement for schools to purchase careers services from organisations with the Matrix accreditation; the Quality Standard in Careers accreditation; EHC Plan process requirements such as holding annual reviews; statutory requirements such as two careers 'interviews'; and the use of the Future Skills Questionnaire (FSQ) and implementing PALS (Provider Access). Collectively these should all amount to a qualitative approach to early career development but we all need to keep vigilant on a regular basis. Destination reporting also provides a prompt to ensure destinations are improving year on year.

Summary of key points

At the end of the day, what you want from your key stakeholders is that they all hold the core belief that young people with additional needs have the right to whatever an optimum career outcome looks like for them. They also need to achieve connectivity, joining together to reinforce a career development process that results in improved outcomes whether family, schools, external organisations, the Careers Hub and local authority. Career development in school should be a *system* of experiences and planning resulting in improved outcomes. Finance always plays a part, and it can impact the level of support available, but often the key aspects of career development are not about the financials. The quality and standard of career development have improved beyond recognition since the changes in 2012 and special schools often outperform their mainstream peers, but destinations need to catch up. Career ready, yes; opportunities provided, not always.

Resources

www.gov.uk/government/publications/area-send-framework-and-handbook/area-send-inspections-framework-and-handbook

www.careersandenterprise.co.uk/careers-leaders/careers-leader-training/

GUEST CONTRIBUTOR – NICOLA HALL, DIRECTOR OF EDUCATION AT THE CAREERS AND ENTERPRISE COMPANY

The exceptional progress made by schools of all types is in no small part due to the powerhouse that is exemplified by Nicola. Treating education as the key client was pivotal in this acceleration and Nicola led the charge on this. Being the 'guardian of quality and impact' has led to a deeper understanding of what is required for young people with additional needs or who are vulnerable and/or disadvantaged. (I do feel there is a Marvel film and costume in here somewhere!)

As the national body for careers education, the Careers and Enterprise Company has the privilege of being the guardian of quality and impact; the ability to reach the education system at scale is significant in this quest and the ambition is to ensure that all young people are reached with equity and inclusion. The key to unlocking this further and faster is the effective use of a well-connected infrastructure.

The Gatsby Benchmarks offer a well-recognised framework for world-class careers guidance and rightly this is universal in its intent and adoption. When I consider inclusion, I must also be clear about our intent. At the CEC, our aim through the lens of inclusion is to ensure that young people with special needs and disabilities can access at least the same level of quality of careers guidance, be that in a mainstream setting or a specialist institution. But of course, I know that some learners need more. More tailored strategic planning, more personalisation, more targeted careers experiences and encounters, more preparation, and more specialist personal guidance.

The statutory guidance for careers guidance and the Gatsby Benchmarks are permissive in their approach to enabling schools and colleges, facilitated by strategic careers leadership to be responsive to the needs of every learner in their cohorts. It is therefore within your gift, as an education leader, a careers leader, enterprise coordinator, Careers Hub lead or indeed employer to make the necessary arrangements to ensure that the learners who do need more get it!

This is why I have taken a systemic approach to the quality and continuous improvement of careers education through development of the Careers Impact System. The system is proven to raise standards through the interrogation of themes in your school, college or special school. Through an internal leadership review against a careers maturity model (underpinned by the Gatsby Benchmarks), you can ask yourselves whether your careers provision is meeting the needs of each and every learner. This approach enables all the actors involved in the development and execution of a careers learning journey for a young person with SEND, including them and their parents, to be empowered and enabled to ensure that the provision is appropriately tailored, evaluated and impactful. If it's not, then changes and adjustments can continually be made.

To really drive continuous improvement every part of the national system needs to work together. This is why the second part of the Careers Impact System is delivered through a series of Careers Hub-led peer-to-peer reviews, a process which sees careers development professionals and school leaders working together and processing their own 'lightbulb moments' through the sharing of critical friendship and best practices.

Some of the most innovative and embedded practices we see in careers education is to be found in special schools. This is now well supported by a national network of SEND-trained enterprise coordinators and much progress has been made against the Gatsby Benchmarks. Special schools on average score nationally slightly higher than mainstream secondary schools. There is still much more to do though; there will always be more to do if we collectively aim for every young person irrespective of their circumstances to access an effective and impactful careers guidance programme for them.

In the spirit of the words of one of my favourite quotes from Helen Keller 'together we can do so much'; together with the network of Careers Hubs, well-engaged employers and driving a culture of quality that permeates every aspect of school life, i.e. taking careers from the margins of education right into its heart and making it the responsibility of every member of a school community and wrap-around support team. Then, together we can do so much *more* for those learners who need more.

My little checklist – Top tips to develop more inclusive career development processes

Improve your understanding of the organisation of career development	Top tips to improve your understanding of the organisation of career development	Planned action	Tick action completed
Could you name all the stakeholders that contribute to the career outcomes of young people with SEND in your school/special school/college?	Create a map of all the stakeholders that you have currently and any that you think would add value that you don't currently engage with.		
Do you have a sense of which stakeholders are critical to the continuous improvement of the young person's career experience?	Use your stakeholder map and list them in priority order in terms of their actual or potential impact on the improvement of career outcomes.		
Could you describe the level of engagement with each stakeholder on the map?	Create a scale of engagement, maybe RAG (red, amber, green), and using your priority list, identify who you would like to improve engagement with and how you could achieve this.		
How well do you know the careers governor, and how aware are they of the issue of (often) poor outcomes for young people with SEND?	Make a point of getting to know them and ensure they are fully aware of your careers strategy for young people with additional needs. Ask for a 'critical friend' challenge.		
Do you articulate the student's career journey through school in ways they can understand it?	Think of the careers offered from a student's perspective, year by year. Add in other 'supporters' like parents/carers/families and look at their planned experience.		
How often do you look for continuous improvement opportunities?	Once you have the student and supporter experiences mapped out, look for improvements to the delivery of the student and supporter experiences.		
Do you regularly look for funding support locally or nationally?	Make a point of checking for funding that might support additional careers support for students.		

Improve your understanding of the organisation of career development	Top tips to improve your understanding of the organisation of career development	Planned action	Tick action completed
Do you look at your Compass results from the perspective of improving outcomes?	As well as congratulating yourself on your results, of course(!), think about each benchmark in terms of how it could influence an improved outcome and add that to your analysis.		
Do you check that careers organisations from whom you purchase products and services have the matrix accreditation?	Check!		
Do you look at destinations year on year in terms of improvement?	Establish the improvement in the range of destinations and the numbers achieving a better-quality outcome.		
How aware are you of the Local SEND Area Inspection changes?	Check out the link in the 'Resources' section.		

The career development process

- Understanding the career development process
- Raising aspirations
- The importance of starting early and young people with SEND
- The career development process in detail
- Guest contributor – Dr Deirdre Hughes, Associate Professor and Co-Founder of CareerChat Ltd

Introduction

This might sound like heresy, but one of the aspects of the Gatsby Benchmarks, numbers 1 to 8, is that it can lead people to view career development, especially in the early days, as isolated events rather than a process. A process is a series of activities which should link together to produce something of value at the end, if there is a defined end. Again, careers are often described as a verb whilst in education and as a noun when a career proper starts. However, if everyone starts to treat career development as a lifelong process, it can start to mitigate the incredible stress young people feel about making career decisions if they are encouraged to look at it as a process.

Having said that, young people in Career SEND Group One may not be able to envision their future much further than the short term, and the long term could be a very stressful concept for them. It can also be a very stressful event for parents/carers and family to anticipate. The clue here is to engage them as early as possible and build their confidence. For students in Career SEND Group Two, there is such a diversity of starting points, but all these young people need a career development process very similar to their peers but delivered differently.

This chapter outlines the career development process in terms of ages and stages and activities; aspiration raising; planning; and aligns this to each Career SEND Group. Note: this is a chunky chapter that needs equally chunky biscuits!

Understanding the career development process

Career development is a process that can start as early as possible and is proportionate to the stage and age of the person taking part. It works like a double helix (as my son Kit, who is a data scientist, informs me!), which means it is a continuous coil that comes back on itself but goes forward overall. Take career exploration; you won't just do it once, but you will repeat it at different times in your career development journey at different ages, and the focus might be different each time.

The career development process should start as early as possible, ideally in early years, and extend throughout education and into the workplace through training, the first role, second role and lifelong career development. The different components of career development are:

- understanding what career development is and its importance
- qualifications and their contribution to career success
- appreciating the influences and influencers on career decisions, both positive and negative
- understanding our own career orientation
- exploring careers that align with individual career orientation
- career planning and decision-making, including external drivers, e.g. application deadlines
- creating a CV/vocational profile and making applications
- personal development – soft/'intrinsic skills' needed for work and life, including travel training, working with a job coach, advocacy, reasonable adjustments, disclosure
- employability skills development and what employers want – needed for work and life, work insights, work experience, part-time jobs
- appreciation of the development of skills needed in the future
- learning how to compete for the career of choice – personal brand and how to stand out, differentiate ourselves positively
- social purpose – social action projects, volunteering.

At different ages and stages, different components of the process will have more or less significance as they will be driven by when a career decision must be made.

Raising aspirations

Many young people with additional needs may not have met or be conscious of other people 'like them' who have achieved career success, whatever that means to them. There is an expression – 'If you can't see it, you can't be it'.

The Ambition Institute identified five 'tips' from an aspiration project:

- keeping aspiration at the heart of your work
- developing student resilience

- creating a culture where young people get multiple chances
- having solution-focused conversations and celebrating success
- promoting wellbeing. It is interesting that this list was published from a project in 2018, pre-Covid, and how much of that has become integral to many schools as a matter of course today.

The Education Endowment Fund looked at research on the benefit of delivering an 'intervention' to raise aspirations and described the evidence as being 'surprisingly weak' but did mention that ensuring students have the knowledge and skills to progress is more effective potentially than an actual intervention. Career development, when viewed as a systematic process, would support the delivery of this.

> ♥ Young people who have had to struggle navigating barriers of different sorts and maybe never had anyone believe in them, including the people who should have supported them, are probably not going to be buzzing with aspiration. Think about the expression 'walk in my shoes' and imagine how you might feel. We all need to recognise we live in a careers village.

The importance of starting early and young people with SEND

The CEC says, 'Career-related learning in primary schools is about broadening pupil's horizons, challenging stereotypes, and helping them develop the skills and sense of self that will enable them to reach their full potential'. This combines aspiration raising and the reasons for starting career development as early as possible clearly. Research shows that stereotypes and socio-economic backgrounds influence children's views of potential careers from as early as five years old. This is just as applicable to children with special needs as those without and arguably even more important for their parents, carers and families. Free careers resources are available including the Primary Futures programme for primary schools. See the paper from the Education and Employers organisation www.educationandemployers.org/research/primary-futures-connecting-life-and-learning-in-uk-primary-education/

The career development process in detail

This is a very chunky section with lots of content, but it's necessary if we are to really appreciate the full nature of the career development process and be able to subsequently create effective pathways to better outcomes. Let's approach it the same way as eating an elephant, one bite at a time. Sorry veggies, I couldn't think of a sufficiently big alternative.

Understanding what career development is and its importance

It is important to inculcate a feeling of positivity and potential around career development; that it is the young person's choice in terms of their potential career destination and that it should be an exciting journey with lots of enjoyable activities along the way. Aspiration raising is key here. Ultimately you are encouraging them to take responsibility and to become their own career manager. But this will seem scary if this concept is introduced too early. Being proactive and ensuring that young people have career development opportunities in good time is important. Many adults totally underestimate the fear, stress and anxiety young people feel about making career choices and decisions.

For some young people whose lives are being disrupted by factors outside of school, they may not even be able to engage in career development but still try in short bursts when things feel calmer; always have a plan in your back pocket. Sometimes I call this 'opportunistic' career development; maybe only five minutes. Structuring a programme that is proactive and has lots of time is necessary for all young people but particularly those with additional needs. For young people in Career SEND Group One, it will depend on their pathways, but from Preparing for Adulthood, a programme delivered across the country by the NDTI, there is lots of information about how to introduce the concept (www.ndti.org.uk/projects/preparing-for-adulthood).

Qualifications and their contribution to career success

Career SEND Group One will often take qualifications that employers do not understand in terms of what can be achieved by the young person as opposed to GCSEs and A levels, which are immediately recognisable. This is problematic in several ways. Firstly, employers are busy and won't necessarily take the time to understand what particular qualifications will enable a young person to do. Secondly, they may 'lump' all young people with special needs together and make erroneous assumptions about individuals, which means that potential opportunities may not be available to a young person.

I often talk to our special schools about qualifications that employers may recognise in terms of making more positive assumptions about learners. For example, sports coaching, first aid courses, food, health, and hygiene courses required for food and beverage environments; Duke of Edinburgh, Jamie Oliver Cooking Courses; and the Peter Jones Foundation Enterprise Tycoon competition. What these all have in common is that they are recognisable brands with positive associations that employers can buy into and give a sense of what a young person *can* do.

You could argue this is subjective, but if it gets a young person further along the application route, it can only be helpful. Career SEND Group One will take qualifications at a range of levels depending on their career pathway – formal, semi-formal, pre-formal.

> ♥ There is a **new Personal, Social and Employability Skills Qualification** in development and I was lucky enough to be part of the development team aimed at Career SEND Group One. It is currently out for consultation at the time of writing and will be in classrooms in 2027. There are three levels all below Level 2 and it will be much clearer for employers to understand what a young person can do in an employment context. Talk about it extensively!

Career SEND Group Two will or could take Level 2 qualifications/GCSE and/or higher levels. They may not take them at the traditional Year 11/16-years-old timeline. Lives may be too chaotic, their education might have big gaps so they are not ready or they might be moving around. They may have had health/mental health challenges which have interrupted their progress. However, they may be students who are very well able to take and succeed in their exams but need other forms of support. As careers practitioners, there is a need to have accurate and up-to-date information for all young people with additional needs so they can fully engage in their stage of career development. Even if some are not taking their exams at the 'usual' time, a clear 'what comes next' is important to avoid the possibility of becoming NEET or the transition breaking down. Understanding the full range of support mechanisms available for students in a wide range of situations is also important, including deadlines for applications. Ensuring that there is connectivity between result publication timelines and application deadlines is also important.

Understanding our own career orientation

Ensuring that career plans are ambitious, realistic and align to our inherent career passions is a tricky threesome! There are several tools that can help young people work out what their career orientation is. As a rule of thumb, young people with special needs in Career SEND Group One probably benefit from externally identified career ideas and making choices from those. For example, Talentino has a resource that was created by researching the jobs that people with learning difficulties actually do. This was then developed into a symbol set of different careers that students can look though them and identify what interests them. At the time of writing, there are 137.

Students in Career SEND Group Two can benefit from using tools which enable them to identify their career orientation from tools which look 'inside'. There are free-to-use tools and paid-for tools and I have included a range in the 'Resources' section.

Career exploration – exploring careers that align to individual career orientation

Young people in Career SEND Group One will have different challenges understanding influences on their career decisions. The word 'realistic' is often a challenge. For example, 'I want to be a pilot', but academically they will be working below GSCE levels. Early on in our work, a group of students in Brookfields came up with an analogy which I use often, and I'll share with you. They came up with having a 'money job' and a 'dream job', something many of us can share! The money job was rooted in reality and enabled them to have a positive life; the dream job was just that.

Career planning and decision-making, including external drivers

There are strict deadlines for submitting applications to training schemes – apprenticeships, supported internships, accessible apprenticeships, FE colleges, universities – and other scheme places as well as funding. There will be dedicated processes for making applications for different opportunities, locally and nationally. Knowing where to find the information, when to make an application, when the deadline is, when the decision is published, what the appeals process/contingency process is and what the next steps are crucial. You should be able to get help from SENDCO, careers leaders, careers advisers and online. Some of these dates are published annually so checking early is vital. Ensuring parents/carers and families know early too is vital. You need to pay close attention to the processes for making applications for funding, new or continuing funding and sources of support from existing organisations and future destinations.

Vocational profiling

Vocational profiling is a process used to assess a young person's skills, interests, abilities and preferences to determine the most suitable career or vocational pathway for them. It can enable a young person to be clear about their skills and preferences as well as provide potential employers or learning institutions with the information they need to get to know the young person better.

Vocational profiling can be particularly beneficial for young people with SEND as it can help them identify and recognise career options that accommodate their unique abilities and challenges. By understanding their strengths and preferences, individuals with SEND can pursue fulfilling and rewarding career pathways that suit their needs and abilities.

Supporting young people with SEND to make informed decisions about their future career paths will maximise their potential for success and satisfaction in the workforce.

Personal development

Personal development happens in so many ways and can be inhibited in so many ways. It is also a lifelong process. I always think it is ironic to call intrinsic skills 'soft' as they can be some of the hardest to develop. Soft skills include communication, negotiation, teamworking, influencing, time management, organisation and planning, managing change, adaptability, flexibility, creativity, empathy, problem-solving, maintaining a positive attitude, personal responsibility, self-motivation, self-esteem and self-confidence.

Career SEND Group One will need particular development opportunities which could include travel training, working with a job coach, advocacy, reasonable adjustments, disclosure, and social skills including rehearsing being in a working environment.

Career SEND Group Two may need additional personal development opportunities such as advocacy, reasonable adjustments, disclosure and social skills including rehearsing being in a working environment, in addition to being supported by other professionals to work through, for example previous trauma, anxiety or poor mental health. Both groups are capable with the right support to gain additional and/or improve personal skills. These opportunities can be delivered through employer engagement, enterprise opportunities, dedicated personal coaching and mentoring, and well-trained and experienced careers advisers. It is worth mentioning too that therapeutic initiatives outside of school will contribute to personal development.

Employability skills development and what employers want

Employability skills articulated by employers in terms of what they are looking for will include the skills identified in the personal skills development section but in addition they are looking for skills such as understanding how to behave in a working environment, understanding how businesses work at a simple level, using the phone correctly (which doesn't sound difficult but lots of young people hate making phone calls), awareness of the importance of customers, numeracy, literacy, IT literacy, self-regulation, and being a self-starter.

These skills can be developed through employer engagement experiences like employer insights, work experience and part-time work (what I used to call Saturday jobs in the old days).

Young people with special needs need these experiences and they increase the possibility and probability of paid employment. Young people in Career SEND Group One who can expect an employment outcome need multiple and authentic employer engagement experiences to 'prove' their value to employers and reduce the anxiety some employers feel.

Young people in Career SEND Group Two may need reasonable adjustments to be able to fully participate. They may need more time, more employer preparation, more preparation and confidence building. This may also focus on their personal and social development as preparation to develop employability skills in a working environment. For some students this might start with very basic challenges like extended introductions, rehearsing, turning up on time and staying for short periods which increase over time. They may need practical support like help with travel/travel costs, clothes to wear at work that are suitable and even personal hygiene products. Think creatively about what the barriers might be and address them sensitively.

How to compete for the career of choice – personal brand and how to stand out

Some factors, like high levels of NEET among young people, fewer opportunities, rising entry levels and access to certain opportunities becoming scarcer, mean young people may need to take on board the concept of competing for their career and this is particularly pertinent for young people with SEND. The names of special schools, PRUs and APs are often recognised locally, and some names may carry with them, however unfair this is, a certain reputation which sets up a question mark in a prospective employer's mind. Even FE colleges can be guilty of this. Without creating anxiety, introducing an element of understanding ourselves better, our 'personal brand' and what 'I stand for', and identifying a list of differentiation activities which can help a young person stand out for the right reasons are excellent ways to tackle any preconceived notions of local employers.

Social purpose – social action projects, volunteering

For highly competitive roles and where students may not be offering the highest level of academic results, and for pure personal and social development, a social action project or a short project/work experience with a social purpose, or volunteering or supported volunteering are all great ways to develop personal and social skills including personal confidence and self-esteem. Look for opportunities available locally or generate them yourself. They could also include an enterprise project (see Chapter 6). They make great content for CVs and vocational profiles.

Summary of key points

There is a huge amount of detail in this chapter, which I won't repeat here, phew! Suffice it to say, if you apply a 'systems' method of thinking to the creation and delivery of career development in your setting with clear objectives and outcomes, you won't go far wrong! Use the Gatsby Benchmarks to identify where you can improve across the key eight areas or deepen your practice. Plot your current careers guidance activities against a framework like the CDI Framework (link in 'Resources'), and across all year groups like a matrix. Make sure you identify how you are raising aspirations and improving outcomes in the objectives of your programme. Your own school career development plan will have focus, purpose and be well understood by all key stakeholders. Make sure you create a version for students so they know what they can expect every year too. It is not unusual for young people to not recognise they are having careers lessons/experiences. You can use the #differentandbetter model in Chapter 8 too, which I know you haven't got to yet unless you like to read a book starting with the end.

Resources

- CDI framework – www.thecdi.net/resources/cdi-framework
- CICO – https://cico.talentinocareers.co.uk/
- CICI – https://cicichat.co.uk/about/
- CEC primary career resources – https://primary-careers.careersandenterprise.co.uk/
- National Careers Service, Explore careers – https://nationalcareers.service.gov.uk/

GUEST CONTRIBUTOR – DR DEIRDRE HUGHES OBE, ASSOCIATE PROFESSOR AND CO-FOUNDER OF CAREERCHAT LTD

I first met Dr D, as I fondly call her, at a meeting in the Black Country in 2016. I was in awe of her extensive background and experience and remember thinking 'don't say anything silly!' The person I found was warm, knowledgeable and eager to share and improve the careers landscape and Deirdre is that same person today. Thank you for sharing your perspective with us, it's really appreciated, including the use of AI in careers guidance.

Career development process for vulnerable young people and adults

Career development is a crucial journey for everyone, but it can be particularly challenging for vulnerable young people and adults. These individuals may face a range of obstacles, including socio-economic disadvantages, special educational needs, disabilities and limited access to resources. Effective career development processes must be inclusive, supportive and tailored to meet the unique needs of these groups. Integrating innovative technologies, such as AI-driven chatbot technology, can significantly enhance the effectiveness of these processes, providing personalised and accessible careers information, advice and guidance.

Barriers

Vulnerable young people and adults often encounter numerous barriers in their career development. These barriers can be broadly categorised into personal, social and systemic challenges:

1. **Personal challenges**: Individuals with special educational needs or disabilities (SEND) may require specific additional support and accommodations to thrive.
2. **Social challenges**: Vulnerable individuals may lack a supportive network, face discrimination or experience socio-economic hardships that limit their opportunities and access to career resources.
3. **Systemic challenges**: Inadequate educational and vocational training programmes, as well as systemic biases, can impede the career progression of vulnerable individuals. They may encounter a lack of accessible services and support tailored to their specific needs.

Opportunities

To support vulnerable young people and adults effectively, career development processes should be comprehensive, flexible and empathetic. Here are some key strategies:

1. **Personalised career planning:**
   - Developing individualised career plans that consider the unique strengths, interests, and aspirations of each person.
   - Regularly updating these plans to reflect their evolving goals and circumstances.

2. **Skill development and training:**
   - Providing access to skills training and educational programmes that are inclusive and accommodating of diverse needs.
   - Offering tailored mentorship and coaching to build confidence and resilience.
3. **Supportive services:**
   - Ensuring access to holistic careers guidance, counseling and wellbeing services to address personal challenges that may affect career development.
   - Facilitating connections with employers, colleges, universities and training providers to provide a highly personalised and tailored support system.
4. **Inclusive work environments:**
   - Promoting inclusive hiring practices and workplace accommodations to ensure that vulnerable individuals can thrive in meaningful experiential learning and work opportunities.
   - Raising awareness and providing training to employers about the benefits of a diverse workforce.

Role of AI-driven chatbot technology

AI-driven chatbot technology, powered by large language models, is revolutionising the career development landscape. Advanced systems such as CiCi, an innovative curated careers chatbot in the UK, offer numerous benefits, particularly for individuals with SEND, enhancing accessibility, personalisation and continuous support.

Benefits for individuals with special educational needs and disabilities

1. **Accessibility**:
   - AI chatbots can provide 24/7 support, ensuring that trusted careers exploration is always available when needed.
   - They can be programmed to deliver information in various formats (text, voice, etc.), making it accessible to individuals with different preferred learning styles.
2. **Personalised support**:
   - Chatbots can tailor their responses based on individual inputs, providing customised advice that aligns with the user's specific needs and goals.
   - They can adapt their communication style and pace to match the user's preferences, ensuring a comfortable interaction.
3. **Confidentiality and comfort:**
   - Interacting with a chatbot can reduce the anxiety that some individuals may feel when discussing their career concerns with a human adviser.
   - The confidential nature of chatbot interactions encourages users to open up about their challenges and aspirations.
4. **Continuous engagement:**
   - The opportunity for ongoing interactions, offering consistent support and motivation.

- They can monitor progress and provide timely reminders and encouragement, helping users stay on track with their career development plans.

Implementation in career development processes

Integrating AI-driven chatbot technology into career development processes involves several key steps:

1. **Designing user-centric chatbots**:
   - Ensuring that chatbots are designed with a deep understanding of the needs of vulnerable populations.
   - Incorporating feedback from users with SEND to refine and improve the chatbot's functionality and usability.
2. **Training and calibration**:
   - Training chatbots on large datasets that include diverse scenarios and user profiles to enhance their ability to provide relevant and accurate advice.
   - Continuously updating the chatbot's knowledge base to reflect the latest career trends and opportunities.
3. **Integration with human advisers**:
   - Combining chatbot interactions with human advisers to provide a blended 'humans in the loop' support system.
   - Using chatbots to handle routine queries and administrative tasks, freeing up human advisers to focus on more complex and personalised support.
4. **Monitoring and evaluation**:
   - Regularly assessing the chatbot's performance and user satisfaction to identify areas for improvement.
   - Collecting data on user outcomes to measure the effectiveness of chatbot-assisted career development.
   - Ensuring the chatbot is prompt engineered to adhere to a professional code of ethics designed to do no harm.

Conclusion

The career development process for vulnerable young people and adults requires a comprehensive and empathetic approach that addresses their unique challenges. By integrating AI-driven chatbot technology, career development services can become more accessible, personalised and effective. For individuals with special educational needs and disabilities, these technologies offer significant benefits, providing continuous support and enhancing their ability to navigate the career landscape. As we continue to innovate and improve these tools and develop new approaches in local places and online spaces for career development, we can empower vulnerable populations to achieve their career aspirations and build fulfilling, successful lives.

My little checklist – Top tips to develop more inclusive careers practices

Improving the career development process	Top tips to improve your career development process	Planned action	Tick action completed
How do you approach career development – activity-led or a systems thinking?	Map all the activities you offer and establish how they link or could link to form a process. Create a matrix year by year, SEND group by SEND group.		
Do you use a framework or planning template for your career development offer?	Are you happy with it? Check out the CDI Framework recommended by the DfE in 2023.		
Raising aspirations – do you have a detailed plan of action across the year groups and for different SEND groups?	Consider the factors which can negatively impact optimal career outcomes and generate a plan which is hinged to the SDP/SIP.		
What are the key influences (overt/covert) on career decisions in your setting?	Try to analyse this annually and look at the potential link to levels of individual aspirations.		
At what age are your students making their first career decision? How is that decision informed?	Offer students the opportunity to better understand their career orientation using exploration tools like CICO/CICI.		
Ofsted recently said the objectives for career development at Year 7 and for KS3 are often not clear enough.	Check yours and amend if necessary.		
Do students understand what they need to do to stand out to compete for their chosen career?	Create a list of differentiation activities, publicise them and explain why they might need to think about this.		
Developing skills is an important aspect of career development, so students recognise the skills they need to develop?	Have a clear skills development plan in place and ensure students recognise which skills are important now and in the future.		
The National Careers Strategy and the recent Ofsted Thematic Review of Careers cited that personal career plans are important	How is individual career planning approached, how involved is the young person's voice and what are the outputs?		
What aspects of your career development offer could be carried through life?	Highlight the activities which could be carried forward and ensure students are aware of them.		

Chapter 5
The career journey of a young person with SEND/ additional needs

Career pathways and destinations explained – Career SEND Group One and Career SEND Group Two

- Career pathways
  - Career SEND Group One
  - Career SEND Group Two
- Career destinations explained
  - Career SEND Group One
  - Career SEND Group Two
- Guest contributor – Amanda Cheney, National SEND Education Manager at Talentino

Introduction

It is fair to say that our focus is often on career destinations and how to enable optimal career outcomes to be achieved, but the pathway towards those destinations is important to consider too. For each Career SEND Group and the groups within those two groups, the pathways will look very different. This chapter looks at the different potential pathways and the key things to think about.

Career pathways
Career SEND Group One

Within this group of young people, there are three career pathways with discrete sets of outcomes for each pathway. Special schools name them in different ways, for example formal, semi-formal and pre-formal; or academic, vocational and experiential. Some will use terms which have no relationship to either academic ability or learning style, using colours for example.

Each pathway refers to several features and can give us a sense of the potential destinations. The features could include:

- level of academic ability
- level of support required
- level of independence
- possibility of achieving employment in the future
- having an EHC Plan in place
- local supply and demand
- attitude of parents and families.

For the sake of our discussion, let's use the terms formal, semi-formal and pre-formal for the pathways.

Young people in the formal pathway will be expected to achieve employment/supported employment in the future. They are likely to have an EHC Plan in place. They could access a supported training scheme like a supported internship or accessible apprenticeship in the future, subject to what is available locally.

Young people with learning difficulties in this group are unlikely to travel far to work or college. They may have travel needs such as requiring funding for transport, or if they can't travel independently, transport. FE college is a potential destination too. Young people in Career SEND Group One, if they are in a special school, may be at school until they are 19 years old, in Year 14. If they have an EHC Plan, they may get support until they are 25 years old.

The career journey of a young person with SEND/additional needs

The learning style of this group will require a lot of repetition and familiarity with previously unknown concepts. Multiple work experiences and rehearsing for work will be a feature of their career development journey.

Many special schools, which are where most young people in Career SEND Group One are educated, have excellent career development programmes comprised of:

- careers leader in place
- classroom-based careers curriculum
- employer encounters/work insights
- work experience
- career planning via their EHC planning reviews
- opportunities to experience enterprise
- parallel training for parents, carers and families.

Examples of career pathways for 'formal' students could look like:

From Year 7 to Year 14 – school-based careers programme
All through school – independent living skills, communication skills, employment skills
From Year 10 to Year 14 – employer encounters, multiple work experiences
Year 9 Transition Review and annual reviews thereafter
Extended transition visits to FE college in Years 11–14 depending on the leaving year
Qualifications taken throughout the senior years
Pre-internship training programme Year 12–Year 14 accessed via school
Supported internship programme: 6 months to 1 year duration, typically for individuals from 16 but more often from 18 years old, can be accessed via a school programme or via a training provider
Accessible apprenticeship from 16 years old but more often from 18 years old, accessed via a training provider
Leave school from 16 years to 19 years to go to FE college, potentially up to the age of 25 years
Leave school at 18 and go into supported employment with a job coach
Leave school at 18 and go into employment without a job coach
Leave school at 18 and take a supported self-employment qualification
Leave school and become a supported entrepreneur

♥ It may be that the timeline is longer to the eventual destination, so some students might leave school at 18, take a supported internship for a year and then take up paid employment from the employer who has provided the training. By the time they are 19 or 20 years old, they have already started their employment journey. Others may need more time, so they may stay at school until they are 19 years old, go to an FE college, then take a pre-supported internship programme before moving on to a supported internship and taking a paid role when that finishes. They might be 23–25 years old before they are ready for paid work. It is very individual. Embrace all versions!

Pathways for the **semi-formal pathway** through Career SEND Group One could look like the 'formal' strands but will require more support throughout and into the eventual destination. The level of academic learning that takes place will be lower than for the formal strand students, and the amount of support may well be higher. The eventual destination may not be full-time employment; it may be part time. A work placement might be offered prior to employment being considered, so there is an extended 'rehearsing for work' period. There may be more emphasis on activities in the community and a focus on leisure and health-driven activities. FE college may form more of a focus for longer for these students, as well as more time spent on building independent living skills.

Learners in the **pre-formal pathway** will not usually be destined for employment, but there will be a greater emphasis on preparing for life after school. There are some people who believe there is a job for everyone, which is laudable, but for our purposes here let's look at the more usual pathway for these learners. College could well be a destination after school where there are courses that offer value to these students.

These young people will need the highest level of support and will be learning at an experiential level. Pathways leading on from school include fully supported living; activities and participation in the community; residential specialist colleges; and opportunities available and publicised in the local offer. Families, friends and relationships are vital to this group to avoid isolation and ensure that a life as positive as possible can be achieved. Advocates will be important for these young people, enabling them to anticipate change and be part of making choices for their own lives.

Career SEND Group Two

Within Career SEND Group Two, there are three membership groups. Academically, all are capable and either could or will be taking GCSEs in Year 11, in addition to potentially higher-level qualifications later. The timing of sitting exams will influence what comes next. Most young people with SEND go to FE college, and it might be that further or even first GCSEs are taken when the learner has left school.

When working with a virtual school, I met a young woman who would have had a very high ACEs score and had not taken GCSEs in Year 11. However, she took them at 19 and by 26 had graduated and was on her way to doing a PhD. It is worth mentioning the challenges of care experienced (looked after children) and young people concerning university. There can be some considerable systemic barriers, for example having to take a housing offer in the place they live or losing it if they go to university in another town. Not the case everywhere but what choice would you make?

The career journey of a young person with SEND/additional needs

Those with an EHC Plan could access a supported internship/accessible apprenticeship. Ultimate career destinations are the same as their peers without SEND. The difference is that they do not achieve at the same level en masse and are often earning less for many years after leaving school, as evidenced by various outcome reports, as well as being more likely to be unemployed. There is no doubt that anything and everything that can be done is done whilst the learner is still at school to ensure they have a solid career development plan and are supported to transition effectively and stay in the destination following school, often FE college.

Academically able and well-supported students can leave school knowing what support is in place for them. Many universities will have additional support for disabled students or care experienced young people, for example. Interestingly, the budget for disabled students is often underspent through students not making claims for support.

Reasonable adjustments are a legal right, and employers must provide them. Learners who don't have the same level of support at home or elsewhere need your support to ensure they can follow a solid career path with a well-executed transition process.

Career destinations

You will find the following notation after each destination indicating if the destination is suitable for Career SEND Group One pathway formal (1F), semi-formal (1SF) or pre-formal (1PF); and Career SEND Group Two indicated by a 2; or either indicated by an E.

Paid employment: Working 16 hours or more for an employer weekly with a contract in place. E

Supported employment: Paid employment utilising personalised support, e.g. a job coach, enabling a disabled person to sustain paid work (Access to Work funding). 1F, 1SF, 2

Higher education: University education – full/part time, open learning – from age 18. 2

Further education college: Full/part time from age 16 upwards – ranging from functional skills to degree level and beyond. 1F, 1SF, 1PF, 2 – depending on the course

T level: T levels are new vocational qualifications introduced in September 2020 that follow GCSEs and are equivalent to three A levels. These two-year courses have been developed in collaboration with employers to ensure alignment with the needs of industry and aims to prepare students for work. T levels offer students a mixture of classroom learning and 'on-the-job' experience during an industry placement of at least 315 hours (approximately 45 days). They will provide the knowledge and experience needed to open the door to skilled employment, further study or a higher apprenticeship. 1F, 2

Specialist college: Specialist further education and training colleges for students with learning difficulties and/or disabilities, sometimes residential. 1SF, 1PF

Apprenticeship: A combination of work and study by mixing on-the-job training with classroom learning and being employed to do a real job while studying for a formal qualification, usually for one day a week either at a college or a training centre. 1F, 2. There have been some changes introduced in August 2024 including more flexibility around entry criteria checkout.

Supported apprenticeship: A combination of work, study and support by mixing on-the-job training with classroom learning and employed to do a real job while studying for an Entry Level 3 Functional Skills for young people with an EHC Plan, or other formal needs assessment offered on a case-by-case basis. 1F, 1SF, 2

Pre-supported internship: An education-based training programme created for students locally who are not quite ready for a supported internship which includes work experience and educational content. 1F, 1SF

Supported internship: Supported internships are a structured study programme based primarily at an employer. They enable young people aged 16–24 with a statement of SEN or an Education, Health, and Care Plan to achieve sustainable paid employment by equipping them with the skills they need for work, through learning in the workplace. Supported internships are unpaid and last for a minimum of six months but can be longer. Wherever possible, they support the young person to move into paid employment at the end of the programme either with the employer offering the internship or another employer. Alongside their time at the employer, young people complete a personalised study programme which includes the chance to study for relevant qualifications, and English and maths if appropriate. *Note there is a current project due to finish in 2025 where 200 young people with SEND but without an EHC Plan are accessing supported internships, which is great.* 1F, 1SF, 2

Traineeships: Funding for traineeships has now been withdrawn, but there a few examples where similar schemes are being funded.

The career journey of a young person with SEND/additional needs

Own enterprise: The young person creates their own business, which could be a social enterprise focused on improving other lives in some way and which they run themselves. 1F, 2

Self-employed/entrepreneur: The young person works on a self-employed basis either for themselves or for another employer and will be responsible for generating their own work, paying their own taxes and looking after themselves. 1F, 1SF, 2

Supported self-employment: The young person is supported to effect their own employment on a self-employed basis either for themselves or for another employer, and will be supported to generate their own work, pay their own taxes and look after themselves. 1F, 1SF, 2

Supported volunteering: Supported volunteering aims to provide the support necessary to encourage confidence building and engagement in volunteering activity by people experiencing mental health problems, people with learning disabilities and other complex needs, and can lead to other career outcomes. 1F, 1SF, 1PF

Extended work placement: The young person receives a longer period of work experience providing essential work skills improving employability and providing a real understanding of the workplace. Some colleges offer bursaries for travel, subsistence etc. and can work alongside a vocational course, for example. 1F, 1SF

Therapeutic environments: An example could be a specialist residential college that offers a wide range of therapeutic services/opportunities for young people aged 19–25 with complex needs. 1PF

Supported independent living: This might be part time, respite/short breaks or as support to move into independent living and will be organised in conjunction with the relevant agencies and families. 1F, 1SF, 1PF

Advanced British Standard: This is a new L3 qualification being phased in as of 2024 to replace A levels with additional study hours and time on maths and English. 2

Summary of key points

For both Career SEND Groups, career plans and development experiences need to be individualised and well supported. On paper, there are lots of potential destinations, but knowing that things get in the way, such as supply and demand issues; support or lack of it; employer confidence or anxiety; and family support/engagement.

💻 Resources

Pathways Poster: https://resources.careersandenterprise.co.uk/sites/default/files/2024-01/Pathways%20%26%20Options%20Poster.pdf

> ♥ Plan early, provide high levels of support, put the young person centre stage, and always listen to their wishes in terms of their career goals, don't assume. I use the word 'career' to mean you learn new stuff over a period of time. For some young people it will take longer to achieve their optimum career destinations; for others they might need several 'chances' repeating exams, taking exams later than others of their age; others might need lots more support; some may not be ready and that's OK too. Having a career development plan as well as an EHC Plan helps to have a timeline and plan and plot career goals, development activities and necessary support.

The career journey of a young person with SEND/additional needs

 GUEST CONTRIBUTOR – AMANDA CHENEY, NATIONAL SEND EDUCATION MANAGER AT TALENTINO

I have known Mrs Cheney (in joke) for over 10 years. We met during the reign of the incredible but now dearly departed Alan Chapman at Catcote Academy. (Alan's biggest regret by the way was not being able to show Holly Willoughby the theatrical stuffed snake he had wrapped round him during a fundraiser on This Morning *a few years ago.) Amanda has 30 years of deep knowledge and experience of SEND and now shares that knowledge around the country. A pragmatic, passionate, Amazonian warrior for better outcomes, thanks AC.*

One of the most significant features of any career pathway is understanding and applying the different types of support.

All pathways can include continued training and access to further education depending on the availability of courses with the required tailored approach to learning including a blend of study, work experience and work skills building.

The structure and destination planning for each pathway need to start as early as possible for both young people and their parents/carers and families to ensure a clear understanding and time to recognise and manage the changes during the transition journey from education to the workplace and independence.

Support possibilities: Support for young people with SEND within either Career SEND Group comes from multiple sources and may include vocational profiling, job coaching, access to work funding, and engagement with the local offer. It is crucial to provide tailored support that addresses their specific needs, builds confidence and raises aspirations, empowering them to succeed in the workplace. Tailored support is pivotal in nurturing their potential and developing independence.

Community engagement: The role of community engagement in supporting young people with SEND in their career journeys, including opportunities for networking, mentorship and participation in community-based activities related to their interests and aspirations.

Tokenism and authenticity: Token gestures have no place in our approach. Authenticity in career pathways ensures that opportunities are meaningful and aligned with young people's interests and abilities.

Individualised and tailored approach: Embracing the diversity within the widely varying groups, advocate for an individualised and personalised approach to career development which requires an ongoing assessment, flexibility, and responsiveness to their evolving needs and aspirations.

Evaluation and feedback: Ongoing evaluation and feedback mechanisms are vital for assessing the effectiveness of career pathways and support services for young people with SEND. Gathering input from *all* stakeholders, monitoring progress and making necessary adjustments to ensure continuous improvement.

Discretion over choices: Empowering young people over their career choices is paramount, as it increases autonomy and self-determination. Recognising decision-making empowers them to pursue paths that align with their goals and aspirations.

Engagement in different ways: Young people with SEND may engage with career pathways in diverse ways, at different times depending on their communication and learning preferences. Providing multiple avenues for participation ensures inclusivity and accessibility.

Community engagement: Community engagement plays a crucial role in supporting young people with SEND, providing networking opportunities, mentorship and participation in community-based activities aligned with their interests and aspirations. This level of engagement can open doors and offer opportunities to young people they may not have considered previously.

Levels of support: Support levels vary depending on their abilities and support needs. Providing tailored support ensures that everyone receives the help they need to succeed in their chosen career pathway. It is equally important for support to be reduced to offer opportunities for further independence. Support staff such as qualified job coaches, coaches or mentors understand this and are trained to reduce the level of support over time where relevant and beneficial.

Financial impact: The financial impact of career choices must be considered when supporting individuals, as access to resources and financial support can significantly influence their ability to pursue their desired career paths. Simple things like the cost of travel and clothes for work, and possibly food and drinks during the day must be considered. It can also increase anxiety within the family if the financial 'best interest' calculations highlight a reduction in the household income. This can in turn affect the motivation to consider the widest possibilities available if it reflects negatively on finances.

Conclusion

Pathways, destinations and support are all closely linked, and they all need to be considered if we are to maximise the possibility and probability of an optimal and sustainable career outcome.

My little checklist – Top tips to enhance your knowledge of ALL career pathways

Pathways	Thinking about pathways	Action	Tick
How do you describe the different pathways for your current groups of students?	Think about the range of destinations your students might achieve and identify ways to describe the potential pathways. Check them with your career guidance activities to see if they align.		
Can you articulate the different pathways for your current groups of students?	Interrogate the pathways, see where there are similar and different aspects, and check them with your career guidance activities to see if they align.		
Does your careers strategy reflect the breadth of pathways and destinations?	Is this reflected in your Gatsby Benchmark 1?		
What is the impact of parents/families on navigating a successful pathway?	Parents, carers and families are brilliant enablers of career aspirations but, for entirely legitimate reasons, can block too. Be honest and look at each family one at a time to identify ways to bring them onside early and sustainably.		
Can you describe the external factors on the choice of destinations and the pathways to them?	Do a little exercise looking at historical destinations and see how often the phrase 'I always do it like this' emerges, then challenge it.		
What is the mechanistic link between the different career planning opportunities?	EHC Plans, statements, individual career plans and planned pathways all need to have connectivity and reinforce each other. Ofsted may look for this.		
How do you manage career pathways that cross year groups and Key Stages?	This brings in the question of transitioning, but having a dedicated pathways process, document or diagram can help.		
Thinking through the different support mechanisms that deliver a comprehensive pathway, what do you currently offer?	Consider the list in this chapter and identify what you do well and what you could start to do in addition.		
How are students made aware they are on a career pathway towards a positive destination?	Review this process and improve it if necessary.		

Career destinations – discuss!

- Destinations – key questions – the challenge!
    - What is considered a 'good' destination?
    - Who decides a destination is 'good'?
    - When is the decision being taken that a young person has a 'good' destination?
    - Can proposed destinations be questioned?
    - Who decides on a proposed destination?
- Supply and demand
- Travel
- Infrastructure
- Recording destinations
- Guest contributor – Dame Christine Lenehan, Director of Council for Disabled Children (Retired)

Introduction

We've just covered destinations; I hear you, but well not quite . . .

Why the title and exclamation mark? Well, destinations are not as simple as the word implies. Yes, all young people with or without additional needs will arrive at a destination after leaving school or college, but there are some critical questions to consider, and I will attempt to tackle them in this chapter. At the very least, I want you to ask yourself these questions and, at best, make plans to enable your students to achieve the *optimum* career outcomes or destinations. The word 'optimum' is a way of describing the most favourable destination for an individual, and these destinations will vary widely.

The shortfall of the word 'destination' is that it describes an endpoint, whereas for young people it is only the first stop-off point in the career journey. I use the term 'career' to mean 'learning new stuff over a period of time', not doctor/lawyer/teacher, so it can apply to all young people and is an inclusive term when explained in this way. There is a large industry in terms of the collection of destination data fraught with all sorts of barriers, some legitimate and some made difficult through misunderstanding GDPR data limitations. Schools and local authorities collect destination data locally, and it is uploaded nationally to provide national datasets. Data collection almost seems to dominate discussions around destinations, and although it is important, it is the actual quality of the destinations or how favourable they are to an individual's future that is key.

> ♥ Gird your loins and go into this chapter with your virtual challenge sword and make sure the pertinent questions are being considered!

Destinations – key questions – the challenge!

Destinations are about the individual learner achieving the most favourable outcome, or as the Careers and Enterprise Company describes it – the 'next best step'. There are some key questions to ask about destinations including:

- **What is considered a 'good' destination?** Being contentious, is it just about not being NEET (not being in education, employment or training) at the point of leaving school? The Youth Futures Foundation published a report in December 2023 and cited two risk 'cluster' groups more likely to become NEET in its report *Risk Factors for Being NEET*. The first cluster was young people with SEN without qualifications above Level 1 – our Career SEND Group One in fact. The second group was young people who have a limiting disability and poor mental health. So, I know the students we are working with are at significant risk of becoming NEET. It is worth reading this report (see https://youthfuturesfoundation.org/news/new-research-identifies-the-key-risk-factors-for-young-people-becoming-neet/).

- **Who decides a destination is 'good'?** This is linked to the previous question, but on a local level it is worth examining where the locus of decision-making around potential destinations is taking place: Is it the young person (with or without support/advocacy), parents/carers, other agencies that are involved? Local authorities? Is it related to funding/personal or family budget issues?

- **When is the decision being taken that a young person has a 'good' destination**? When it is planned, e.g. in June/July, once they have started or six months in? This is why tracking is so important. Best practice identifies that tracking for three years after leaving school is ideal and many schools do this and learn so much in terms of what good destinations look like.

- **Can proposed destinations be questioned?** Two things spring to mind here, both around who is questioning and the legitimacy or otherwise of the questioning. For Career SEND Group One, the question of realism often crops up. Young people with learning difficulties have dreams the same as everyone else, but will not have the granular understanding of what is required. A group of students at a large special school I worked with came up with a good model quite by accident that has helped many careers professionals. They talked about their dream job and their money job. Dream job might have been an airline pilot and money job was something closer to the ground like working in the café at Ikea (real example!). There are also some occasions where parents/carers can question destinations which can seem at odds with a proactive careers programme.

- **Who decides on a proposed destination?** The obvious answer here is the young person, but there will be many people giving advice and opinions, and some will be louder than others. It goes without saying that the young person's voice should dominate the discussion and be informed by experts around them not drowned out. Everyone around the young person should have the highest aspirations on their behalf as, ideally, they will have for themselves.

Supply and demand - what influences destinations?

There are 10,000 leavers from special schools annually in England and there are not enough employers offering training, employment and supported employment opportunities at the school gate. There have been increases in the number of supported internships and there is a project for supported internships for young people without EHC Plans, which is brilliant as most young people with additional needs do not have an EHC Plan. The (Supported) Internships Work project delivered by DFN Project Search, BASE and the NDTI aims to double the number of supported internships to 4,500 by March 2025. Accessible apprenticeships, which work in a similar way, are not well known by employers and more could be done to publicise them. Changes in the way apprenticeships will be offered beginning in August 2024 might increase supply too.

> ♥ Both training schemes achieve a very high rate of employment after training, between 65% and 100%. This is significant when you know that anecdotally the employment rate from FE college is 27% and much higher after a structured employer training scheme.

For those living in rural areas, there may be fewer opportunities and self-employment may be a possibility. The Samee Charity has a new qualification involving supported self-employment (see https://samee.co.uk/nvq-courses-alternative-provision/self-employment-for-education/). You can influence destinations locally by bringing employers into your school/college enabling them to see their potential workforce.

Travel
Destinations can be influenced by travel requirements such as distance. For example students in Career SEND Group One are unlikely to travel far to work and will stay local in all probability. Travel costs may be high if starting/training salaries are low and may prohibit accepting a potential destination. Some students will need travel training whilst still at school and that is often an additional cost as students may not live near the school. Travel companies will sometimes provide passes for people with additional needs, but these may start outside of the rush hour when most people start work. Hybrid working can help. However, Lord Shinkwin recently reported that a tiny percentage of jobs offered in the civil service were work-from-home as mentioned earlier.

Infrastructure
Local training providers, supported internship providers, supported employment services and job coaches all need to be explored before destinations are decided upon. The Greater Essex County Council's project – Inclusive by Design – has brought together all the key stakeholders needed to improve the employment of young people, with additional needs driven by the employer-led LSIP.

Recording destinations
Most schools and many colleges are using the Compass+ tool supplied for free by the Careers and Enterprise Company locally via the Careers Hub, with 90% of schools belonging to date. All schools have to report data to their Local Authority including those at risk of becoming NEET. The DfE's new Unit for Future Skills set up in 2022 aggregates and publishes data annually on destinations of learners from Level 2 and higher which would include Career SEND Group Two. There is some early evidence being published of pathways too (www.gov.uk/government/groups/unit-for-future-skills).

Summary of key points
When thinking about destinations there are some key questions, and it can feel like you never get to a clear answer. This is fine, as it should be a process of continuous improvement. The important thing is to continue to ask the questions:
- What is considered a 'good' destination?
- Who decides a destination is 'good'?
- When is the decision being taken that a young person has a 'good' destination?
- Can proposed destinations be questioned?
- Who decides on a proposed destination?

You also need to be not just aware of the supply and demand for post-school opportunities but also think about how you and your data can drive up the availability of local opportunities. Other aspects like travel and support need to be considered. Young people in Career SEND Group One may well not travel long distances for work or training, either independently or otherwise.

Resources

https://resources.careersandenterprise.co.uk/resources/support-students-risk-neet

https://resources.careersandenterprise.co.uk/resources/collecting-intended-destinations

https://resources.careersandenterprise.co.uk/resources/compass

> ♥ Go in to debate and discussion about destinations with clarity and a questioning mind, and there is no doubt you can make a difference to a range of good quality destinations being available, accessed and sustained.

The career journey of a young person with SEND/additional needs

 GUEST CONTRIBUTOR – DAME CHRISTINE LENEHAN, DIRECTOR OF COUNCIL FOR DISABLED CHILDREN (RETIRED)

Everyone knows Christine – policymakers, government, charities, families and young people. I remember queuing up to meet her and thinking did I actually know how to curtsy?! (She would laugh at that.) Christine is direct, empathic, deeply knowledgeable and most of all devoted to changing things for the better. Thank you for coming out of retirement to contribute (although I don't think you will be taking on my celeriac challenge as I can't see you and retirement in the same sentence).

It is my delight to add my thoughts to this excellent resource.

The heart of our work in children's services is to ensure that young people enter adult life as full members of the community and can reach their potential. Unfortunately, over the years I have heard from many young people who have had their ambitions and enthusiasms curtailed when I know so many of them are keen to be active contributing members with much to offer. I know I need to start in early years to promote belief and self-worth, working in partnership with both children and their families to build aspirations, confidence, and an enthusiasm for taking risks and opportunities.

I also need to test ourselves against our own beliefs and limitations. Destinations can have many meanings and a single route to full-time work, while perfect for many young people is only one of many. I have been pleased to work with schools and colleges in the past who support young people with very complex needs with a goal of being an active part of their community, by volunteering locally, by working with businesses, and with the local authority and health services. I have worked with others who do not share this vision. Parents can also be, and often are, the greatest champions for their children, but, as with all teenagers, young people need the space to be themselves, take risks and do things their parents wouldn't always approve of. This process of becoming an adult can be so much more difficult for young people with significant additional needs and requires a positive system of support and challenge. What often holds people back is not the practicalities of placements but a deep-rooted belief that these young people are not capable or would not welcome the choices. The days of the old adult training centres where adults were paid a pittance to do commercial contracts are long gone and young people themselves are clear on the value they place on work and themselves.

Part of the approach must be about making young people part of the change process. I have been really inspired by young people's determination to create change, often in the face of adversity. I now have some strong role models of disabled young people who lead the way and achieve in their areas of expertise. Look for examples at https://councilfordisabledchildren.org.uk/

resources/all-resources/filter/education-and-learning/tomorrows-leaders-world-beyond-disability.

The Education and Training Foundation has a resource celebrating success and achievement. Examples of success are critical, and SEND has not been a world which has been good at celebrating achievement and helping turn the narrative and expectations of success. The medical model of disability where young people are seen to have an illness has held us back, We need to see disability as a positive difference where, with the right support, young people can have the same expectations as their peers. In a meeting recently again the result of a local consultation with young people was the desire 'to have a job, have a relationship, have a life'.

My little checklist – Top tips to improve destinations for everyone

Destinations	Top tips to improve your SEND careers practice – destinations	Planned action	Tick action completed
How do you define the word 'optimal' for your students?	Having this discussion totally underpins the 'raising aspirations' component of the career development process.		
Could you define the two groups of optimal career outcomes for Career SEND Groups One and Two?	Ensure you identify the full range for each group and that all staff are aware of the potential destination possibilities.		
How is a 'good' destination defined in your educational setting?	Identify, discuss and challenge if necessary. There should always be a range too.		
Who decides what is a 'good' destination?	Think about staff, young people, parents/carers/families, the local authority, careers advisers, and other stakeholders.		
When do you collect destination data?	This will have an impact on the outcomes, i.e. if it is a planned destination, or when it starts, or sometime after the start date – or all three!		
How do you use the destination data?	Acknowledging GDPR, the data can be anonymised and shared with all interested parties and used to incentivise the improvement of both the range and access to (and potentially supply of) different destinations.		
What is the impact of travel on potential destinations?	Think about independent travel, travel training, costs, access and locations of potential destinations.		
How broad is your definition of 'destination'? What about students with more complex needs? Are their destinations dissected enough?	These young people might access opportunities via the local offer, and their destination might be a combination of supported volunteering, leisure activities, engagement in the community and new relationships.		
What role do parents, carers and families play in supporting the achievement of optimal career outcomes?	This can be degrees of challenging for various reasons, emotional, perceived financial loss/impact and a lack of understanding about what is possible. Therefore, involve them as early as possible and stay connected.		
Do you compare destination data with other schools locally?	It may be you could both learn from each other about how to improve the probability and possibility of better destinations.		

Youth voice – hearing from young people

- Oracy
- Billy
- Emily
- Guest contributor— Laura-Jane Rawlings MBE, CEO of Youth UK

Introduction

'Youth voice' is a simple term; however, when it comes to young people with additional needs, it is one of those things that could make all the difference to the young person's destination and, of equal importance, the understanding of other stakeholders who can influence their outcomes.

Young people with additional needs fall into many groups, as we know. A young person might need encouragement to articulate their thoughts and opinions, they might need the support of an advocate, they might need to build confidence to voice their opinions, and they might need communication aids like adaptive technology, symbols or communication loops.

Young voices are often brought together in groups, for example youth councils at school; oracy schools such as those in Voice 21; national youth groups like the Careers and Enterprise Company's Youth Advisory Group; and charities such as the Council for Disabled Children, which has a Youth Matters conference annually co-developed and co-delivered by FLARE, a group of young disabled people who are also an advisory group to the Department for Education. Disability Rights UK has a young Disabled Apprenticeship Network.

Locally, young people can participate in politics through the Young Mayor scheme. Youth voice can also be corralled through different interest groups such as care experienced children and young people. These include A Natural Voice operated by CORAM, and the Children's Society, whose group provides input on the experience of being excluded.

In our career development context, needing to ensure that a young person can communicate what they need and want when it comes to career planning and decisions is key. Establish what barriers could be in place and find ways to mitigate them too. There are processes in place where their voice needs to be heard, for example at annual reviews, career planning reviews, making choices and career decisions, and PEP meetings. But informal and opportunistic communication is important too. Sometimes formal processes can feel too intimidating to a young person, so being able to engage with them when they are ready to communicate is important too.

> ♥ You can get distracted by all sorts of aspects of youth voice, but remember, understanding what is important to a young person, what their aspirations are, how they want to develop, what is working and what is not working, and the support they want is central to generating a valuable career development experience that results in an optimum outcome after school. And don't forget stakeholders; they need to hear young people's voices too.

Oracy

Oracy is gaining accelerated prominence, and this fundamental skill for young people, enabling them to gain confidence and the ability to speak in powerful ways, has the widest range of positive impacts, including building employability skills, self-confidence, self-awareness, social and emotional and interpersonal skills, resilience, and transferring across all areas of life. It may become part of the National Curriculum, so develop your oracy offering to students, especially those with additional needs. Think about it in terms of its contribution to career success too for both Career SEND Groups.

The next section has been written by two young people – Billy, who would have been a Career SEND Group Two student, and Emily, who would have belonged to Career SEND Group One. They have both contributed their very different voices. Billy has approached the challenge by describing what he feels stakeholders should know, and Emily has described what her current career looks like and the advice she would give others. Enjoy!

💻 Resources

Annual Youth Voice Survey 2023: www.youthemployment.org.uk/dev/wp-content/themes/yeuk/files/youth-voice-census-2023-report.pdf

Council for Disabled Children Youth Voice Matters annual conference: https://councilfordisabledchildren.org.uk/what-we-do-0/evidence/involving-young-people/our-projects-and-programmes/making-participation-3

CORAM Exclusion report: www.childrenssociety.org.uk/information/professionals/resources/youth-voice-on-school-exclusions

Timpson report on exclusion: https://assets.publishing.service.gov.uk/government/uploads/system/uploads/attachment_data/file/807862/Timpson_review.pdf

Oracy Framework Voice 21: https://voice21.org/wp-content/uploads/2019/10/The-Oracy-Framework-1-1.pdf

YOUTH VOICE – BILLY

I met Billy in 2018, and it was really apparent that he had huge potential. He has a very high ACEs score and, at the time was working as a teaching assistant in the AP school where he attended as a pupil. You will have met him in Chapter 3 if you saw the video made when he was a careers champion for the Careers and Enterprise Company. He has an expression which I love, which is 'Don't define me by my past', and he is a living testament to this. Billy doesn't have conventional qualifications like maths and English GCSEs, but he has put himself through an, at times, gruelling one-year residential social enterprise course in Sweden, along with other international learning and voluntary experiences along the way. He is currently waiting to start an alternative education course in Denmark as he wants to help other young people like him and delivers talks in schools like the ones he attended.

I asked him to contribute in his own words what he would like careers leaders, careers advisers and particularly employers to think about. In his own words, this is what he said:

> Before reading you need to have in mind that every person can achieve the same as the greatest humans that have walked this earth. People just need the right circumstances to help them get to that point.

Every human looks for security in their lives in some shape or form. In young people, this security tends to come in the form of parents or caregivers. Naturally, when we grow up, we start to rely less and less on the security of our parents and gain much more independence. This isn't the case for everyone. Young people with additional needs require *additional* care and security. Some young people will have not developed to the point where they don't continue to require this security from a parent or a caregiver when their careers journey gets going and low self-esteem and in turn low self-worth follow. So, because of this as an employer, you must accept that in some way you will become this security and caregiver for the young person with additional needs. You also need to accept that this is a big-time investment. Foundations need to be laid in the initial interactions with any young person, but this is especially true for those with additional needs.

As an employer, you may ask, how can I help develop a secure relationship to help develop the young person and how can my business benefit all at the same time? I see this question as a short series of steps. Only once you figure out how to build a secure relationship, can you then develop the person and once you have developed the person you will harvest the rewards.

- **Step one – Develop a secure relationship.** I'd highly recommend reading about attachment theory as I believe it will give a perspective on young people that you probably didn't have before.
- **Step two – Create an authentic and consistent relationship.** Forming a secure relationship takes a lot of time and consideration. Authenticity in your approach is paramount; they may not feel able to be authentic so

you approaching in such a way may feel warm to them. Your authenticity will be tested if this young person is not so trusting of people. So, the next most important thing is to be as consistent as possible. This will show that you are to be trusted to be who you portray yourself as. Consistency also allows for a sense of security to grow because there are fewer variables.
- **Step three – Avoid surprises**. The unknown can be scary for anyone particularly young people who don't feel a secure attachment in the early days of your relationship.
- **Step four – Create safety**. This comes from all the steps being combined. Feeling physically safe is a must but equally emotional safety is just as important. Safety in knowing that you won't judge them, you won't take advantage of them, you'll support them, you won't abandon them. Some young people will not realise they worry about these factors because they don't have that emotional and social development yet but it may show through their behaviour.
- **Step five – Relationship foundation**. You have now laid the foundation for a successful relationship but this needs to be continually 'tended'. Young people whose trust has been broken for much of their lives will not believe something good and better can happen and you will need to continually prove this to them until they start to believe it themselves.

Benefiting your organisation – employers: Companies in the modern world strive to stand out in all industries. How do you stand out in this world when there are competitors everywhere doing the same as yours? You innovate! A young person with additional needs has most likely had a different way of being taught in their education and therefore learnt differently. This means these individuals will have a different mindset from other young people. Once you have made them feel secure, they will explore how it is to work for your company and create. There's a wealth of untapped potential your company can harness and profit from while also helping society develop and more importantly changing a young person's life for the better. Your next best innovator could be just round the corner!

YOUTH VOICE – EMILY

I first met Emily and her mum, Ruth, at Brookfields School in Reading where she was a student. Always positive and engaging in everything around her, you can also spot Emily in the Brookfields video link in Chapter 3. These are her (unedited) words describing her career:

> When I was younger, I always liked to bake and cook and make puddings from different countries. Whenever I had my annual review, I always said I love cooking and baking. I wanted to be a patisserie chef in the future at the Hilton Hotel.
>
> I did work experience at Café active when I was 17 years old one day a week and I used to make hot drinks using coffee machines restocking drinks and fridges check dates and making light lunches. I went to Foxes Academy to get the qualifications to work in hospitality and catering sector and I learnt lots of different skills working at different events and in the hotel. The qualifications I got were food hygiene English-speaking distinction in English. This gave me so much confidence to work in this industry.
>
> I have a paid job at the National Trust I've been working here since September 2022. I work in the shop and in visitor reception this involves scanning cards and welcoming customers.
>
> My tips for employees are to have a job coach and to have someone to come to the interview with you. Employers should provide interview questions beforehand provide task cards if needed in your new role. Speak to the manager if you have any problems and have someone to support you if you need them.
>
> I also have a volunteer opportunity at Sheeplands on Monday. This is where I use my cooking skills. I go to Berkshire College of agriculture on a Friday I do cook and doing online baking course. In the future I'd like to work at the Hilton Hotel and be a patisserie chef.
>
> I am very confident at doing all tasks I've been given with a big smile on my face. I am good at talking to customers and like to bring joy and happiness to their day.

GUEST CONTRIBUTOR – LAURA-JANE RAWLINGS MBE, CEO OF YOUTH EMPLOYMENT UK

Laura-Jane was recently awarded an MBE and rightly so (loved the hat). Her single-minded mission to ensure the voices of all young people are heard and by policymakers is legendary. Thank you for enabling us to understand more about your work and its value to young people.

As this book highlights, young people have very different experiences and needs as they transition from education into employment, but generally throughout life we all experience things very differently and very personally.

It is why listening to people and learning about them as individuals is so important. It is far too easy to make general assumptions or allow your own experiences or first impressions to determine what a person may need or want. But it is often the case that these assumptions and first impressions are unreliable and will rarely provide you with the information you need to deliver support, a service or opportunity with the best results.

At Youth Employment UK I have spent more than 12 years finding ways to bring the voices and experiences of young people into our work. It has not always been perfect, and I have learnt a lot about what works and does not work over time.

In 2024 our youth voice activity is stronger than ever and the impact that I can have because of it is something I am deeply proud of.

Annually I lead the Youth Voice Census, the biggest survey of 11–30-year-olds in the UK, which explores a range of issues from place to education to training and employment. Young people have learnt to trust us as an organisation, and they know that the information they share with us will be used in ways that can make a difference. I see this in the volume of young people engaging with the Census each year, but also in terms of their characteristics. Many young people who are often reluctant to share their experiences do so in the Youth Voice Census.

In addition to the Youth Voice Census, I have run a volunteer Youth Ambassador Programme since 2013. The programme supports around 40 young people a year aged 16–25 and provides them with training, support, opportunities to connect to others, and opportunities to share their views and experiences across a range of platforms, including national and international conferences and at government events.

I work hard to ensure that Youth Ambassadors are supported in both personal and professional capacities, that they get more from us than they give. And by understanding their career aspirations I can tailor opportunities to help them develop their skills and experiences. Through this commitment I have seen many Youth Ambassadors share with us that their volunteering experience has changed their lives, developed their confidence, sense of belonging and allowed them to feel like they have made a difference to an issue they care about. In turn our Youth Ambassadors have helped shape our strategy, influenced the services I provide and more times than I can count have helped us to shift the dial (sometimes minutely and on occasion significantly) at a policy or employer practice level.

It is through the Youth Voice Census, Youth Ambassador Programme and our other youth voice activity and research that gives us such confidence in being an expert youth employment organisation. By understanding young people, where they are at, who they are and what they need I can better inform employers and policymakers, closing quite significant gaps in expectations versus reality.

There are many layers to creating meaningful youth voice opportunities, and those colleagues working with young people should spend time really developing a framework that works for the setting, service and the young people themselves. Too often youth voice can feel tokenistic, where conversations or workshops are had with young people but there is little post-session action that reflects what was really said. Your setting or service needs to be ready to hear and act on what young people want to tell you.

Small can sometimes be better too, trying to scale up youth voice work from ground zero can often result in a poor experience for everyone involved. Whereas taking it slowly and building on what works and adapting the things that do not work can create a much better foundation to build on.

There are lots of different approaches to youth voice participation, but often the best start with an honest and open conversation with young people themselves about what they would want the participation to look and feel like. Co-creating a youth voice framework with young people is where the magic can really happen.

My little checklist – Top tips to include youth voices

Youth voice	Top tips – How to improve youth voice	Planned actions	Tick action completed
What in-school youth voice groups currently exist?	There might be small informal groups or more formal school council-type groups.		
Would your school benefit from more youth voice groups or better communication/oracy skills at an individual level (or both)?	Think about the current youth voice groups you do hear from and those you would like to hear from. Talk to your students about how they would like to become involved in others hearing about what is important to them.		
What communication/oracy skills training could your students benefit from?	What oracy skills could you arm your students with? Could you become a Voice 21 school – see https://voice21.org/register/		
Are there particular concerns/issues that your students could become involved in and form a group to tackle them?	Young people have strong views about a wide range of subjects, for example climate change. As a precursor to maybe sharing views that are more personal to them, could you orchestrate a youth voice group around a particular subject, developing oracy skills here?		
Are there external groups your students could belong to, ensuring they are part of a collective voice of groups like them?	This is another way of bringing Youth Voice into school, where young people are already used to speaking about subjects they are passionate about or interested in. They could enable other students to find out more.		
Does your school/college contribute to the annual Youth Census organised by Youth Employment UK?	This is underway at the time of writing, but the report from 2023 is available in the resources section. It is well worth reading and encouraging your students to participate next year.		
Do you proactively secure feedback from your students?	Within the career development processes you facilitate, do you have an ongoing dialogue with students, or is it confined to specific junctions? How could you create more opportunities and a continuous flow?		
What communication and feedback processes do students have access to?	This is relevant to the point above, and it might be helpful to create a communication map of where and when communication takes place outside of the conversational. For example what/why/when/how, and then how well it works, looking for improvements		

Youth voice	Top tips – How to improve youth voice	Planned actions	Tick action completed
Have you researched youth voice toolkits?	www.activepartnerships.org/news-tags/youth-voice Check out 'Engaging Young People Toolkit'.		
Have you considered the safeguarding aspects of your youth voice activities?	www.childnet.com/resources/youth-voice-in-online-safety-toolkit/		

Chapter 6
Increasing employer engagement, enterprise and skills

Increasing employer engagement

- Why aren't employers engaging in the numbers needed?
- What do special schools, schools and colleges want from employers?
- How to attract more employers
- Training for employers
- Employer standards
- Getting ready for the challenge!
- Guest contributor – Julie Grant, Employer Engagement Manager at Brookfields Special School

Introduction

In our experience, the number one request from special schools of all types is to provide support with finding more employers to engage with to provide work insights and work experience for their learners. I think the reason for this is employers are people and many people are anxious about diversity and disability; not excuses in my experience.

I know that are lots of things that get in the way, and I will highlight some of them and include some mitigation actions to try to get over them. I will share what other special schools have done to woo more employers. And I will mention some things that don't work like cold calling (average response rate 4%!).

Why aren't employers engaging in the numbers needed?

There are lots of reasons including the people who could make it happen lack confidence or are anxious. Organisations don't always understand the needs of young people per se let alone young people with special needs; assumptions can be made about what people can't do instead of what they can. Some companies think there are major adaptations and costs involved they can't deliver or afford, they think they can't offer anything of value to this cohort, they don't know how to reach out to special schools/schools, or they think they are out of their depth and lack experience working with a diverse workforce. They might be missing information about the availability of job coaches or Access to Work Funding, which can pay up to circa £50,000 annually to help with additional costs of adaptations, travel, etc.

There is no statutory imperative or 'quotas' to hire people with additional needs so it is left to the employer's discretion.

Many employers don't know about the business benefits of employing a more diverse workforce, which can include lower recruitment costs, better retention, positive impact on staff morale, improved customer reputation and attracting the purple pound. So it makes sense whether you are an economist or come at it from an ethical perspective.

Size matters here too. Large corporations often plan well in advance so they may not have the capacity to support you when you knock on the door. Most organisations, over 90%, in the UK are SMEs with under 250 staff members and there are a significant number of microenterprises with fewer than 10 staff members. They might be your first port of call for they may be fertile ground as they exist in much higher numbers.

What do special schools, schools and colleges want from employers?

I think I know what is wanted in general terms from employers. But I think it is about flipping the question and asking what would an employer gain from working with our students before I return to what I want.

What would an employer gain from engaging with your students? This could include free Equality, Diversity and Inclusion (EDI) training which could benefit their existing staff, helping them improve their reputation and business locally, connecting with a future talent pipeline and opportunities for staff development. You need to look at it from the employer's perspective; it is a transaction and you want to effectively 'sell' something to them so they 'buy' it.

What special schools and schools want from employers are real engagement and understanding around students' potential and who they are that can lead to authentic work insights, work experience, work placements, and the possibility of supported training places after school like supported internships or accessible apprenticeships. Maybe mentoring or coaching opportunities which certainly enable learners in Career SEND Group Two to settle in and have a more positive experience.

Ways to attract more employers – what can you offer employers?

- Let's give them clear information on who our students are using the Career SEND Group One and Two model (see Chapter 3). It is my belief the number one barrier to opportunity is a lack of understanding about who these young people are and the cycle of anxiety that establishes.
- Help them with language and communication advice – what do I say, what do I call them, what's 'wrong with them', I don't have Level 1 roles.
- Be clear about who your students are, what their potential career outcomes could look like and what they could do given the opportunity.
- Find out if the employer knows anything about supported internships or accessible apprenticeships and how they work, how flexible they are, and the funding that is available.
- Ask if they have heard of job coaches or Access to Work funding.
- Offer free EDI training.
- Offer employers the opportunity to visit the school to meet students. A tip here – you may have students with a wide range of needs (and this is in no way meant to be disrespectful), but to build the employers confidence, try to start their journey with students who are able to communicate with employers about their aspirations, talk about their careers lessons, maybe what they want to do when they leave school and perhaps any enterprise they have been involved in. Prior preparation for the students is key here.
- Inviting a few employers to an employer tea and getting students to make cakes and serve the tea is a great start. At this stage, I would gently outline ways employers can get involved; some will be totally sold, whilst others will need more time, and that's fine.

♥ In my experience, schools always want 'lots' of employers, but they all need managing and if you don't engage with them quickly once they commit, they may drift off. It might be better to start with a handful to whom you can really give your attention. Look at Brookfields and its video in the case study and read Julie Grant's contribution at the end of this chapter just bursting with ideas.

Training for employers

You may have already delivered EDI training, but if you haven't, reach out. There will be a school nearby that has. If not, consider putting a short training session together. Alternatively you could have a look at a case study from the Birmingham Careers Hub which you will find on the CEC Resource Directory (https://resources.careersandenterprise.co.uk/sites/default/files/2022-07/Birmingham%20Case%20Study%20FINAL_0.pdf).

A recent three-year project called DIVERSO had to recruit 50 SMEs in London's growth sectors to offer employer engagement experiences to 1,000 young people with SEND at 10 FE colleges in London. The key learnings from the recruiting employers were to:

- be very gentle
- respect their starting points wherever that was in terms of previous experience or lack of it
- provide training upfront (a SEND Masterclass of one hour was offered to employers even if they were just considering joining the project)
- hand-hold throughout the process to build confidence, including checking ideas and materials for employer encounters
- reward contributions (cupcakes went down well)
- stay in touch with newsletters, etc.
- look at their recruitment practices, check their understanding of supported training schemes.

Employer standards

Thousands of employers are engaging with schools, special schools and colleges all over the country. The new CEC Employer Standards have been published and you can find it at www.careersandenterprise.co.uk/employers/employer-standards/.

Getting ready for the challenge!

It is not easy but my goodness it is rewarding when you see the light go on and another employer joins your network. Use every resource at your disposal – your own network, your school's network, your staff's network, your enterprise coordinator and enterprise adviser, local business groups – or go hunting like Julie Grant did at Brookfields Special School. It held an employer launch event, students made and served food, the governors came, local press took photos, the local MP came and spoke, but not one employer turned up. Undeterred, Julie physically visited lots of local businesses and spotted people who she thought would be good to approach. Ten years later (yes it doesn't happen overnight) she has 60 employers and has closed her books to new ones. These employers are invited to termly afternoon tea parties where students make and serve food. Employers are pitched against each other with a competitive awards ceremony where they can win bronze, silver or gold awards. They come back to the school to recruit and train students who also have multiple opportunities to experience work and engage with employers. Brookfields is a four-times Ofsted outstanding school with Career SEND Group students, with an employer-led destination rate that far exceeds the national average.

Summary of key points

Employer engagement takes time and precision; you need to look through the employer's eyes at what would compel them. Training is key, and the quality of any engagement is important too. Don't expect overnight success, but when it comes, it will be sustainable, and your network will keep growing until you must close it like Julie!

Resources

Brookfields Video – use it with employers they love it!

www.talentinocareers.co.uk/special-schools.html

GUEST CONTRIBUTOR – JULIE GRANT, EMPLOYER ENGAGEMENT MANAGER AT BROOKFIELDS SPECIAL SCHOOL

Julie (or M'Julie as I like to call her her) is the original and the best when it comes to employer engagement. She has almost mystical powers in this field. Julie took Brookfields from 1 to 70 employers and closed her books. Her students benefit from multiple employer encounters, work experiences and employment-related opportunities. Julie is a guru in this field; bring her top tips to your practice; they make all the difference to outcomes.

Increasing the number of employers to work with SEN students

Employer engagement and employer encounters are a powerful source of career development for SEN students.

Employer encounters offer students the opportunity to learn about what work is like and what it takes to be successful in the workplace. Every encounter with an employer helps students to acquire social and cultural capital.

It is particularly valuable if you can introduce students to new and different people who will tell them interesting things.

Evidence suggests that the quantity of these encounters is important, so you need to ensure that there is a wide range of different things to choose from and that they are meaningful, some having more impact than others.

In my experience, the more encounters a young person gets, the more benefits they receive from them. Although quantity is not the only thing that matters; it is equally important to focus on the quality of the encounters you offer.

There are lots of different ways to approach employer engagement, but it takes lots of time and energy to organise. Having a network of employers is critical to your ability to being able to offer a high-volume, learning-focused, varied selection of opportunities.

In our school we are always looking to increase the number of well-designed employers encounters that maximise both quantity and quality. It is important to understand which employers you have around locally and have current LMI. I have over time built up a strong network to ensure all students routinely have them as part of their experience of school. This can be through work experience, mock interviews, onsite and offsite encounters, career talks, career fairs, enterprise competitions, mentoring, and employer involvement in the curriculum are just a few examples.

You can also offer them in different ways – face to face, online and virtual. The encounters always need to have a clear learning outcome and be monitored to ensure they are high quality and involve a two-way interaction between the student and employer, ensuring they are prepared and understand who they are meeting and why, and will have the best chance of making a positive impact on them.

I record all students' participation in career guidance activities so I can see what they have accessed and how they felt about them, which helps us plan going forward recognising the diversity of our learners.

It is good practice to engage parents and carers in the careers programme and employer engagement, as they have a wealth of contacts and connections and play a significant role in their child's career plans and future.

My top tips:

- Remember you are linking education to the real world of business which are still very different, so be prepared, things may take time.
- Listen to businesses and what they are saying.
- Don't be afraid to keep trying if you have a knockback.
- Don't stop networking.
- Think creatively and outside the box!
- Share experiences with employers.
- Build your reputation and what you offer.
- Set expectations.
- Build relationships.
- Invite employers into your school/setting.

I would work in the same way to develop an employer's network in both a mainstream and a SEN setting. The differences may include managing the expectations of the employers (this is a positive thing, usually higher), discussing the level of support needed and the appropriate level of communication. I also believe it is our job as career practitioners and job coaches to work with and support the employers for these relationships to be a success.

Employers don't know what they don't know, so it is important to spread the word remembering that we aren't trying to shoehorn our young people into their business, but show to them how extraordinary they are and what they have to offer.

My little checklist – Top tips to improve employer engagement

Improving employer engagement	Top tips to improve employer engagement	Planned action	Tick action completed
Which employers are in your network now?	Could you use them as 'teaser mares' to attract other employers?		
Have you explored the networks of staff?	Cold calling has a success rate of 4% apparently. Use a warm network like your staff; they will have friends in their networks who are employers, probably local. Get them to see if they might be interested in having a conversation. Keep it light at this stage.		
Have you explored the school's network, for example companies that provide services?	Think about groundskeepers, catering, cleaning, maintenance, tech, HR services, transport, local authorities, booksellers, stationery companies, decorating, flooring, furniture, any company that you buy from, in fact.		
Have you been creative about exploring your local employers?	Have you visited them instead of emailing? Could you take some cakes made by students?		
What are your next steps when an employer looks like they want to engage?	Can you offer them EDI training? Can you put something together or use other's resources. Can you offer it at their site or at school?		
When you are delivering, do you explain clearly who your students are and what their potential career outcomes could be?	The point of this question is to focus on the 'I can' not the 'I can't'. Keep positive and inform that the time for talking about additional needs is when reasonable adjustments are being discussed.		
Do your employers know how supported internships and accessible apprenticeships work?	Make a point of explaining these opportunities and discuss (lightly) what they are and how they work for employers.		
Do your employers know about the business benefits of a diverse workforce?	Make sure they *do*. Use Mencap to help you: https://www.mencap.org.uk/resource/fact-sheet-2-benefits-hiring-someone-learning-disability-your-workplace		
How are your employers doing?	Once they have signed up, introduce the Employer Standards to be clear about standards and expectations.		

Improving employer engagement	Top tips to improve employer engagement	Planned action	Tick action completed
How do you sustain employer engagement?	Accept there might be a natural lifecycle but keep employers interested with lots of communication, lots of engagement with students (and lots of cakes!)		
How many employers should I recruit|?	As many as you need, but appreciate there will be turnover, so it is about having a pipeline, and that is a positive thing. Extend tenure as long as possible.		

The value of enterprise for young people with SEND

- The essence of enterprise
- Enterprise and entrepreneurship/intrapreneurship
- Enterprise skills
- Enterprise and SEND
- How to bring enterprise into your school, special school and college
- Guest contributor – Bill Muirhead, Managing Director of the Peter Jones Foundation

Introduction

Many young people in Career SEND Group One are not competing for jobs and training places with qualifications that employers understand in terms of what they *can* do. This puts them at even more of a disadvantage. Equally, those young people in Career SEND Group Two or who are disadvantaged or vulnerable may not be able to deliver the L2 results they are capable of because of a variety of barriers, for example education that has been interrupted. Or they may not be taking exams at the conventional time (i.e. in Year 11) or lack of engagement for whatever reason.

Bill Muirhead, Managing Director of the Peter Jones Foundation, says of working with young people with SEND and the new Tycoon Talentino SEND Enterprise Competition:

> It's been truly inspiring to work with an organisation as impactful and passionate about supporting SEND education as Talentino. Our partnership with them to make the Tycoon Enterprise Competition more accessible for SEND providers has been a huge success, not only in significantly increasing participation but in ensuring that the learning experience is more engaging and meaningful. The feedback I have received from teachers and students alike has been nothing but positive, with many identifying the programme's success in helping learners develop their self-confidence as well as their employability.

Enterprise is an opportunity for a young person to develop their self-confidence and self-esteem; a better sense of their self-identity is the value of enterprise.

The essence of enterprise
'Enterprise' is a verb and a noun; you can be *enterprising,* and you can have an *enterprise* which can be small and short-term or grow into a significant operation. The essence of enterprise is about originating an idea, putting something in place that is needed, generating revenues and making profit. However, you can have a social enterprise, too, where the 'profit' is less about a financial benefit for its own sake and more about a social benefit for a designated group of young people.

Enterprise and entrepreneurship (intrapreneurship)
Often enterprise and entrepreneurship are strongly linked together. According to a YouGov poll in 2017, 82% of young people from disadvantaged backgrounds perceived barriers to succeeding in business, including a lack of resources, networks and opportunities; and 80% wouldn't know where to start. Yet, 54% would like their own business, and 39% had ideas about products and services they wanted to develop. Stephen Bartlett, a well-known entrepreneur at 29, is worth £68 million but was expelled from school because of a 30% attendance rate. However, a subsequent teacher 'unexpelled' him because he was doing deals for the school and making it money, then went on to encourage his entrepreneurial activities. Jane Hatton started Evenbreak as a disabled person herself to enable other disabled people to apply for jobs with disability-positive organisations.

Entrepreneurs would generally be developing enterprises from their own ideas and creating a new enterprise, whereas intrapreneurs apply the same thinking and behaviours but inside an existing organisation to innovate or improve products, services or processes.

Enterprise skills
What really strikes me from among the Peter Jones top skills for entrepreneurs is that the majority are not hard-nosed business skills (or perceived as such) but skills for life, skills for becoming a more considerate human being, maybe skills that have not had the opportunity to develop if a young person is disadvantaged and facing barriers. They include:

- having a vision
- making a commitment
- aiming for results
- build confidence
- act
- timing

- being flexible
- influencing
- perseverance
- using intuition
- being caring.

As much as these skills can be applied externally to developing an enterprise, they have significant value when looking inward, particularly if a young person has had to face disadvantages and/or other barriers. Enterprise provides a unique opportunity to develop these skills. (Note: I would also like to add networking to this list, probably one of the most valuable skills for the future.)

Enterprise and SEND

There is no doubt in my mind about the value of enterprise for all young people, but especially those with SEND/additional needs. If our purpose is about improving outcomes, then young people who maybe don't present to prospective employers in the way that other young people do – predictable qualifications, experiences and backgrounds – can use enterprise to bridge that gap, at least perceptually.

> ♥ Imagine a young person who isn't competing with qualifications employers are familiar with (i.e. not GCSEs), *but* they can talk about customers, sales, production, marketing, the skills they have developed and the understanding they have of business. Think through the enterprise curriculum so that it enables students to express their knowledge in a way that is compelling to employers.

Quotes from schools engaging in Tycoon Talentino SEND Enterprise Competition show the value they believe enterprise can bring:

- Gary Smith, Head of Department at Waverly School expressed, 'The students were given a fresh incentive to learn more skills such as developing independence, communicating confidently with customers, serving drinks, and raising funds to reinvest into the business'.
- Students at the College of West Anglia received a goodwill loan of £100 to start their business Candle with Care. Learning Support Offer, Tiff Marsh commented, 'Just like the candles they have made, our students have shined brightly throughout their entrepreneurship'.
- 'Our setting is a CAMHS setting, and supporting young people in crisis. The Tycoon in Schools Competition has been invaluable to developing our student's self-confidence and self-esteem. Thank you so much for your support and the opportunity'.

How to bring enterprise into your school, special school and college

Enterprise can be developed on a small simple scale or a much grander, larger scale. It might be that your careers governor is an employer or entrepreneur who would like to bring their knowledge into school in a practical way and support the development of enterprise. Your enterprise adviser, part of the local Careers Hub, may also be able to support you.

Enterprise can be small, such as making and selling cappuccino cupcakes every Tuesday morning in the spring term. It might be larger, like creating a physical café that offers opportunities for ongoing work experience. It might be a one-off, like a charity event. One special school organised a Valentine Evening dinner for parents, as their scope for a night out was very limited. Their children participated in the marketing and food prep with the school kitchen team and acted as the wait staff too, a very special night. Catcote Academy developed a set of enterprise skills not just for students but which also applied to staff too and everything was delivered through the enterprise 'commandments'.

Whatever the scope and scale and longevity of your enterprise, you will need to create a business plan and I have included a template for you to use. You might need to bring in other people or organisations like the Peter Jones Foundation, Young Enterprise and The Princes Trust.

You will need some start-up resources, usually including money. Talentino and the Peter Jones Foundation together created the Tycoon Talentino SEND Competition where you can apply for up to £1,000 of start-up funding which is only repayable if you make a profit.

The key thing at the start is to have an idea for enterprise which solves a problem. I remember hearing Peter Jones say on *Dragons Den* 'the worst thing you can do is create a solution for a problem that doesn't exist' – ouch! Try not to think too big . . . at first. One school I worked with wanted to have an upcycling stall at the local market. Great, free stock you sell for a profit, but what about the school holidays, what about customers' expectations in terms of seeing you there every week (or not), what about the support students will need? Who will organise the licences, what safeguarding arrangements need to be in place? The school day is six hours long and the students must travel in this time too. So, customers only have a four-hour window to purchase. What about market regulations and so on? Exploring what the idea could impact is as important as planning for success.

Planning is everything and 'my little checklist' is essentially a start-up list to create your own enterprise so it looks different in this chapter.

The last word here goes to staff – they will have skills and knowledge you never knew they had; ask them what they would like to create. And don't make staff the only paying customers; they have small purses and will run out of motivation if they are being constantly nobbled, however lovely that 'Rolling Scone' is. (Thanks to Fairfield School for that brilliant name for their scone business! Their students are aged 3–19 with severe and profound learning disabilities in Batley, West Yorkshire.)

Summary of key points

Enterprise and opportunity are complementary. All young people but especially those with additional needs can benefit from enterprise both from a knowledge and skills perspective and importantly from their improved ability to enable employers to understand what they *can* do. Enterprise is hugely enjoyable and can work well for students who are disengaged. Enterprise can 'qualify' under Gatsby Benchmarks 5 and 6. Young people who do not have additional needs can be brought in to co-create multi-ability enterprise teams to enable them to learn and accept a more diverse group of young people and to understand their value and perspective.

Enterprise is exciting, delivers a huge cost–benefit ratio, can exist at every size and scale. You can organise yourselves or bring in others to help you. I believe it is one of the most underutilised career guidance activities and I should all be shouting the benefits of enterprise from our proverbial rooftops!

Case studies

- Catcote Academy: www.catcoteacademy.co.uk/mini-enterprise-project/
- Charlton Park Academy: www.youtube.com/watch?v=uCyM0IFnTEM
- BBC: www.bbc.co.uk/teach/teacher-support/articles/z42bf4j
- Peter Jones Foundation SEND Tycoon Enterprise Competition: https://cico.talentinocareers.co.uk/wp-content/uploads/2023/11/Peter-Jones-Foundation.pdf
- Character education: https://assets.publishing.service.gov.uk/media/5f20087fe90e07456b18abfc/Character_Education_Framework_Guidance.pdf

GUEST CONTRIBUTOR – BILL MUIRHEAD, MANAGING DIRECTOR OF THE PETER JONES FOUNDATION

I met Bill in a bar on Pancras Station about seven years ago; no it is not one of those stories! He has led the Peter Jones Foundation to increase support for more young people with SEND/vulnerable/disadvantaged and last year offered opportunities to 50% more young people. Bill is clear on the value of enterprise from employment to happiness. Love that.

Enterprise can be a misleading word, and in education, I have found it means different things to different people. At the Peter Jones Foundation, I define it against a framework of eight core skills. For us, to be enterprising is to be competent in communication, creativity and innovation, teamwork, digital skills, financial skills, leadership, resilience, and self-management as well as problem-solving. It's a definition that is not a million miles away from the Skills Builder approach that has been adopted by many providers and, as they do, I argue that these competencies are essential; a crucial toolkit that should be developed through the curriculum rather than marginalised to extra-curricular enrichment or off-timetable challenge days, as is so often the case. I would love to live in a world where enterprise is thought of in the same way as health. Just as no one would question the importance of a healthy diet and regular exercise, I should always be looking after and nurturing our skills, whatever our age or circumstance. Enterprise skills are all too often linked to employment or self-employment and of course I could leave you with a hefty in-tray of reports showing their value to recruiters and demonstrating their vitality in the DNA of entrepreneurs. But it is bigger than that – strong enterprise education is about helping young people find happiness as much as it is an ingredient to success in the world of work.

For me, this is even more indisputable when it comes to talking about enterprise in SEND education. A few years ago, I met a group of eight young people with severe and complex learning needs who had set up and ran a small gifts business through one of our programmes. They had taken a £380 goodwill loan from the foundation and turned it into a £2,794 profit, demonstrating and developing all the skills I have mentioned along the way. What struck me though was how their teachers eulogised the programme, developing their confidence and self-esteem. Yes, they had developed their skillset but more than that, they had developed self-belief. In a world where there can be a lot of 'can't do' (often unspoken), strong enterprise education is very 'can do' and can be a significant springboard towards raising aspirations and realising opportunities in later life. Also of note is that enterprise education is often rooted in practical, project-based learning and, as such, provides a noticeably clear example – whether that is in a CV, an interview or simply working away as a powerful mnemonic reference point – of a young person's competence. The other thing that struck me about that group of eight SEND students was their smiles. They had enjoyed the experience of setting up and running a small business and were rightly proud to be telling me about its success. What I have come to call the three courses of good enterprise education – strong skills development for starters, a main of self-esteem and sweet happiness to finish – were there for all the see.

My little checklist – Top tips to build an Enterprise in your special school/school/College

Harnessing the value of enterprise	Improving my practice – creating an enterprise in my school/special school/college	Actions	Tick action completed
What is the idea of your potential enterprise?	One sentence		
What is the vision?	What will you see happen because of your Enterprise?		
What is the mission?	What will you do to deliver the vision?		
What problem does it solve?	What would continue to be a problem if your Enterprise didn't happen?		
How long will it last?	Is it a day/term/one off event/longer?		
What resources would I need (non-financial, e.g. people)?	Which students and staff and people outside my school?		
What start-up funding would I need?	Where will it come from? How will I pay it back?		
Would it benefit my enterprise to engage with an external enterprise organisation?	Consider Peter Jones Foundation Tycoon Competition, Princes Trust, Young Enterprise		
What skills and knowledge do I have already?	Who else has the knowledge / skills the enterprise needs?		
When do I get started/how long will the Enterprise last?	Does it matter when the Enterprise starts, do you have enough term time to deliver it?		
What is our brand?	What does the Enterprise stand for/exemplify?		
How do I market/promote it?	What marketing / social media marketing is necessary to promote it?		
How do I sell it?	What are the revenue channels?		
What does the cash flow look like?	Are you spending money before any sales are made?		
How do I accept money for sales?	Is it cash, card, other, e.g., green barter?		
Where do I keep the money?	Bank account, dedicated charity bank account, safe, jam jar?		
How do I get started?	Make a specific date to start and finish		
Which staff are involved?	You need a motivated team both inside and possibly outside school		
How do I engage local businesses?	Who do I need, who do I know, what do I want?		
How do I engage the local community?	Who do I need, who do I know, what do I want?		
How will I know if it is a success?	Social impact, profit, use of funds, other		

Skills and skills development

- Explore the difference between skills, knowledge and behaviours
- Skill development levels
- Explore different skills frameworks
- Skills focus for each of the two Career SEND Groups One and Two
- The impact of disadvantage on the acquisition of skills, positive and negative
- Planning for skills and ways in which skills can be developed
- Guest contributor – Tom Ravenscroft, CEO and Founder of Skills Builder Partnership

Introduction

Skills are a significant and integral part of everyone's development before, during and after school no matter who you are. Young people are often criticised by employers who say young people don't have the skills they need; they are not work-ready, and even general opinion can reflect a derogatory view of young people, describing them as 'snowflakes' among other things. What these adults fail to realise is that young people embarking on their first tentative steps after school have never had such a challenging situation, post Covid, with education and personal and social development seriously interrupted combined with the huge changes in the workplace.

NEETs have increased to 12% as of April 2024 so it is incumbent upon us as careers practitioners to arm young people with the skills they need before leaving school. This is even more critical for young people who are vulnerable or disadvantaged in some way.

As careers practitioners, we need to be granular about the development of skills, how they can be developed and to what level. Even coming back to basics and identifying what is a skill, what is knowledge, and what are behavioural competencies or intrinsic/soft skills.

Explore the difference between skills, knowledge and behaviours

Many people group skills, knowledge and behavioural competencies together, however, they are discreet and not the same thing:

- Knowledge per se is about understanding a subject and it is the application of knowledge that creates a level of skill/skills, e.g. learning to drive.
- Skills is the practical application of knowledge which enables someone to carry out a task successfully/apply their knowledge to a specific situation. The acquisition of skill is the first step towards being competent, and the development of competence comes through practising or rehearsing skills. This is especially important for Career SEND Group One who will need multiple opportunities to rehearse and practise skills.
- Behavioural competencies are commonly called 'soft skills', although many would argue they are anything but soft as they can be hard to acquire. They could include skills such as communication, negotiation and influencing.

Skills development levels

Whether the focus is on the acquisition of knowledge, skills or behavioural competencies, there are three levels of acquisition:

- Entry level – introductory, beginner level which starts with building an awareness
- Development and application – the early stages of developing and starting to use a skill
- Mastery – achieving competence in a skill

Exploring different skills frameworks

Everyone has an opinion on what skills young people should develop whilst at school. I have brought several of them together over the next few sections to identify where there is agreement and difference. It is up to you to form your own opinion and skills development approach. My information came from Skills Builder, STEM Learning, Talentino, Peter Jones Foundation, Mencap, Youth Employment UK, UNICEF, CIPD, and World Economic Forum (see the upcoming table).

Interestingly, although the language might be slightly different, there is a lot of agreement across these different skills frameworks. If I think about knowledge/skills and behavioural competencies, irrespective of the Career SEND Group, whether One or Two, there are common skill areas which every young person needs to develop. The skills highlighted in gray scale in the following table are those most often mentioned. The following table is a further suggestion of the core skills you could think about enabling your young people to develop, grouped in clusters.

Increasing employer engagement, enterprise and skills

Skill	Skills Builder	STEM Learning	Talentino (MORE)	Peter Jones	Mencap	YE UK	UNICEF/World Economic Forum	Talentino Future Skills	Employers (CIPD)
Have a vision									
Listening									
Speaking/oracy									
Problem-solving									
Creativity									
Staying positive				Make a commitment					Work ethic/reliable
Aiming high				Aim for results					
Leadership									
Teamwork/collaboration									
Digital literacy									
Build confidence									
Using initiative				Act					
Organisational/time management									
Resourcefulness									
Making choices									
Working under pressure/to deadlines				Timing				Stress tolerance	
Ability to learn/adapt								Manage change	
Openness to change									
Communication/interpersonal									
Using adaptive tech								Tech adaptability	
Influencing									

The Big Inclusive SEND Careers Handbook

Skill	Skills Builder	STEM Learning	Talentino (MORE)	Peter Jones	Mencap	YE UK	UNICEF /World Economic Forum	Talentino Future Skills	Employers (CIPD)
Negotiation									
Valuing difference and diversity									
Professional networking									
Personal /social development									
Resilience and EI				Perseverance					
Mental health awareness									
Use intuition									
Social/emotional competence					Empathy				
Ethical responsibility and social awareness				Be caring					
Effective working practices									
Critical thinking									
Entrepreneurial mindset									
Continuous employability development									
Career management skills									
Continuous lifelong learning									
Building relationships									
Self-advocacy /disclosure									
Daily living skills									
Independent travel									

If I identify the highest scoring skills and group the others under the highest scoring skills, I get some interesting competency groupings. Some of the skills identified by Mencap could easily be transferred into an environment for young people without learning difficulties too. It is worth mentioning too that the detail in terms of the interpretation of each of the skills will have different nuances according to the creator. However, for our purposes grouping at face value offers a way of considering multiple skills frameworks so you can decide how you want to develop and plan yours if you aren't using an existing framework. Obviously, the cluster titles are skills in their own right too.

Problem-solving
- Creativity
- Using initiative
- Resourcefulness
- Critical thinking

Staying positive
- Have a vision
- Aim high

Teamwork/collaboration
- Professional networking
- Entrepreneurial mindset

Digital literacy

Organisation and time management
- Leadership

Ability to learn/adapt
- Making choices
- Openness to change

Communication and interpersonal
- Listening
- Speaking/oracy
- Influencing

- Negotiation
- Personal/social development
- Building relationships

Adapting to technology and use of adaptive technology

Effective working practices

- Continuous employability skills development
- Career management skills
- Lifelong learning
- Daily living skills including travel training

Resilience/emotional intelligence

- Use of intuition
- Social/emotional compliance/self-regulation
- Build confidence
- Working under pressure and stress tolerance
- Mental health awareness
- Self-advocacy/disclosure

Ethical responsibility and social awareness

- Valuing difference and diversity

Skills focus for Career SEND Group One

There are three broad pathways that comprise Career SEND Group One – (1) learners aim for employment; (2) employment/supported volunteering could be options; and (3) supported independent living, leisure and activities in the community as well as FE college may be the goal. I identified the list from Mencap on the large table that can be calibrated in terms of delivery for each pathway, and it is also worth considering others that are relevant including effective work practices, adaptability/flexibility and managing change, building self-confidence, and staying positive and aiming high.

Skills focus for Career SEND Group Two

There are three membership groups – those who need some type of reasonable adjustment; those whose context around them impacts their engagement with career development, and those whose adverse childhood experiences may have interrupted their development which impacts the possibility of engaging too. The clusters of skills are relevant to all three groups, but you could pay particular attention to the following skills to enable these young people to participate as fully as possible in career development opportunities: staying positive, aiming high, digital literacy, organisational and time management skills, making choices, openness to change, personal/social development, negotiating, building relationships, effective work practices, build confidence, stress tolerance, mental health awareness, and social/emotional self-regulation.

The impact of disadvantage on the acquisition of skills, positive and negative

There is an assumption that disadvantage has a totally negative impact on young people, and this is largely true. A recent COSMO study (Covid Social Mobility and Opportunities 2021) found young people from disadvantaged backgrounds felt less likely to be in control of their futures than young people from better socio-economic backgrounds. They also found that the qualifications of parents were a factor as although they might want their child to do well at school, they might be less likely to be engaged with the school to see how things are progressing. Young people from households where families were long-term unemployed felt they had fewer chances in life.

> ♥ So, when you think about skill acquisition, aiming high, building confidence, and staying positive are great places to start. Don't assume skills aren't present because other things have been missing in a young person's life.

However, there is also evidence that amid some of the challenges faced by disadvantaged young people, and although the method is not ideal, they can develop resilience, perseverance, and be more empathic and creative. I remember working with a group of 50 young carers and I asked a random sample of adults, who were not known to them, what characteristics they would ascribe to a young carer. All of the words were good to superlative in nature. I wrote them on cards and stuck them to the wall before the start of a three-day career workshop. On the third day, I told them what the words meant, and they were all really surprised to learn how people thought of them and their skills, and I had seen many examples over the three days.

Planning for skills using the Gatsby Benchmarks

A robust career development programme that meets the Gatsby Benchmarks (GBMs) is a great vehicle through which to develop skills for the future. You can see next some ideas for the clusters I have identified and the individual Gatsby Benchmarks. I have also highlighted activities which sit slightly outside to generate discussions in your planning for both Career SEND Groups One and Two.

GBMs	Planning for skills	Skills – many skills can be developed within each Gatsby Benchmark	Skill development ideas for Career SEND Groups One and Two
1	Careers strategy – All skills need to be identified within an overall Skills Development Plan ideally linked with the LSIP in your area.	All, but differentiate the levels – awareness, building, mastery at different year groups	Think about in school, out of school, use of mentors, coaches, enterprise and offer multiple opportunities.
2	LMI – Through direct relationships with employers, LSIP and other sources of LMI, you can identify the skills employers value locally, enabling students to better understand what the market is looking for.	Digital literacy	Use the skill alignment tools such as Skills Builder, Morrisby, Talentino CICO to align skills to notional career goals.
3	Personalised – individual skills development plans as part of an individualised career development aligned to notional career goals and pathways.	Career management, making choices, openness to change, communication skills, staying positive, aiming high, building confidence, speaking/oracy	Personal career development plans offer an opportunity to specify how personal, social and emotional development skills can be built either in individual or group initiatives.
4	Curriculum – look for ways to overtly include skill development across the curriculum.	Problem-solving, communication skills, using initiative, critical thinking, creativity	Most good teachers will do this naturally, but highlighting what the skill is and how it is used at work can be developed early and the advantage that brings.
5	Encounters with employers and employees	Professional networking, employability skills, ethical responsibility, valuing difference/diversity	Benchmarks 5 and 6 are bursting with opportunities to find out about the skills employers value and young people need.
6	Experience of workplaces	Employability skills, building relationships, daily living skills, traveling independently, working under pressure/stress tolerance, use adaptive technology, self-regulation, adaptability/openness to change, resourcefulness	Work experience, virtual work experience, work shadowing, internal work experience, enterprise in school/out of school, work skills competitions, volunteering, supported volunteering, social action projects, part-time jobs, networking (e.g. LinkedIn), do something new, improve your online presence, take a short online course, improve self-awareness.
7	Encounters with destinations after school/FE, HE	Continuous lifelong learning	Really important in the transition process.
8	Personal guidance – Interestingly, in the recent Ofsted Thematic review of Careers, it said careers advisers should be talking about skills.	Personal/social development, career management	Make sure that the careers adviser is fully briefed about local skills that are needed and your broader skills plan.

Summary of key points

In this chapter, I have explored the difference between skills, knowledge and behaviours, and appreciate that they are different from each other. To acquire a skill, you first need to learn about it, become more aware of it, then develop it through repetition/rehearsal until you secure competence within that skill. There are lots of different skills frameworks and views about skills, and I identified nine different approaches to identifying what skills are most valuable/pertinent. From this, I created clusters of the skills most frameworks had identified as important and then correlated these skills to the Gatsby Benchmarks, identifying some planning and development ideas for each of the two Career SEND Groups. Understanding the impact of skills development, or a lack of, for young disadvantaged people is important, and I noted that some young people will develop skills because of negative experiences. Skills need to be overtly factored into your planning processes, identifying the skills, how they will be developed and when. For young people with SEND who are at such a disadvantage, the development of skills is an advantage and a differentiator.

Resources

Skills Builder Framework: www.skillsbuilder.org/universal-framework

Mencap: www.mencap.org.uk/advice-and-support/employment

World Skills: www.worldskillsuk.org/

Peter Jones Foundation: www.tycoon.com/

GUEST CONTRIBUTOR – TOM RAVENSCROFT, FOUNDER AND CEO OF SKILLS BUILDER PARTNERSHIP

If you cut Tom in half like a stick of rock, it would read Skills Builder Universal Framework. He has been the most persistent, consistent, constant advocate of the contribution skills make to the development of all young people over the last 12 years. It is a massive achievement; well done Tom and thank you for your contribution.

For more than a decade at Skills Builder Partnership, I have had the privilege to work with learners with diverse needs across mainstream primary and secondary schools, colleges, and in alternative provision and specialist school settings too.

Essential skills are just that – the glue that connects foundational skills and learning with their application in the real world. I think about them as highly transferable skills that support the application of technical skills and knowledge. These skills are widely talked about, covering interpersonal and collaborative skills, the ability to be creative and to solve problems, effective communication, as well as being able to set goals and work towards them.

Every learner is unique, particularly when they have additional educational needs, and I do not presume that there is any 'average' profile. Different learners will make progress more easily than some while facing meaningful barriers in others. However, all benefit from the more detailed understanding and recognition of those skills that the Skills Builder Universal Framework offers.

The framework defines eight essential skills: teamwork, leadership, creativity, problem-solving, aiming high, staying positive, speaking and listening. It then takes these broad skills – like teamwork – and breaks them down into more achievable steps, sequenced to support progression. Teamwork includes being able to contribute ideas, complete an allocated task or order tasks effectively. Similarly, listening includes being able to listen without interrupting, recall instructions and then relay instructions to others.

This helps to identify and address the needs of individuals, and we've seen these steps helping to structure a focus on essential skills as part of Education, Health and Care Plans (EHCPs); vocational profiles; and individual learning plans.

More broadly, we've seen six principles as being transformative for building essential skills for individuals across the education institutions we've worked with:

- *Keep it simple*: There is huge value in helping learners to understand the essential skills by referring to them consistently across school or college

life. This might mean the eight skills I focus on being up in classrooms or celebrated in assemblies or class.
- *Start early, keep going*: I see the value of building essential skills to set learners up for their lives, but they also support learning, so it is important to start early and maintain their focus throughout education.
- *Measure it*: Given the diversity of learners, it's important to understand the essential skills of each learner and their individual priorities for development. Using the Skills Builder Universal Framework can help to measure these through observation and self-assessment.
- *Focus tightly*: There is an important role in directly teaching these skills – they all have elements which can be directly taught so learners are not left to work it all out for themselves.
- *Keep practising*: These skills become intuitive and honed through practice in lots of different settings – whether through arts, sports or other hobbies.
- *Bring it to life:* To help learners see the value of these skills and to support their transferability, I encourage giving learners real-life projects and challenges to put their skills to use.

By taking this approach, we've seen that young people can see their essential skill strengths and the opportunities these open. They can then, with teacher support, identify where they want to hone their skills further – thus setting themselves up for the careers they aspire to.

My little checklist – Top tips to improve the development of skills for all

Planning for skills development	Top tips to improve your understanding of skills planning and development	Planned action	Tick action completed
How does my school/special school/college currently approach the identification of skills?	Check out the current careers strategy, how skill development is captured by teaching staff, and whether you use a skills framework formally or informally.		
Do my team and other staff understand the difference between skills, knowledge and behavioural competencies?	Run a short training session to enable staff to recognise the difference and the different ways in which they can be developed.		
Does the careers strategy capture the skills plan?	If not, when you carry out your annual evaluation of careers, you can ensure you incorporate a skills plan, having first identified the skills you want learners to develop.		
Does your LMI include references to skills wanted by employers locally?	Find the LSIP and which employers are involved and the skills they are looking for. Ensure they are cross-referenced with your (new) skills plan.		
Do your learners have individual career development plans? Do they include skills development?	Work with your students to identify their notional career goals in Year 8 if possible (you can use CICO to do this). Identify the skills that are pertinent to that career and ways in which they can be developed across the year groups.		
Have you identified disadvantaged and vulnerable/SEND learners?	Focus on the personal/social/emotional development needs of this group and how their confidence can be built, and aspirations raised.		
How many methods do you use currently to develop skills?	Identify what they are and then think creatively about other ways skills could be developed.		
How do you measure the development of skills through the three stages – awareness, build, mastery?	You could use skills tests or behavioural competency frameworks and aligned questions such as 'Tell me about a time when you…' Use a fun way is to engage in competitions like World Skills.		
Do you use enterprise to develop employability skills?	Check out the Peter Jones Tycoon Enterprise Competition with £1,000 of free start-up funding for each enterprise, with new Talentino SEND Enterprise options.		
Do you consider what skills might be needed in the future, and how they could be developed?	Create a workshop with Year 11 upwards to generate ideas and cross-reference them with your own research.		
How do you currently enable learners to develop skills for the future?	Using the data generated from above, work together with an employer and students' group to identify methods.		

Chapter 7
Making the difference

> Suggestion – a big cuppa and a plentiful supply of your favourite biscuits to start this chapter!

Transition and why it is vital to get it right

- The importance of getting transition right
- What happens when transition goes wrong?
- Different types of transitions
- Preparation for transition – Career SEND Groups One and Two
- Support and reasonable adjustments
- Parents, carer and family perspective
- Post transition
- How to ensure transition goes well
- Guest contributor – Brandon Mills, Head Teacher at Brookfields Special School (Retired)

Introduction

> ♥ 'Transition' is an easily understood word – moving from one thing to another – but in a careers context, especially for young people with additional needs/SEND, it has lots of potential trip hazards along the way. Transition is most often used to describe the move from school to the next step, but transition occurs multiple times in our lives and careers. At a macro education level, transition takes place when we first go to school, move through different key stages in school, move from school to school, move to the next destination after school and so on. For some young people, transition happens and it has a huge impact at a micro level – understanding what comes next in a sequence, understanding and anticipating change, moving from a familiar environment to an unfamiliar environment, meeting new people. Broadening our understanding of what transition can mean at different levels to different young people with (and without) SEND is an important contributor to increasing the probability of an optimal career outcome.

The importance of getting transition right

If you think about transition for your students with additional needs, a successful transition process needs to:

- secure great family support and engagement
- deliver information in a timely fashion between all parties
- ensure full information is being shared between the outgoing and incoming organisations to which the young person will 'belong'
- provide sufficient time for the preparation of everyone involved
- organise support mechanisms and be in place on time
- provide rehearsals in terms of what comes after transition to familiarise the young person with the impending changes
- engage the young person so they are fully knowledgeable, fully committed and excited about the next steps.

For young people in Career SEND Group One, transition can pose challenges for both the young person and their parents/carers. Some pupils may have been in the same school since early years, and early and effective preparation for everyone, especially parents and families, is very important. Preparation needs to start years before the potential leaving date with parent/carer/family workshops and extensive preparation on every aspect that will change for young people – (see section 'Different types of transitions').

For young people in Career SEND Group Two studying at the GCSE level, transition is driven by specific process timelines, such as exam times, publication of results, application deadlines, school leaving age and mandatory school leaving age. Specific groups will have their own challenges and may not be ready for change/transition at the times at which the changes have to happen. They may not be ready emotionally either. Care experienced children/looked after children may have to change their living arrangements at 16 years of age. Young carers may be torn between accepting a housing offer or losing it if they choose to go to university outside their town.

What happens when transition goes wrong?

Transition is not free from stress even at the best of times. However, if problems ensue, anxiety escalates for everyone. Most young people are probably affected by changes like feelings that affect their sense of belonging or experience a disruption to friendships and relationships with school staff and the wider community which, in turn, can negatively impact confidence, self-esteem and even attainment.

Different types of transitions

Transition for many young people can include changes – stops, starts and differences to how things are for them now. For young people with special needs, this can be alarming, considering the range of challenges they could face. These changes could involve travel arrangements, the level of independence and making choices, handling money and owning a budget, making new friends and relationships, generally having to be more responsible including for own personal safety, and making good choices concerning health, fitness, diet and leisure activities.

Preparation for transition

At the centre of any transition planning is the young person and their parents/carer/family. There are common denominators for both Career SEND Groups one and two however there will be a different skew for each group.

Career SEND Group One

Students who attend special schools and are working below Level 2/GCSE can fall into three career pathways, each of which will influence the transition process that will be determined by the range of potential career outcomes broadly split into:

- Pathway One – training and employment, possibly supported employment
- Pathway Two– supported employment, supported independent living, supported employment
- Pathway Three – transition to adult services and activities based in the community and leisure activities

All pathways can lead to/include FE college depending on the availability of courses. There are questions about EHC Plans, funding and benefits that I don't have space to cover here, but these will be of paramount importance to parents/carers and families so make sure they have support. Useful websites are www.entitledto.co.uk/ and www.disabilityrightsuk.org/. Publish a huge handbook annually on benefits.

Transition processes for each pathway all need to start as early as possible for both young people and their parents/carers/families and must be personalised. There is the opportunity to make more formal plans via the annual planning review if the student has an EHC Plan.

Pathway One – formal needs to be able to offer multiple opportunities for work experience, work insights and rehearsing for work, getting comfortable in a working environment, communication at work, 'soft skills' training, enterprise experience, working with a job coach, preparation for working such as travel training, managing increased independence, handling money, making choices, making friends, and personal safety. Becoming familiar with the designated FE college is important too. All of this can be organised as part of the school's careers programme and start as early as possible. Familiarisation and training need to start early for parents, carers and families including siblings. Once the young person is in the training/employment/education environment, the transition process should continue until everything is settled, so this needs to be built in too.

Pathway Two – semi-formal will have very similar elements to Pathway One with additional support built in plus an increased focus on developing independent living skills with lots of rehearsal. Many special schools have a room dedicated to this with a bedroom area, kitchen area and bathroom area. Once the young person is in the training/employment/education environment, the transition process should continue until everything is settled, so this needs to be built in too.

Pathway Three – pre-formal will look very different to Pathways One and Two but the essence will be the same: familiarising the young person with what is coming next, trying to reduce the anxiety that change brings, lots of rehearsal, providing support/advocacy for the next choices, and lots of support for parents/carers and families.

Career SEND Group Two

Again, transition needs to start with the young person and plans created from their perspective. There will be big differences between the various groups of additional needs, for example a disabled young person who is heading to university needs to ensure they have researched the support available, but a looked after child/

care experienced child will have to manage potentially leaving care and questions of housing and the impact of their choice of university, incomprehensible in many ways. Young carers are often in a dilemma over their care 'responsibilities' and leaving home to go to university. I put this in quotation marks as I personally should not be expecting the 800,000 children and young people from five years old to undertake this. Young people who have little support at home, have not made the 'expected' academic progress, or maybe have had one or multiple adverse childhood experiences need really careful support at this time as school. Even if they profess to dislike school, it may be the only solid thing in their lives.

This section in no way describes the range of situations you will encounter but if you start transition early, put the young person in the centre of your planning, assume every individual is different and unique and their journey will be too. Aim to build their confidence and reduce anxiety. Ensure you have together explored the widest range of options and support available and set a positive path. That is a great start.

Support and reasonable adjustments

There are too many supports and adjustments to list here and you need to carry out some local research including your local authority. But following is a selection of the main types; please do your own research.

Proactive support: For example the Sutton Trust Higher Education courses for disadvantaged students during the school holidays to encourage university attendance (www.suttontrust.com/?gad_source=1&gclid=EAlaIQobChMIwLar7J7 BhQMV_5IQBh37fAuhEAAYASAAEgJKc_D_BwE).

Employment: Job coaches via Access to Work funding including for two weeks' work experience and when in employment www.gov.uk/access-to-work. Job carving is a method used to create parts of a job that can be done by someone with additional needs.

Under the Equality Act, the young person could be entitled to '**reasonable adjustments**' at school, college or work, which could include allowing flexible working, the provision of aids such as screen reading software, alterations to premises, adapting workplace policies, reviewing job duties, or allowing time off for medical appointments (www.gov.uk/reasonable-adjustments-for-disabled -workers).

Study at university/apprenticeships: There is a huge amount of information on the UCAS website about support for students with the widest range of additional needs (see www.ucas.com/undergraduate/applying-university/individual-needs/disabled-students).

Parents, carers and families perspective

Shift in roles and responsibilities: The transition from school to work signifies a shift in roles and responsibilities for both young people and their parents. While in school, parents are actively involved in their child's education, often advocating for their needs and collaborating closely with the school team. However, in the workplace, the dynamics change, and parents may find themselves navigating unfamiliar territory where their involvement is more limited. Very often, once the young person has left school and is in employment, the family may continue to reach out to the school with issues and problems encountered in the workplace, seeking its advice and support or to resolve any issues.

Uncertainty and anxiety: The uncertainty surrounding their child's future employment prospects can be an overwhelming and emotionally charged experience for parents, as well as for the young people themselves. Parents may experience a range of emotions, including anxiety, fear and sadness. They may worry about whether their child will find and maintain a suitable job, receive the necessary support, thrive in the workplace environment, establish social connections, and achieve a sense of fulfilment and purpose in their chosen career path. This uncertainty can lead to heightened anxiety and stress during the transition period.

Lack of familiarity with workplace culture: Parents may not be familiar with the expectations and norms of the workplace environment, especially when it comes to accommodating individuals with learning difficulties and additional needs. They may have concerns about how their child will be perceived by employers and colleagues, and whether they will be able to successfully understand the social and professional aspects of the workplace. Transitioning to the workforce means relinquishing some control over their child's environment, which can be difficult for parents accustomed to advocating for their child within the school system. Unlike the structured support networks available within the school setting, parents may feel isolated when trying to understand the complexities of the workforce

Managing expectations and building understanding: It is essential for educators and leaders in special schools, as well as careers advisers, job coaches and employers, to work in partnership with families to support their understanding that the relationship with their child's workplace will be different from the relationship they had with their child's school. Inadequate partnership working, planning and coordination of post-school transition services can exacerbate the challenges families face during the transition from education to employment.

Without a clear roadmap and career plan for their child's future, parents may feel overwhelmed and uncertain about how to best support their child's transition into the workforce. This lack of planning can lead to missed opportunities, delays in accessing essential support services, and increased stress for both the individual and their family members.

Post transition

Transition is anticipated, takes place and then what? It can be difficult to stay in touch with young people, however, there is a range of ways of doing it (legally) bearing in mind GDPR limitations! Here are some ideas to see how transitions have gone and learn how to effect even better transitions for the future:

- invite students back as alumni to talk to other students
- set up a leavers group on social media
- ask students' permission to stay in touch before they leave and stay in regular contact
- organise activities/contact during the summer holidays before the change takes place to ensure they take up their place
- contact students at 'danger' times like October, December and New Years when they may be feeling low
- stay in touch with parents/carers and families.

Summary of key points

You may have expected transition to be a fairly low-key area of career development, but I expect you are now thinking it is absolutely loaded and it is. Getting it right changes lives no doubt. It happens at a macro and micro level and could upend or transform a young person's experience and life outcome. It needs to be started as early as you can; Year 8 is good as it avoids starting in Year 7 which is already a huge transition. Potentially the summer term of Year 7 can work well too depending on the cohort. Personalisation and individualisation is critical; talk to the SENDCO too if you have one.

Transition has three stages: preparation, the transition itself and post transition. Treat it as a three-stage process, not just the main event. There will be different transition pathways for each of the Career SEND Groups One and Two and personalisation within the pathways. Think about the level of potential impact, for example looked after/care experienced children may have to make decisions about housing at the same time (remember when you were 16–18 years old, could you have taken that on too?). Explore and factor in as much support and different support mechanisms as you can. And as our guest contributor Brandon Mills has pointed out in detail, the engagement of parents, carers and families at every step is vital. After transition has taken place, keep in touch as much as humanly possible; it will reap dividends for the young person, their family, and your learning and careers practice.

💻 Case studies

- Year 7 Transition Programme and resources: https://resources.careersandenterprise.co.uk/resources/transitions-guide-started-yr-7
- 'Transition programmes for young adults with SEND: What works?' from the Careers and Enterprise Company: www.talentinocareers.co.uk/cec-transition-programme-what-works.pdf
- Preparation for Adulthood – although this is an audit tool for local authorities, there are lots of questions posed which are useful to consider in our careers practice, particularly in our careers practice for Career SEND Group One: www.ndti.org.uk/resources/change-development-project/post-16-transition-audit-tool

My little checklist – Top tips to improve transition at every level for all

Transition	Improving transition	Planned action	Tick action completed
Who are the groups of students who will transition? (Clue: all your students!)	Try to group the students in a matrix which identifies their broad additional needs and optimal career outcomes. This won't be exact at the start but will be refined the nearer they get to leaving school/college.		
If you have students who have been excluded and come to you before they are reintegrated (which is never an exact science), imagine their experience and the impact on them. What are your conclusions?	Carry out a transition triage with them if you can without triggering and agree on an outline plan together or potential options, rehearsal activities, support mechanisms, notional career goals and feedback/reviews/check-ins.		
Think about what transition means in your school/college. Does it address macro and micro transition elements?	Design an outline macro and micro transition process for all year groups and all groups of additional needs – involve students too.		
Can you design a better pre-transition process?	Develop your macro and micro transition plan to involve the pre-transition phase.		
Can you design a better transition process?	Develop your macro and micro transition plan to involve the actual transition event.		
Can you design a better post-transition process?	Develop your macro and micro transition plan to involve the post-transition phase.		
Do you feel you know enough about the range of support that is available for students with additional needs?	Carry out your own desk-based research and make it available to young people and their parents/carers and families.		
Do your employers understand the impact of transition and why some young people may not appear 'ready'?	Carry out a training webinar for employers to discuss career readiness when young people join them and what could be done to improve this.		
Who needs to be involved in the new transition process?	Communicate your ideas and plans to the wider staff; secure volunteer transition champions.		
How will you engage parents, carers and families throughout their child's school journey using the ideas in this chapter?	Ensure you engaged with this group in the research and design of your new plans;, and share with existing and new parents.		

Engaging parents, carers and families

- Guest contributors Hardeep and Eshan Rai
- Why is it vital to engage parents, carers and families to improve outcomes?
- Further ideas for effective parent/carer/family and young person engagement
- Models of engagement – Dr Naomi Dale
- What schools could put in place to improve engagement

GUEST CONTRIBUTOR – HARDEEP RAI, PARENT

OK, I am going to break with tradition and start the section with a guest contributor. Hardeep Rai tells us about his son Eshan and he describes in aching detail his journey with Eshan, who is profoundly disabled. If you have lived experience, much of what he says may resonate, even if you don't, what Hardeep describes is felt by many parents of special needs children.

The 18th of November is a day I will remember for the rest of my life . . .

'Don't worry, soon you will hear your baby cry', said the nurse as she closed the doors in the operating theatre where a crash caesarean was about to take place.

I waited and waited, but that cry never came. Some moments later, I caught a glimpse of a nurse rushing along the corridor with a limp baby and an oxygen mask on his face.

I felt sick to my core, and I immediately knew something had gone horribly wrong. Eshan was going to be the only chance of a child that we had.

When I look back at my time and the days, weeks, months and years after Eshan's last-minute birthing complication, I could never have even begun to experience the trajectory that my life would have taken.

I had to battle my heart and mind to accept that I had become the parent to a severely disabled child. All my original hopes and dreams for my son and his future were shattered. I had to learn how to mourn the son I had lost and welcome a new son into a life that I didn't recognise or understand. I had to learn to overcome the fact that I wasn't a failure, even though deep down, I felt I was.

I had to wrestle with the government for many years for them to understand and acknowledge the severity of Eshan's condition and give him a care package that was commensurate to his needs. I am extremely grateful to say, we were successful and for the last 10 years of his life, he has been in a residential care home.

I had to learn to accept that I was slowly becoming alienated by some of those around me that were supposed to be my family and my friends. Because they didn't 'understand' disability, they judged it unfairly, just as I did, until it entered into my life in the guise of Eshan.

I had to learn to face unfair judgement and treatment in the workplace, where people made assumptions about my capabilities, without asking me first. Those that trusted me before, started to doubt me, and those that were my friends, found it hard to ask me how my new life was.

Perhaps the hardest thing for me to accept at the time, was that my marriage was probably over. Because we didn't have the strongest foundation, Eshan's challenges drove us further apart, as opposed to bringing us closer together. This was something I didn't expect, but I did understand.

My next fight was then against the residential health care system in the UK. Finding a way to trust and believe in a system of care, that was inherently flawed.

Finally, my hardest battle was with God. I asked myself over and over and over . . . why me? Why did this have to happen to me. I questioned my faith.

The above paints a bleak picture from one perspective. However, there is another perspective too. That perspective is a realisation that our children with disabilities are innocent and untainted souls, who entered this world the way they did, for a reason. That reason was to show their parents and those around them that there was something unique and beautiful in difference. That love still exists but in a different plane, one that is almost more unconditional and beautiful, because of its purity innocence. I know that my son inspired me to redefine my purpose in life and find a new way forward. Through him, we have set up a company that can help other people with disabilities find their purpose in life.

As for Eshan and his development, it has been far greater than I could ever have imagined. I still recall the day I was told he wouldn't be able to do anything in life and would be a 'vegetable'. Harsh words from the doctor who at the time was trying to convince us to switch off Eshan's life support machine.

Although he has a list of over 20 conditions, and at the ripe old age of 17 may be significantly developmentally delayed, he can inspire people more than words can describe and place a sense of serenity and peace upon anyone that can meet him. He loves nature, bird sounds, the wind in his face, and people singing to him and classical music.

As for me, in my heart and soul, I am at peace, and I am content, and when I say that, I really mean it. Eshan is my greatest gift and my life teacher. Sure, I went through five years of depression, mental health challenges and suicidal thoughts because of how I was initially judged by so many that were around me, especially those in my Asian community. But that time passed. In my personal experience, the most important word that helped me was quite simply 'acceptance'. I accepted my new way of life. I accepted my new career. I accepted my new friends, and I accepted my new son.

I had to somehow find the strength from within, first, to deal with things my way, and only then, could I face the world.

♥ I defy you to have read Hardeep's contribution and not be really moved. Of course, not all parents of disabled children or children with special/additional needs have experienced such a harrowing journey. But elements of his story will resonate for many: the battle to get the right support and education, the isolation, relationship breakdown. When you come up against an apparently feisty parent, remember that they are probably war weary, love their child beyond measure and are driven by doing what they believe is the right thing. Be empathic, supportive and informative; stay alongside.

Introduction

One of the (many) recent education secretaries said (and I paraphrase) the most important people to engage with in terms of career development and career decisions are parents, carers and families. But you cannot legislate for this, literally! The BBC did a survey a few years ago that identified that 80% of career decisions are influenced by parents. Parents of any young person are usually going to be very invested in the career decisions their child must make. For those with children with additional needs, this is arguably even more fraught.

For young people following a conventional mainstream path, there is a certain amount of tacit knowledge around the exams a young person will take (i.e. GCSEs), and the potential destinations after school (e.g. apprenticeships, college, university) and the process that needs to be followed and when. For young people with an EHC Plan, there are annual reviews which generate these discussions.

For parents and families whose own education and employment history (or otherwise) might have been patchy, or parents who may have special needs themselves, understanding 'what comes next' can be very challenging and fraught with emotion. Young people with special needs in Career SEND Group One may be in the same school for many years and the fact they must leave doesn't surface for a long time and still comes as a shock when parents realise this, and they can get caught in a double loop of grief and loss. Concerns about their child's safety, wellbeing and even loss of financial benefits can all come into play. For young people who have parents/families who do not or cannot for whatever reason get engaged with the child's next steps, this is a huge loss too.

The next section is split into two: firstly, you can find the parent/family engagement models by Dr Naomi Dale, and secondly, what schools could consider putting in place to improve communication and engagement.

The models of engagement with parents, carers and families are described in terms of decision-making, who is considered to be 'the expert', how the protagonists are engaged together and each has pros and cons. The professional could be from school, a careers adviser/leader, specialist of some kind, maybe a medical/therapist or someone from the local authority.

The Expert Model: The professional is seen as the 'expert', and makes decisions based on their expertise alone. The young person and family's role is to accept the decisions made by the expert leading to a power imbalance between the professional, the young person and the family.

The Consultative Model: The professional will actively seek input and information from the family and may seek the young person's input, but the professional will still make the decisions.

The Joint Partnership Model: The professional and the family are seen as equal partners in the young person's education and care and include the views of the young person. Decisions are made collaboratively. This model recognises that the family is constant in the child's life and therefore has a unique insight into the young person's needs and strengths.

The Empowerment Model: This model aims to empower the young person and their family to take an active role in transition planning. The professional provides support and resources to help the young person and their family develop the skills and confidence they need to make informed decisions, and if necessary, the parents advocate for their child.

The Collaborative Engagement Model: This model focuses on encouraging collaboration between schools, young people and families. All parties engage in decision-making processes concerning the education, aspirations, support needed and overall welfare of the young person.

The Ecological Model: This approach considers the many contexts and systems, including family, school, community and wider societal issues that impact on the young person. This model highlights the interdependence of different systems and promotes a creative and dynamic approach to problem-solving so the young person's transition from education to employment is successful.

The Strengths-Based Model: This model encourages identifying and capitalising on the strengths and assets of families, schools and communities to support young people with SEN. By recognising and building upon these existing strengths, this approach seeks to empower young people and their families and promote positive outcomes for young people.

Cultural Competence Model: This model calls for educators and professionals to understand and respect the cultural beliefs, values and practices of families. By ensuring that interventions and support strategies are culturally responsive and inclusive, educators can build stronger relationships with families, thereby facilitating improved outcomes for their children.*

Trauma-Informed Model: This approach emphasises sensitivity, empathy and understanding in interactions with families and young people. Acknowledging the potential impact of trauma on young people and families, this model pursues an approach that creates safe and encouraging environments for support, resilience and positive relationships. By recognising the signs of trauma and responding with compassion and understanding, schools and professionals can cultivate an atmosphere that fosters trust, safety and belonging for all young people and their families, preparing them for a successful transition from education to employment.

These models illuminate how decision-making processes work and it is useful to review how decisions are being made about careers for young people with SEND/additional needs.

As a careers leader, you could build a brilliant parent/carer/family engagement strategy from the information on the next few pages. This is reinforced in the next 'My little checklist'.

Further ideas for effective parent, carer and family engagement

Foster open communication channels: Establishing open communication channels with parents and families is crucial in understanding their aspirations, concerns, and expectations regarding life after school, including:

- The Person-Centred Annual Review is one of the essential processes that can foster this partnership.
- Open-door policy
- Scheduling regular review meetings
- Utilising communication apps opening online reporting to families
- Encouraging parents to share their insights, experiences and goals for their child's career path to ensure that everyone is on the same page regarding the young person's needs and the reasonable adjustments needed
- Help parents understand and have realistic expectations for their child's performance in the workplace, emphasising growth and progress rather than perfection.

*Note: Joe Mintz is Associate Professor in Education, IOE – Learning & Leadership at the University College London. Later this year, he will start research concerning the cultural competence model.

Collaborative goal setting: Collaborate with young people, parents/families and employers to identify and prioritise the development of essential skills required for employment such as:

- For a specific job
- Communication, social skills, independence skills, time management and job-specific competencies.
- Implement individualised education plans (IEPs) that integrate vocational training, job shadowing, internships, and work-study programmes tailored to the child's abilities and interests.
- Consider how families and young people can collaborate with the school's careers team or job coach in identifying specific goals to be developed within the context of work experience placements such as getting their work clothes ready, personal hygiene, travel skills, making a packed lunch, following instructions, etc.

Person-centred vocational profiling: For pupils from Year 6 onwards, discussions should begin to focus on the young person's aspirations for life after school and the identification of the specific stepping stones (EHCP Outcomes) that will support the young person in developing the skills and knowledge to enable them to achieve their aspirations. It is essential that the focus for the outcomes is based on the young person's aspirations for employment, independent living, community inclusion and health (Preparation for Adulthood, NDTI). Encourage and support parents to actively participate in setting realistic and achievable employment goals.

Provide resources and information: Equip parents with resources and information related to expectations, vocational opportunities, your CIAG (Careers Information, Advice and Guidance) and careers programme, and the support services available for individuals with SEN.

- Collaborate with job coaches, supported employment providers, social care, supported internships, employers, and community organisations to provide comprehensive guidance and support to parents and young people.
- Support families to understand the differences, as it can be a huge shock to them when their child starts work – they will no longer have their child's teacher on hand to address and resolve concerns or worries, and the workplace may not be as flexible as the young person's school might have been.
- Connect those parents and families with those who have already experienced this process to share their advice.

- Offer parents detailed information about the transition process, including the types of support available, employment opportunities and the expectations of the workplace. This can help alleviate some of the uncertainty and anxiety surrounding the transition.

Encourage independence and self-advocacy: Empower parents to foster independence and self-advocacy skills in their child by encouraging autonomy, decision-making and problem-solving.

- Provide opportunities for the young person to practise self-advocacy skills in various settings, which will empower them to develop independence and the skills that will serve them well in the workplace.
- Encourage parents to foster and develop these skills at home and to reinforce them through practical experiences and role-playing scenarios.

Promote community engagement: Set up opportunities where parents and young people can engage with local businesses, employers and community organisations to explore internship opportunities, job placements and vocational training programmes. Organise job fairs, career exploration events and networking opportunities to facilitate meaningful connections between students and potential employers.

Celebrate achievements and progress: Celebrate the achievements, milestones and progress of young people in their journey towards employment. Recognise the efforts of both the young people and their parents in overcoming challenges, acquiring new skills, and embracing opportunities for growth and development.

Parent workshops: Organise regular workshops specifically focused on employment preparation for young people with special needs.

- Cover topics like vocational profiling, supported employment, supported internships, travel training, CV building, job search strategies, work experience, interview skills, how the world of work is different from that of a school, and workplace adjustments.
- Invite guest speakers including job coaches to explain their role, employers who have experience employing individuals with special needs, and young people who have transitioned into employment and their families can provide valuable insights and inspiration to parents.
- These workshops will support parents' understanding of the workplace culture, rights and responsibilities of employees, and strategies for supporting their child's transition to work as well as how they will be supported in work.

- Provide practical tips and resources to empower parents in advocating for their child's needs in the workplace.

Individualised career planning sessions: Offer one-on-one sessions with parents and their child to discuss their child's strengths, interests and career goals. Together, create personalised career plans that outline steps for skill development, vocational training and job placement. Providing resources and guidance tailored to the young person's abilities and aspirations can empower parents to take an active role in their child's career development.

Job shadowing opportunities: Collaborate with local businesses and organisations to arrange job shadowing experiences for both young people and parents. Allowing parents to observe different workplace environments first-hand can help them better understand the types of jobs their child may be interested in pursuing and the skills required for success in those roles.

Networking events: Organise networking events that bring together families, young people, educators, employers, supported employment and community members. These events provide invaluable opportunities for parents to connect with professionals from various backgrounds, learn about job opportunities and expand their support networks. Encouraging ongoing communication and collaboration among all stakeholders can foster a supportive community dedicated to enhancing employment outcomes for young people with SEN. Create opportunities for parents to connect with other families who have gone through similar transitions or are currently navigating the process. Peer support can be invaluable in helping parents feel less isolated and more confident in their ability to support their child's journey into the workforce.

Resource library: Create a resource library or online portal with information on destinations, vocational training programmes, success stories, job search websites, disability rights laws and other relevant resources. Empowering parents with access to comprehensive and up-to-date information will help them make informed decisions and advocate effectively for their child's employment needs.

Peer support groups: Facilitate peer support groups where parents and family members can share their experiences, challenges and successes related to their child's employment journey. Connecting with other parents who are facing similar circumstances can provide validation, encouragement and practical advice. Encourage open dialogue and mutual support within these groups to foster a sense of community and empowerment.

I would like to thank Brandon Mills for his contributions to the previous two sections on the models of engagement and what schools can do to improve engagement. Brandon was the Deputy Head Teacher along with Sara Attra at the first special school I worked with and taught me so much about SEND and inclusion and the art of what's possible. Thank you, B.

Summary of key points

I agree that there is a *huge* amount in this chapter, but the challenge of engaging parents, carers and families is always in the top three of items careers practitioners want to improve along with employer engagement and work experience.

> ♥ I would urge you to plough through the last few pages and pull together a detailed engagement strategy rather than organise yet another coffee morning. Sorry that sounded trite, I didn't mean to, but we have to dig deeper into this and stay alongside for longer. Parents, carers and families are the biggest influencers on potential career destinations, and they need to be totally engaged.

Understanding that most parents, carers, and families want what is best for their child/children and that the nature of the engagement process plays a vital part is a great starting point. The models of engagement exist to show us what is possible and a way to analyse what happens now and what you design for the future. Parent/carers/family engagement is *vital* to ensure optimum career decisions are made, support mechanisms are identified and provided, and all stakeholders feel fully informed and involved, confident in their child's future.

> ♥ Suggestion – big cuppa and plentiful supply of your favourite biscuits at this point!

Resources

Working with Families of Children with Special Needs: Partnership and Practice (Routledge, 1996). Author Naomi Dale outlines several models of engagement that professionals can use when working with families of children with special needs.

Talking Futures: https://resources.careersandenterprise.co.uk/talking-futures

My little checklist – Top tips to improve partnerships when working with parents and families

Partnership working with families	Top tips to improve your practice in engaging parents/families	Action	Who
How would you describe your current model of engagement with parents/families?	It might not just be within the careers team that you look for models of engagement. Talk to your SENDCO, pastoral care team, year heads, other staff too.		
Short question – does it work?	Identify what is working and what needs more attention.		
Who else is currently involved in achieving good engagement?	Which groups of people – staff, professionals, advocates, employers, careers advisers, for example? What roles do they 'play'?		
Looking at each engagement model in turn, establish one that describes most closely how you can engage from a careers perspective.	It may be that different models operate at different times and you describe this.		
Look at the engagement models and decide if one style may enable you to work more effectively with parents/carers/families.	Analyse which models currently exist and what you would ideally like to develop to improve engagement.		
How do you currently communicate?	What methods – online, offline, multiple, hybrid, face to face, written materials, symbol language?		
Using the ideas to improve engagement, choose three that you would like to try and how you will implement them.	1		
	2		
	3		
Accept that for different groups of students you may have to adapt models or take elements of models and assemble them purposefully.	Design an engagement strategy that has the potential to reach all families and test its acceptability with small groups first and refine.		

Evaluating the impact of your careers programme: answering the question, 'so what?'

- What are you evaluating?
- Who are you evaluating for?
- How are you evaluating?
- Why are you evaluating?
- Ways to secure evidence
- Nesta's Standards of Evidence
- What will you do with the data?
- Guest Contributor – Dr Emily Tanner, Head of Post-14 Education and Skills at Nuffield Foundation

Introduction

Evaluating the impact of a careers programme is an opportunity to improve outcomes. It is standard good practice to evaluate your careers programme annually. Our favourite question is 'so what?' The way to use it is to think about a careers activity and then ask yourself the question so what; in other words, what is the point of doing that activity. Once you have an answer, continue to ask the 'so what' question of that answer and so on. The point is to establish a connection between an improvement in outcomes and the activity. The process looks something like – inputs, outputs, outcomes and impact. An example could be:

- Input – organise work experience.
- Output – work experience takes place.
- Outcome – both employer and student can articulate the value of the experience.
- Impact – the student has improved their work-related skills and knowledge, which has contributed to refining their career goal, and the employer has deepened its understanding of young people with additional needs and has offered training places in the coming year.

Impact doesn't usually happen in a short period of time so don't expect to make impact quickly, but you will achieve outcomes and it is more authentic to describe this than claim artificial impacts. Following a robust evaluation process will help you achieve this.

What are you evaluating?
It can be tempting to think about evaluating huge amounts, the whole careers programme for example. For young people with additional/special needs, it is often the subtleties that make the biggest differences. Think about the specific area you want to evaluate and then consider the questions posed in the following sections.

Who are you evaluating for?
Are you evaluating for a particular person/group or for a particular purpose, for example funding or where to allocate funds or to find out who might benefit the most from the activity/programme. Think about who your beneficiaries are – students, parents/carers, staff, employers.

How are you evaluating?
Basic considerations include when you need the results. Do you need immediate results or is this about long-term outcomes? Which aspects will you focus on, what data will you seek to collect, how it will be reported?

Why are you evaluating? The purpose will determine types of evidence, for example:

- Why – accountability to funders, Ofsted or other stakeholders such as employers that have invested in a project. Evidence could include quantitative metrics and 'stories'.
- Why – improve and/or develop careers programmes. Evidence could include outcome measures.
- Why – maximise impact from limited resources. Evidence can be found by comparing outcomes from two or more approaches.
- Why – assess long-term impacts on young people's outcomes. Evidence can be collected through destination tracking.

Ways to secure evidence
- Measuring outcomes
- Measures completed by teachers, providers, parents/carers about young people based on observation
- Teacher/parent versions of standard tools

- Bespoke surveys, qualitative evidence
- Perceived impact – during, after, later
- Video blogs
- Pictures/photos
- Interviews, focus groups
- Surveys/focus groups with adult beneficiaries to understand the impact on knowledge, attitudes and behaviours
- Structured observation tools to assess engagement with activities
- Creative and visual methods, e.g. choose pictures, photographs
- Case studies of young people or programmes involving insights from different perspectives
- Journey mapping/life story methods

Nesta's Standards of Evidence

Nesta is a very useful method to identify the level of rigor being applied to any evidence. This can then inform the reader in terms of being able of being able to rely on the information and use it as a basis for their own work. They can also make a judgement call on the probability that if they used the information to create similar situations, there is an implication that the probability of achieving the same result would increase as they used evidence from the different levels, e.g. anecdotal, case studies and so on. You can also start with a theory of change. I have adapted it slightly but have included a link to the original model in the 'Resources' section. The levels are:

1. Anecdotal – someone saw or talked about something happening which could be better or worse or no change. This might be recorded or a verbal record.
2. Case study – this is more involved and could be recorded in writing more formally and will follow a structure, something along the lines of overview, baseline, action taken, results analysis, conclusion, next steps.
3. Measured using an evaluation tool created internally – this could be an evaluation tool you have used before or something designed specifically.
4. Measured using an evaluation tool created by an external, reputable organisation.
5. Some type of external evaluation tool like the Future Skills Questionnaire (see link in 'Resources' section).

When thinking through collecting evidence, think about proportionality; you don't need to take a hammer to crack a nut as the saying goes.

What will you do with the data?
You may find that you have generated data which has some findings you were expecting and some you weren't. There are probably many stakeholders who will be interested in these findings. An obvious little reminder is to anonymise data so individuals cannot be identified, and any video/photographic evidence or quotes must have the person's permission.

If you have gone through all the steps, you will know why you are carrying out the evaluation, who it is for, and why and what the purpose is. You will have collected evidence that is relevant to the purpose and know what you want to achieve.

Writing up a simple report first and sharing it with a small internal audience is a good start. A template could include an overview, action taken (your evaluation study with methodology), results, analysis, conclusions and next steps. And remember to put a date on the front; it is amazing how often that gets forgotten.

Recall that I started with the notion that evaluation can lead to improved outcomes, so in the case of young people with additional needs/SEND, the outcomes might seem small at the time, but they can have a significant impact for the individual so don't be disappointed with small changes if that is what you find.

Summary of key points
You can't improve what you can't measure, and we need to really understand what makes the difference to a young person with additional needs/SEND achieving their optimal career outcome. By some standards, these can be small changes but with big impacts. By interrogating the inputs and outputs, we can understand more about the outcomes and impacts. Be very clear about why you are evaluating, what you are evaluating for whom and how you will carry it out. Share results and make innovations/improvements.

Case studies
An example of using Nesta's Standards of Evidence can be seen in the Talentino Social Impact Report (see https://www.talentinocareers.co.uk/social-impact-report.pdf)

Resources
Nesta Standards of Evidence: https://media.nesta.org.uk/documents/standards_of_evidence.pdf

Achieving change/future focus commentary
Future Skills Questionnaire: https://resources.careersandenterprise.co.uk/resources/future-skills-questionnaire

GUEST CONTRIBUTOR – DR EMILY TANNER, HEAD OF POST-14 EDUCATION AND SKILLS AT NUFFIELD FOUNDATION

Emily has always impressed me with her ability to enable the unscientific among us (me) to understand concepts and ideas so we can interrogate our work and develop a better understanding of its impact. Emily has a genuine desire to improve outcomes. Thank you for contributing Dr Tanner, much appreciated.

In essence, programme evaluation is simply the process of testing whether our assumptions of how an activity or intervention would help a young person are borne out in practice. These assumptions may be implicit, based on experience, or explicit, for example when trying a new approach. Either way, evaluation is an essential part of good practice in career guidance, ensuring that limited resources are used to maximum benefit of the young people I support. For young people with SEND, the evaluation principles are the same, but they may need a bespoke approach tailored to communication preferences and career mapping journey.

The term 'evaluation' encompasses everything from gathering feedback on a career talk delivered to a group of young people to meta-analyses of multiple randomised controlled trials testing the same type of intervention on a large scale. *Standards of evidence* can be used to identify the extent to which the findings might be replicated in different contexts and how confident I can be that the intervention caused the outcomes. Practitioners can draw on insight from large-scale studies in designing career programmes and contribute to evidence-generation by taking part, while also evaluating their own work on a smaller scale.

Whatever the scale of evaluation, a good place to start is setting out the theory of change. Following one of the many *guidance tools* available will help to clarify what it is you want to know and why, and then to articulate your target group, the intended outcomes (such as attitudes, behaviours or skills), how to design the activities to best achieve those outcomes, and the factors that will help or hinder. Working through a theory of change will result in a useful output, such as visual representation, that you can use to work out what evidence to gather to test it. But a theory of change is also a process – a means of reaching consensus with colleagues and beneficiaries about what you're setting out to do and then reflecting on what could be improved. Careers Hubs have been developing theories of change over recent years to underpin tailored activities under the umbrella of Hubs Innovation Projects and *careers interventions for disadvantaged young people*.

Theories of change guide the type of evidence to collect. For example, if the intended outcome of a career's intervention is to support the transition to college, then you need data on what proportion of your student group made that transition, perhaps a college view on how well settled they are, and the young person's view on satisfaction with what they're studying and how it fits with their future plans. If the activity is a work experience programme aimed at developing employability skills such as communication, then you may want to collect feedback from the employers and young people taking part, and perhaps include observation data.

Questionnaires such as the Future Skills Questionnaire (SEND version) within Compass+ can be useful for tracking career readiness and providing quantitative data that can be used to compare differences over time (such as before and after an intervention) or between groups (students who participated in a supported internship and those experiencing classroom-based learning). However, sometimes qualitative data collected systematically, such as feedback from young people, parents/carers and employers, or observation data recorded by a careers practitioner can be a more effective way to capture the insight needed.

As well as collecting data on outcomes, it is important to record the process so that you can understand how the intervention was delivered in practice, how many sessions young people took part in and whether there were variations for different participants.

Once the careers interventions have taken place and you have the data, the theory of change provides a way to structure the reflection and improvement process. Some questions that might be used to ask include:

What evidence is there that the activity led to positive outcomes for young people? Was it to the extent that was expected?

What factors helped that to happen or posed obstacles?

Did some students benefit more than others? Why might that be?

What refinements are needed?

My little checklist – Top tips to improve your impact through better evaluation

Evaluation	Top tips to improve your SEND careers practice	Planned action	Tick action completed
What do you currently evaluate and/or measure?	Analyse the current evaluation you carry out from a strategic level – SDP/SIP, careers strategy to the micro individual level currently.		
Have you evaluated anything in the careers field previously?	Analyse a previous evaluation you carried out, and using the list on pages 194–5, identify the rationale and methodology you used.		
What are you evaluating? What are the top three areas you wish to evaluate about career development and young people with SEND?	Think about your SEND or and vulnerable/disadvantaged students in particular and aspects of career development which are key to improving outcomes; prioritise the top three areas.		
Why are you evaluating? Having identified the top three priorities, ask yourself why you are evaluating.	Hopefully, your answer will be about improving outcomes, but it might be about improving aspects of the career development process too.		
Who are you evaluating for? Having identified the student group(s), who is going to benefit from your evaluation exercise?	This might seem obvious but remember to include as many relevant groups as possible and the rationale as to why they would benefit from the knowledge you will generate.		
How are you evaluating? It can be tempting to imagine an evaluation that is very involved, takes a long time and is quite elaborate involving lots of people and cost.	It is important to be realistic when planning an evaluation. If you are new to this, don't be too ambitious. It is better to carry out a smaller but higher quality evaluation than one that is too ambitious at this stage.		
How are you going to secure evidence? Think about a balance between the cost of gathering the evidence and the potential value of the evaluation.	Remember to use the Nesta Standards of Evidence and the different levels starting with anecdotal to case studies to instruments you have designed, and then instruments others have designed and importantly what you need.		
Have you used the FSQ?	This is a free tool offered by the CEC and works with Compass+.		
What will you do with the data? Evaluation is always a balance, and the method needs to be proportionate to the perceived value delivered by it.	Remember, sometimes there can be a huge value to quite a simple evaluation exercise (and vice versa) and it comes back to who will benefit from knowing the information and make positive changes on behalf of the designated beneficiary.		
Think about who might be interested outside of your direct circle.	Your evaluation might stimulate others in your Careers Hub or inclusion group and stimulate them to make changes.		

Chapter 8
The value chain of early career development for inclusion #differentandbetter

> ♥ I feel a drum roll coming on . . . You have read and taken on board an enormous amount of information, been pinged through a slingshot of emotion and I am sure you must be bursting with ideas on how to improve your practice. But I have one last model to present to you – #differentandbetter a value chain for inclusion.

This final chapter will bring everything together highlighted in a way that hopefully helps you create your own value chain of early career development for inclusion – #differentandbetter. There are two case studies illustrating the model at the end of this chapter.

Throughout this book, I have established some **basic principles of early career development** of young people with SEND/additional needs, those who are vulnerable or disadvantaged in some way or just need a little more support for whatever reason. Those principles include raising aspirations; authentic inclusion; opportunities for everyone, starting career development early; significant levels of employer engagement; utilising Careers Hubs and enterprise coordinators and enterprise advisers; deploying the Gatsby Benchmarks; and evaluating the impact of careers guidance in our schools, special schools and colleges.

Look what you have achieved, what you have covered and what you are be more confident about. You:

- know who young people with additional needs/need additional support are, and Career SEND Groups One and Two provide a simple but informative model encouraging the conversation to focus on outcomes, not diagnosis; 'can' not 'can't'
- appreciate these young people can be found in every educational setting and at home, and young people have told us of their experiences
- acknowledge (but don't accept) optimal career destinations are less likely for young people with SEND or who are vulnerable or disadvantaged (and want to change this); and barriers are a combination of systemic, supply and demand issues, and held sometimes within us
- know anxiety can exist around diversity, difference and disability; the reasons (not excuses) for this; and what needs to be done to mitigate this
- understand the impact of poor or ill-informed choices around language
- recognise two discreet sets of optimal career outcomes for each of the two Career SEND Groups
- can grasp the different roles that different stakeholders play such as careers leaders, careers advisers, SENDCOs and, of course, employers
- comprehend what inclusion is (and isn't) and how to create inclusive careers guidance
- understand the different pathways and destinations they lead to
- realise how the Careers and Enterprise Company can provide different types of support
- recognise the need for the youth voice to be heard
- better understand the Gatsby Benchmarks and SEND and the process of career development
- know more about measuring/evaluating progress, which has been a key thread throughout – answering the powerful question 'so what?'
- can see the value of enterprise and how to increase employer engagement
- would want an overt approach to the definition and development of skills
- appreciate how important it is to get transition right at a micro and macro level

- agree the Gatsby Benchmarks remain a solid framework of standards through which to deliver inclusive SEND careers education and are developing further
- and #sameandifferent gives us a model through which to organise early career development for both SEND groups.

> ♥ And I hope you are totally committed to improving career outcomes for the millions of young people who need extra support.

So, how do we put all your learning together?

Whilst it seems almost impossible to bring it all together, something I have been noodling on recently is the value chain of early career development which is a process of linked activities that should lead to improved destinations.

'Value chain' was a term identified by Michael Porter of Harvard Business School and describes 'a flow of inputs and outputs with different actors controlling different parts of the process'. A value chain should lead to improvements in some way; in a business sense it might be costs savings, an improvement in quality or customer service, a product innovation, or saving time.

Our value chain of early career development must be ultimately about improving destinations and enabling all young people to achieve their optimal career outcomes. I know this is not the case for many young people with additional needs so drilling down into the career development process and careers guidance activities to find out what can make the difference and how it connects is key. Career development naturally follows a timeline but is not always viewed as a process. It is sometimes seen as islandic events, for example moving schools, making exam choices, doing work experience, going to a careers fair.

It is vital for young people with SEND/additional needs or those who are vulnerable or disadvantaged to view career development as a process or value chain. I know that when there are hand-off points whether planned (for example moving schools) or unplanned (for example being excluded) there is an opportunity for the value chain to be stretched and possibly broken and never quite put back together.

There is no doubt that career development has improved for young people with additional needs, but there are still some 'amber' areas like parent/carer/family engagement and influence; employer confidence concerning diversity; career readiness of the broadest groups of young people; FE courses that enable employment; and destination data tells us these groups are still not achieving at the same level as their peers.

If all the key stakeholders involved in a young person's early career development examine the process, define the process, identify where it could be brought forward and/or extended for the benefit of a young person, and pinpoint where it is under strain and could break, then ensuring that connectivity is maintained can only help to improve the possibility and probability of an optimal career outcome being achieved. This is where #differentandbetter comes in.

Twenty years ago, I did an executive Strategic HR Management course at Harvard Business School, and I remember saying out loud at the end, 'Is that it?', which has seemed terribly rude for many years. I realise now that whilst it was one of the best courses I had ever done, it had been an experience that was formulaic, rehearsed to the point of any new thinking or creativity being rinsed out of it, and not leaving us with something new, for me that is. So, I am not leaving you with a tired and tested narrative but with a new model to think about – #differentandbetter.

One of the numerous reports last year talked about being more granular, identifying inputs and outcomes, and individualising careers guidance activities and plans. Our new model #differentandbetter which builds on our original #sameanddifferent takes this on board.

The revised and new processes in #differentandbetter need to be thought about as a matrix essentially. Process work along lines gets interrupted by transition points but also meets at junctions where more stakeholders are involved. It is at these junctions where there is potential for things to not go as planned. It is about generating better connectivity, so the career development processes flow up, down and along resulting in improved outcomes.

This is a new model so I will explain it conceptually, but it will grow with your involvement too. The overarching principle is of raising aspirations across all stages. The value chain has within it eight strands or processes all of which contribute to career development and optimal outcomes:

- **Education and learning** from 0 to 25+ and includes qualifications
- **Careers Guidance** which is a collective term for multiple career development activities, which will deliver the Gatsby Benchmarks and more

The value chain of early career development for inclusion *#differentandbetter*

- **Careers Advice** is the advice and guidance delivered by qualified careers advisers
- **Transition** – macro and micro stages when things change during a career s journey
- **Parent/Carer/Family** – those who are responsible and support and are alongside for life
- **Employer Engagement** including different activities such as gaining work experience, mentoring, coaching, training
- **Skills development** – for life, for work, for study and includes 'soft' skills
- **Quality, standards and management information** – Ofsted, Gatsby, DFE, CEC,CDI and others

Explaining the diagram Inclusion #differentandbetter

You will see across the top a timeline from 0 to 25 years+ spilt into educational key stages. On the left-hand side are the eight strands/processes which collectively form career development. Across the middle of the diagram is a wiggly line with spots at the edge of each key stage. The spots represent key transition points. The assumption flowing through this wiggly line is all the eight strands will be working cohesively together towards enabling optimal career outcomes for the individual.

Each of the strands has two lines that run across the key stages. The top line will be a perspective on how well things are working in that area now. I acknowledge this is a blunt way of describing, say, education and learning as there are so many challenges so a kind of generic view is taken. Please feel free to break this line down further with your own experiences and situations. Where the line is broken, it means it is not working as well as it could.

The line underneath the first line is thicker and indicates where we need to make improvements so things 'work even better'. Importantly, they also indicate where the value chain needs to be brought forward earlier or extended later to improve processes and the possibility of a better outcome.

You could probably create your own version of the value chain which would enable you to focus in on where improvements need to be made.

The Big Inclusive SEND Careers Handbook

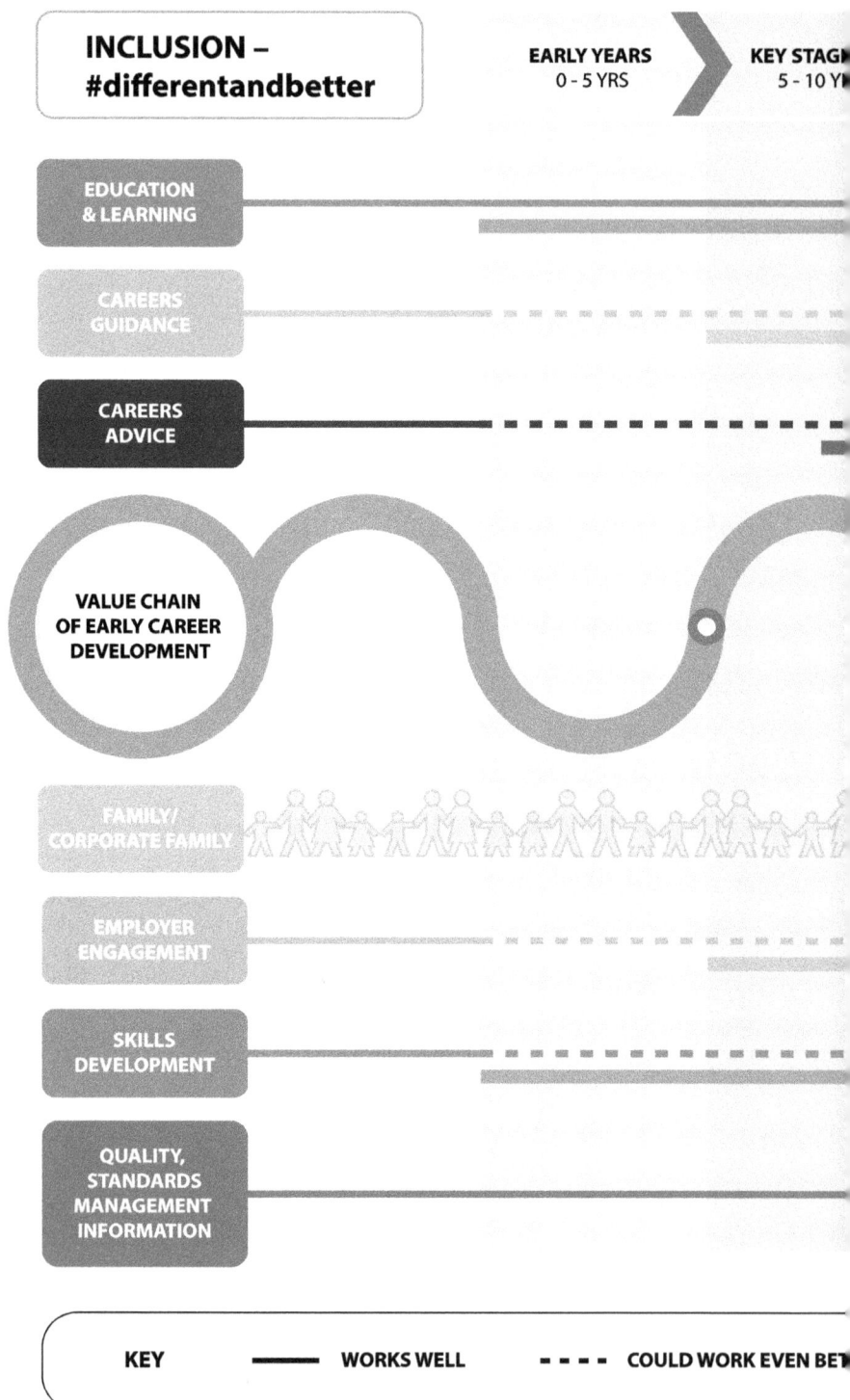

The value chain of early career development for inclusion *#differentandbetter*

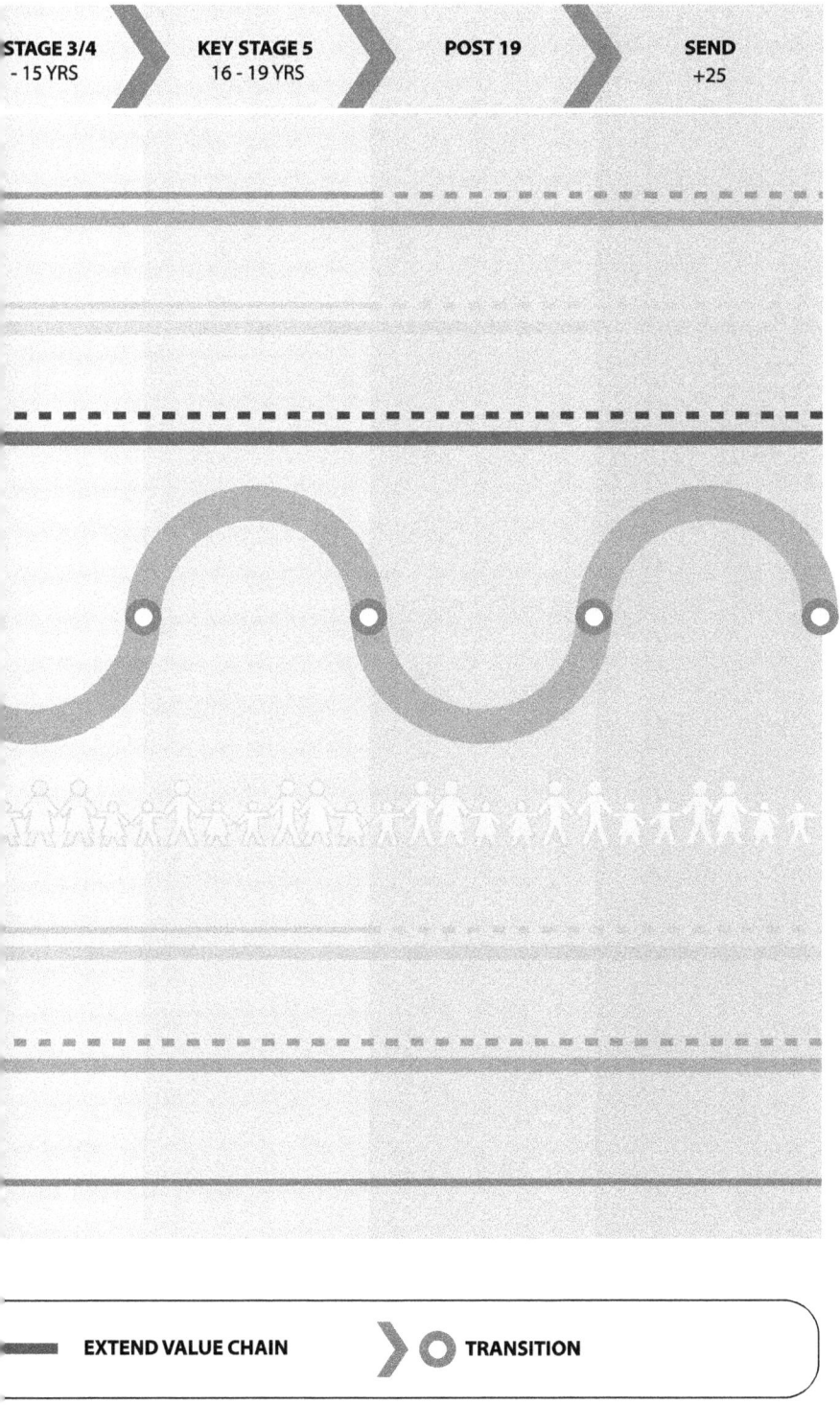

Now that you have had a chance to consider this value chain for inclusion, explore how you could extend the value/contribution of different strands of activities and sub-activities . Where and how could things work even better? What does macro- and micro-transition look like for all stakeholders? I would be really interested to see what your analysis reveals and how you are using the model. Next, we have two contributors who have demonstrated brilliantly their own approaches to creating their own value chain of early career development.

The value chain of early career development for inclusion *#differentandbetter*

 GUEST CONTRIBUTOR – HELEN HANNAM, DEPUTY HEAD TEACHER AT MANOR GREEN SCHOOL

The value chain of early development

At Manor Green School I realised that preparation for adulthood and our careers system had to be the very bedrock of the school for both our students and staff. I also knew, without trying to sound too political, that the very survival of special schools is at risk because of the lack of funding and the ever-increasing level of need of the cohorts we are seeing. With these two elements very clearly coupled, it became important to us not only to ensure our own financial stability but to do so in a way that would benefit not just our own cohort of students but also the local community.

Manor Green School has, therefore, established several provisions turning the school into a successful business whilst also enhancing life chances for students and championing staff development.

Our first provision was The Link. As a special school, our cohort has very complex educational and medical needs. It is very vulnerable and, unfortunately, as a special school it cannot be everything to everyone. Within our local community there was a high number of permanent exclusions for primary-aged students. These students with high SEMH needs were being placed straight back into mainstream placements without anybody trying to understand the reasons behind the behaviours. This was setting them up to fail. As such, I established our own Alternative Provision, The Primary Link, a therapeutic unit for permanently excluded primary-aged students with nurture at its core. I firmly believe that all behaviour is a form of communication and that with the right therapeutic intervention and identification of needs, the students can be reintegrated into suitable placements back into the education system.

The Secondary Link was established at the same time for mainstream-ability secondary-aged students who simply could not cope with the mainstream environment. Our cohort ranges from transgender, high-functioning ASD, PTSD to high suicide risk. Again, therapy is the very core of the unit, and its success has been incredible. About 160 students have attended across both units. One student did not attend her mainstream school for three years and did not leave her bedroom for 18 months, but with emotional therapy and a great school dog not only did she thrive in the Link, but she has also now successfully completed university. Fifteen other Link students have attended university, and three students now work at Manor Green. The Link is now a very successful business. It is non-profit making but benefits Manor Green by employing three full-time councillors, a speech and language therapist, and an occupational therapist who work across the provisions.

The second established provision is called the Hive. Again, I looked at the local community to see the gaps that simply were not being filled. Students with SLD but also with very high medical needs were unable to attend school; there just wasn't anything for them. Tutors employed by the local authorities tend to be mainstream teachers with no experience of complicated special needs. The

Hive aims to take high-level SEN education into the home to work with students who can't come to school, whilst upskilling parents and carers. Our lead teacher is also a qualified conductive educator, and the integrated therapy model is used within the home. Families have been highly appreciative of the service I have been able to offer, and the fact that I can reduce barriers to learning to ensure that the students receive access to the education they deserve is something I am very proud of.

Like most schools, we were hit hard by Covid-19. Although as teachers and professionals we adapted quickly with new ways of working and the use of virtual platforms, the realisation that people could work from home has had a huge impact on recruitment, especially teaching assistants. As a school we employ over 350 people; following Covid-19 we had to run the school carrying 27 teaching assistant vacancies, which was not sustainable. We had been one of the first schools within our local authority to take advantage of the Apprenticeship Levy, however, the quality of the apprenticeship delivery being provided was dire as it was provided by people who had not worked in education and certainly not within special needs. This is where our fourth provision was born: why accept substandard? Why not become an apprenticeship provider ourselves?

As part of the ethos of Manor Green I have always invested in our staff professionally. To date I have trained and qualified 33 teachers. I have taken our best TAs and promoted them to HLTA and our best HLTAs have been put through the assessment-only teaching qualification. This investment has had a hugely positive impact on staff wellbeing and retention.

In 2021 we became an apprentice provider offering level three, four and five apprenticeships for staff. As a business model this has created a significant financial stream for the school, but, most importantly, it solved our recruitment crisis and has enabled high-quality SEN-focused modelling and learning for teaching assistants. We now have over 40 apprentices across eight schools. Staff feel we are investing in them. They are gaining qualifications and recognition, and this has led to promotions within the school. I have now moved on to stage 2 of this plan, which is to roll out the apprenticeship to our student cohort. This leads very nicely into provision five, our College Link.

I find many of our students are reluctant to go to college as locally our college placements are three days with a limitation to the courses they can access. I also see that, regardless of how much preparation for adulthood I have delivered at school through our enterprise curriculum, very few of our ex-students were reaching the employment status they deserved. With a full-time careers advisor at the heart of this, I decided to take the next step towards employability by developing an SEN careers hub for 16- to 25-year-olds with EHCPs, which I have called College Link.

College Link is set up like a job centre rather than a classroom. It provides valuable employability skills such as travel training, banking, money management and ICT as well as work experience opportunities supported by job coaches. This provision has allowed us to roll out our first student apprenticeships and has benefited from the vocational teaching spaces that I have developed. Our industrial-level training kitchen, run by a qualified chef, provides pre-employment education and catering qualifications. Our work experience café sells much of the food produced in the training kitchen and adds customer service training and a barista qualification to the package offered. The addition of construction and engineering is now allowing the school to become a vocational hub, which the local mainstream schools can also access. This, in turn, contributes to school finances, which allows us to further develop our facilities.

Manor Green School prides itself on being a centre of excellence at the heart of the local community. I feel it makes us a *very* special school that enhances the life chances and experiences of so many young people and adults across our local community.

GARETH IVETT, PRINCIPAL AT CREATING TOMORROW COLLEGE

The value chain of early career development

In our journey to understand and enhance career education for learners with SEND, I delved into the concept of the 'value chain'. At its core, I saw it as the entire life journey of individuals with SEND, encompassing their experiences and opportunities for growth. Through this exploration, it became apparent that this journey can be broken down into three distinct sections, each offering its own unique value: school, education immediately beyond school age, and the rest of the person's life.

During the initial stage within the school system, most young people with SEND often receive good value. Schools are continually striving for improvement and are equipped with professionals who understand how to meet the diverse needs of learners. Support services are readily available, ensuring that individuals progress along their developmental path. This period aligns closely with the foundational principles of Maslow's hierarchy of needs, with emphasis placed on fulfilling basic requirements and facilitating personal growth.

However, as learners transition beyond the school environment into the second section of the value chain, a significant disconnect emerges. While some continue their education in settings that provide meaningful input, aligned with the principles of Preparing for Adulthood, others find themselves in courses that merely rehash previously acquired knowledge and skills. This repetition impedes progress towards successful adulthood, stalling personal development and limiting opportunities for growth.

The third section of the value chain, encompassing 'the rest of their life', presents a daunting cliff for many individuals with SEND. As they navigate the complexities of adulthood, particularly in the realm of employment, support services and networks often dwindle or disappear altogether. The transition from structured education to the uncertainties of adult life can be overwhelming, leaving many individuals struggling to achieve their aspirations. Days are filled with activities funded by personal budgets, which, while enriching for some, fail to provide the meaningful engagement and fulfilment that paid employment can offer.

It's crucial to acknowledge that while these life-enriching activities may be appropriate for some individuals, there exists a significant cohort of young adults with SEND who possess the desire and capability to engage in meaningful paid employment. However, without adequate support and guidance, they risk being sidelined from the workforce, unable to fulfil their potential and contribute to society in a meaningful way.

As I navigate the intricacies of early career development for individuals with SEND, it's imperative that I address the gaps within the value chain. By bolstering support systems, fostering inclusive education practices, and promoting meaningful employment opportunities, I can empower individuals with SEND to lead fulfilling and independent lives, realising their aspirations and contributing to the fabric of our communities.

Epigraph

On 5 July 2024, a new Labour government started working. This final section is not about political affiliations but about whether the intentions they have expressed could support the value chain discussed in the previous section.

- Bridget Phillipson, Minister for Education, has stated that the eradication of child poverty is at the heart of the government's mission to ensure background is no barrier to success, and inclusion will be at the heart of mainstream education.
- The policy for SEND and AP will be restructured and come into the DfE Schools group 'to ensure inclusion is a core consideration'.
- The National Audit Office is reviewing DfE support for children and young people with SEND. The report, due in the autumn, asks two questions:
  - Does the current system support a sustainable SEND and AP system that delivers positive outcomes for young people with SEND/AP?
  - Is the DfE taking effective action to deliver longer term systemic improvements in the SEND/AP Improvement Plan?
- **Education and care systems** do not meet the needs of those with SEND, and early intervention in mainstream is key for this group (sic). **Career experience** could become a protected characteristic.
- **A Curriculum and Assessment review** will be carried out by Becky Francis. 'Barriers faced by disadvantaged children and those with SEND in mainstream will be central to the review.'
- There will be a pause and review of de-funding BTECs with a report published by the end of 2024. This is important as many disadvantaged young people secure university places using BTECs.
- **Personal Statements** will be replaced by three simple questions for university applications from 2026.
- **Education law bill by the end of 2024: Early Years** will include breakfast clubs for every child, more speech and language support and a focus on early maths.
- **Skills England** has been created to deliver skills training to unlock opportunities, harness talent and drive growth. This will include skills to support Great British Energy like home insulation; generation of Green Power; industries of the future.

- Careers Adviser will be 'strengthened'; CEIAG is seen as a driver of change within society improving life chances, empowering people who take control of their own lives.
- Disability Employment will be enhanced by more tailored employment support; the new Minister for Social Security and Disability is Stephen Timms; the National Careers Service and The Job Centre will merge; under the new Employment Legislation, employees will have the right to request part-time/flexible working.
- **Absenteeism, exclusion:** All councils will need to keep a Truancy (their word, not my choice) register, with better connectivity among stakeholders. A recent report shows 48% of suspensions and 38% of exclusions are more likely to be young people with SEND – diagnosis not punishment is need. English schools will also have to phase out 'cruel' behaviour management tactics.

Afterword

A massive thank you again to all our guest contributors who were so lovely when I approached them, all of them revered specialists in their fields and yet flattered to be asked. Amazing, so humbling.

Thank you to *you* for engaging with this unconventional careers book. It was worth it. ♥

Thank you to *you* for getting to the end, unless you like starting at the end of a book and some do, in which case you are in for a treat!

Glossary of Key Terms

Ableism Unfairly favouring non-disabled people. In an ableist society, it's assumed that the 'normal' way to live is as a non-disabled person. It is ableist to believe that non-disabled people are more valuable to society than disabled people (SENSE UK).

Access to Work A grant that funds practical support if you have a disability, health or mental health condition to help you start work, stay in work or be able to move into self-employment or start a business.

Accessible apprenticeship Apprenticeships which take into consideration the individual needs of the learner, allowing them to get the most out of their apprenticeship journey. There is also flexibility with the entry criteria increasing access.

ADHD Attention deficit hyperactivity disorder (ADHD) is a condition that affects people's behaviour. People with ADHD can seem restless, may have trouble concentrating and may act on impulse (NHS).

Anxiety What we feel when we are worried, tense or afraid – particularly about things that are about to happen or which we think could happen in the future. Anxiety can become a mental health problem if it impacts your ability to live your life as fully as you want to (Mind).

Autism A lifelong developmental disability which affects how people communicate and interact with the world (National Autistic Society).

Barriers Anything which prevents something from enabling an optimal outcome and can be physical, psychological, systemic, structural, bias, ableist, a process (e.g. recruitment), economic, or educational among others.

BASE British Association of Supported Employment

Career development process A set of linked career activities at different ages and stages which follow a timeline of key career decisions, for example GCSE choices in Year 8/9, transition reviews in Year 9, annual reviews for those with an EHC Plan, and career choices after education driven by application deadlines.

Career management skills Able to alone or with support identify their own career orientation, explore different careers, identify career goals and make plans to develop pathways towards their goal.

Career outcome The next step after the current education or training is completed and could include more education, training, employment/self-employment or supported living.

Career SEND Group One Young people with SEND who will not study at Level 2/GCSE, and for whom optimal career outcomes will follow one of three pathways – formal, semi-formal and pre-formal/sensory. For each pathway there is a discrete set of optimal career outcomes.

Career SEND Group Two Young people with SEND who will or could study at Level 2/GCSE and beyond, and for whom optimal career outcomes should be the same as young people without additional/special needs.

Glossary of Key Terms

Careers advice and guidance Personal guidance delivered to individual young people by a Level 6-qualified careers adviser (in schools) (National Careers Strategy 2017).

Careers adviser Careers advisers provide guidance about career choice, employment, training and further education opportunities to clients, including young people and the unemployed.

Careers and Enterprise Company The national body for careers education in England, supporting schools and colleges to deliver modern, 21st-century careers education. Their mission is to help *every* young person find their best next step by working with primary and secondary schools, colleges and employers to improve careers education and secure better outcomes for young people. Working nationally through a network of Careers Hubs that bring together schools, colleges, employers, and apprenticeship providers and in partnership with mayoral/local authorities to connect with local skills needs.

Careers guidance Any careers activity that delivers the Gatsby Benchmarks (National Careers Strategy 2017).

Careers leader Careers leaders are responsible and accountable for the planning and delivery of their school, special school or college's careers programme. They develop a strategic careers plan, build a progressive careers programme, and track and evaluate the impact of provision. The careers leader needs to be someone who can liaise with external partners, such as employers, learning providers and careers guidance services, as well as manage and coordinate the school's, special school's or college's provision through a stable and embedded programme. A careers leader is not a careers adviser but some combine both roles. These roles are distinct but complementary, and it is common for the careers leader to either manage or commission the careers adviser (Careers and Enterprise Company).

Careers governor An individual on the governing board with dedicated responsibility for careers.

CICI AI-driven careers guidance tool offered by CareerChat Ltd.

CICO® Profiling tool offered by Talentino Ltd.

#sameandifferent A model through which to view career development for both Career SEND Groups One and Two against those who do not have any special needs.

#differentandbetter A model which represents the value chain of early career development for young people with SEND or who are disadvantaged or vulnerable.

Destinations Typically the outcomes of young people when they have left education. The Unit for Future Skills aggregates the data annually (www.gov.uk/government/groups/unit-for-future-skills).

Disability A physical or mental impairment that has a 'substantial' and 'long-term' negative effect on your ability to do normal daily activities (Equality Act 2010).

Disabled Apprenticeships Network A network and online forum for apprentices who are training or who have finished their training. www.disabilityrightsuk.org/disabled-apprentice-network

Education settings Places – actual or virtual – where education takes place.

EHC Plan Education, Health and Care Plan

Glossary of Key Terms

Employability skills Skills which will support successful employment including 'soft' or intrinsic skills

Employer engagement The process of bringing employers into education and the activities they may deliver through Gatsby Benchmarks 5 and 6.

Enterprise Closely related to the role of an entrepreneur, it could be a new business, a small business or a venture with a social purpose and could be carried out by anyone as either their main activity or as a short-term project, in a school for example.

Enterprise adviser A volunteer from business who supports Careers Hubs in a dedicated school in different ways such as employer engagement activities and the strategic development of their careers plan.

Enterprise coordinator Works within a Careers Hub, facilitates the career development of special schools, schools and colleges, and supports employers to better engage in education and improve their careers and enterprise programmes.

Gatsby Benchmarks A standards framework of eight benchmarks through which career development is delivered in over 90% educational settings. Created by Sir John Holman as part of the Gatsby Foundation and now adopted in countries outside the UK too.

Impact is about bringing about change and could be positive or negative or neutral, e.g. the two students' applications were successful and offered apprenticeships which they took up upon leaving school.

Inclusion 100% of children learning and having needs met in high-quality education 100% of the time. Every child, every lesson, every day, every week. Inclusion is aspiration, progression and success for all. It is not about special *v.* mainstream schools.

ISP/IEP Individual Support Plan or Individual Education Plan for young people defined as having a special educational need or disability but who are not entitled to an EHC Plan (Education, Health and Care Plan).

Job coaches Job coaches provide support for the individual to develop on-the-job skills and support for the employer so that the working relationship can develop and prosper.

LMI Labour market information, often related to a particular area, identifies information about the relevant sectors, areas of growth and decline and maybe numbers of opportunities. Gatsby Benchmark 2 is concerned with access to LMI.

Local offer The local offer is the range of opportunities for SEND young people required to be published by the local authority, often aimed at those with more complex needs.

LSIP The Local Skills Improvement Plan (LSIP) is an initiative funded by the Department for Education (DfE), the aim being to put employers at the heart of the skills agenda and build stronger and more dynamic partnerships between employers and further education providers.

National Careers Strategy The National Careers Strategy was published in 2017 in conjunction with the Statutory Guidance published in 2018 which set out the then government's approach to careers and the obligations of schools and colleges. Later papers include the Skills for Jobs White Paper, the Education

Glossary of Key Terms

Select Committee report 2023, and Ofsted's Thematic Review of Careers SEND published in February 2024.

NEET A term used to describe young people not in education, employment or training.

Nesta's Scale of Standards A scale of standards through which to understand the impact of initiatives and report on them and starts with a theory of change.

Neurodivergent Neurodiversity is the concept that all humans vary in terms of our neurocognitive ability. Everyone has both talents and things they struggle with. However, for some people the variation between those strengths and challenges is more pronounced, which can bring advantages but can also be disabling (Genius Within).

Ofsted's Thematic Review of Careers A deep dive into careers guidance in education in England carried out in 2023.

Outcome something happened as a result, e.g. two students met employers, found out about their apprenticeship schemes and applied.

Outcomes The third step in the impact model and example:
  Input I planned to do something, e.g. careers fair.
  Outputs the thing happened, e.g. careers fair.

PAL Provider Access Legislation (see www.careersandenterprise.co.uk/fe-skills/provider-access-legislation/). It is a statutory obligation for schools.

Personal/social development Development of skills relating to personal and social development that supports career development and employability skill development.

Peter Jones Foundation/Tycoon The Tycoon competition is an enterprise competition for schools and the new Talentino Tycoon SEND Competition is focused on young people with SEND and supported by the Peter Jones Foundation.

PMLD Profound and multiple learning disabilities – those with the most complex needs.

Raising aspirations The process of enabling someone, usually a child or young person, to set their sights higher than they might have done otherwise in terms of careers and life ambitions.

Reasonable adjustments Actions taken by any organisation making adjustments to a physical environment, sensory environment, processes and/or policies which enable a person with additional needs and/or disabilities to access education and employment.

SDP/SIP School development plan/school improvement plan.

SEMH Social, emotional and mental health; previously sometimes described as BSD.

SENCO/SENDCO Special educational needs/disability coordinator in schools with responsibility for all SEND students and statutory reporting.

SEND Special educational needs and disabilities

SEND alumni School leavers with SEND who can return to school to carry out careers activities and act as role models for current students.

SEND Code of Practice Legislation introduced in 2014 as part of the introduction of EHC Plans. www.gov.uk/government/publications/send-code-of-practice-0-to-25

Glossary of Key Terms

SEND Gatsby Toolkit An online reference document available which provides a detailed interpretation of how to deliver the Gatsby Benchmarks for young people in both Career SEND Groups One and Two. https://resources.careersanderprise.co.uk/sites/default/files/2023-01/1051_SEND%20Gatsby%20Toolkit%20Refresh%20V8.pdf

SEND Reforms The set of reforms published in 2023 as a SEND and improvement plan. www.local.gov.uk/parliament/briefings-and-responses/send-and-alternative-provision-improvement-plan-2-march-2023

Social/medical model of disability The original and current models through which disability is defined, separated by the issue around barriers being the 'fault' of the individual or the wider society.

Special school A school delivering education for young people with special needs aged 2–19, the vast majority of which will have an EHC Plan, funded by the state or independent.

Stereotypes A way of describing groups as having (usually) negative characteristics and come from (apparently) a basic human need to categorise or make things simpler to explain a world that is more complicated than most can deal with and is 'grounded in the observations of everyday life' (Alice Eagly).

Supported employment Employment supported by a job coach at work.

Supported internship A training scheme involving education and an employer providing training across a number of departments lasting at least six months resulting in improved probability of paid employment open to young people with an EHC currently, but this could change without first needing to have an EHC Plan.

Supported living Living either at home or away from home and receiving support to maintain independence.

Supported self-employment Self-employment supported by a job coach and/or others.

Supported volunteering Volunteering supported by a job coach, personal assistant or other person.

Transition – macro The big junctions in the career development process like leaving school.

Transition – micro The impact on our feelings when we experience a macro transition.

Travel training Instruction for young people with special needs, often learning difficulties, in terms of how to travel on public transport to school, work experience, college and work.

UCAS Disabled Students A service for disabled students applying for university. https://www.ucas.com/undergraduate/applying-university/individual-needs/disabled-students

Unconscious bias Biases which we are unconscious of influenced by our education, experience and socialisation which negatively affect our behaviour towards those who are different from ourselves.

Value chain of early career development The interlinked career development activities and processes that result in improved outcomes if kept intact through connectivity.

Glossary of Key Terms

Vocational profile Similar to a CV, contains additional information on personal preferences/choices and support requirements.
Vulnerable In need of special care, support, or protection because of age, disability, risk of abuse, or neglect. There is a list on page 23 of examples of vulnerable young people (Gov.UK).
Work experience The activity of engaging with an employer either at work or virtually to experience the world of work.
Work placement Extended work experience usually at the employer site.

NEW AND BEST-SELLING FROM TROTMAN

New in 2024

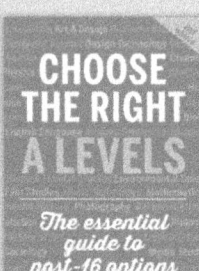

Get into University

Careers Essentials

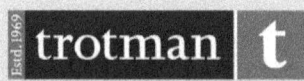

Enhance your careers library with our bestsellers, visit:
www.trotman.co.uk

www.ingramcontent.com/pod-product-compliance
Lightning Source LLC
Chambersburg PA
CBHW040321300426
44112CB00020B/2824